Doing Organizational Ethnography

T0295645

This book presents a new way of understanding organizational ethnography due to its strong emphasis on what the word organizational means in organizational ethnography. In the past five years, a new organizational studies research field has developed involving organizational ethnographies, which is when organizations are studied using ethnographical methods. This development has shed light on the difficulties of organizational ethnography, and yet we argue that confusion remains as to what organizational ethnographical approaches are.

In *Doing Organizational Ethnography*, organizational is defined as polyphonic ways of organizing based on the interactions and co-production of the many voices, discourses, practices, and narratives in and around organizations, thus providing readers with in-depth reflections on what organizing and organizations become when *doing* organizational ethnography.

This volume will offer students and scholars a profound understanding of organizational ethnography by presenting concrete examples, reflections, and discussions of how to understand and adequately conceptualize the word organizational in organizational ethnography by combining *organizational phenomena* (e.g., strategy making, policymaking), *analytical perspectives* (e.g., sensemaking, narratives), and *ethnographical methods* (e.g., texts, interactions, shadowing in fieldwork).

Anne Reff Pedersen is Associate Professor in the Department of Organization at Copenhagen Business School, Denmark.

Didde Maria Humle is a Postdoctoral Researcher at Copenhagen Business School and University College UCC, Denmark.

Routledge Studies in Management, Organizations, and Society

For a full list of titles in this series, please visit www.routledge.com

This series presents innovative work grounded in new realities, addressing issues crucial to an understanding of the contemporary world. This is the world of organized societies, where boundaries between formal and informal, public and private, local and global organizations have been displaced or have vanished, along with other nineteenth century dichotomies and oppositions. Management, apart from becoming a specialized profession for a growing number of people, is an everyday activity for most members of modern societies.

Similarly, at the level of enquiry, culture and technology, and literature and economics can no longer be conceived as isolated intellectual fields; conventional canons and established mainstreams are contested. Management, Organizations, and Society addresses these contemporary dynamics of transformation in a manner that transcends disciplinary boundaries, with books that will appeal to researchers, students, and practitioners alike.

Doing Organizational Ethnography

Edited by Anne Reff Pedersen and Didde Maria Humle

Routledge
Taylor & Francis Group

LONDON AND NEW YORK

First published 2016 by Routledge

2 Park Square, Milton Park, Abingdon, Oxfordshire OX14 4RN
711 Third Avenue, New York, NY 10017

Routledge is an imprint of the Taylor & Francis Group, an informa business

First issued in paperback 2018

Library of Congress Cataloging-in-Publication Data
Names: Reff Pedersen, Anne, 1970– editor. | Humle, Didde Maria, editor.
Title: Doing organizational ethnography / edited by Anne Reff Pedersen and Didde Maria Humle.
Description: First Edition. | New York : Routledge, 2016. | Series: Routledge studies in management, organizations and society ; 38 | Includes bibliographical references and index.
Identifiers: LCCN 2016007460 | ISBN 9781138935594 (hardback : alk. paper) | ISBN 9781315677279 (ebook)
Subjects: LCSH: Organizational sociology—Case studies. | Business anthropology—Case studies.
Classification: LCC HM786 .D65 2016 | DDC 302.3/5—dc23
LC record available at http://lccn.loc.gov/2016007460

ISBN: 978-1-138-93559-4 (hbk)
ISBN: 978-1-138-61700-1 (pbk)

Typeset in Sabon
by Apex CoVantage, LLC

Contents

About the Contributors

Authors of Chapters

Morten Arnfred has a Master's degree in anthropology from Copenhagen University. He has worked as a consultant with user-centered innovation in the public sector and in the private sector with design research and organizational culture. As a research assistant at the Department of Organization at Copenhagen Business School, he has done research in user-centered innovation in health care with a particular focus on the development of new methods. His main research interests include design anthropology, ethnographic methodology, and the theory of science. He has published in the *Journal of Organizational Ethnography*.

Jette Ernst is PhD Fellow at the Department of Language and Communication at Southern Danish University. Her empirically based research centres on the organization of work. She employs multilayered analyses to understand the complexities and dynamic aspects of the relations between work, workers, organizations, and the wider context in which organizing unfolds. She takes a particular interest in how organizational settings impinge on people in organizations and how employees respond to and handle these settings. Methodologically, she employs a wide range of ethnographic tools to advance an understanding of organizational lives and the social aspects of organizing. She has published in *Nordic Journal of Working Life Studies*.

Sanne Frandsen has her PhD from Copenhagen Business School and is currently a Post Doc at Lund University, Department of Business Administration. She uses critical, ethnographic, and narrative approaches to study individual and organizational identity work, stigmatization, branding, and sales. Her research has been published in *Management Communication Quarterly*, *Journal of Organizational Ethnography*, *Journal of Management Development*, and *Tamara*.

Jesper Rohr Hansen is Researcher at Danish Building Research at Aalborg University. His research field is urban planning with a specific focus on leadership, disadvantaged neighbourhoods, collaborative innovation in the public sector, and organizing. Currently he is working on a JPI Urban Europe Project that focuses on urban development in the urban fringes.

The project has a special emphasis on flexible intervention, negotiated regulation practice, public-private risk taking, and emerging counter-segregation strategies.

Didde Maria Humle has her PhD from the Department of Organization, CBS. She is currently working as a Postdoctoral Researcher at the Department of Organization, Copenhagen Business School and the Department of Management and Organizational Learning at University College UCC. Her research fields are narrative organizational analysis, work and organizational psychology. Her empirical work is focused on immaterial and relational work (of e.g. consultants and school teachers). She has published articles in international journals; *Management Learning*, *Nordic Journal of Working Life Studies* and *Tamara*.

Mette Brehm Johansen is a PhD Fellow at the Department of Organization at Copenhagen Business School. Her research field is organizational ethnography, and she has a particular interest in the implementation of organizing processes in health care. Mette's PhD project is empirically focused on patient involvement in quality work in an oncology clinic. She studies how patient involvement work reconfigures relations between patients and professionals, how knowledge dilemmas surface in this kind of work, and how patients' experiences are configured and used in very different ways when involving patients in quality work.

Marie Mathiesen works in the intersection of organizational research and organizational practice. She has worked as a management consultant and following her PhD in organizational studies, she was an Executive Assistant to a Senior Executive at Novozymes, a multinational biotech company. She has written about organizations from a narrative perspective and is interested in the role of strategy in modern organizations. Currently she is Co-founder and Partner at Indblik Inc. – a company that offers tools for analysis in organizations. Their Q&A Relay product is an innovative and interactive question and answer relay system that allows organizations to turn tacit knowledge into tangible data. See www.indblikinc.com for more. Marie can also be found on LinkedIn.

Elisabeth Naima Mikkelsen is Assistant Professor at the Department of Organization at Copenhagen Business School. Her research field is work relationships and collaboration with a particular interest in conflict and conflict management, ethnography, organizational sensemaking, and professional identities. Currently, she works on research projects about interorganizational relations in mental health care and work relationships and social capital among correctional officers in prisons. She has published articles in *Nonprofit and Voluntary Sector Quarterly*, *Qualitative Research in Organizations and Management*, *Community, Work & Family*, *Journal of Community and Applied Social Psychology*, and International *Journal for the Advancement of Counselling*.

Mie Plotnikof is an Assistant Professor at the Department of Management and Organizational Learning at University College UCC. Her research field is organization studies with a specific focus on discourse analysis, qualitative methods, subjectivity and power, and the public policy area of education. She has published articles in international journals, such as the *Innovation Journal* and *Nordic Journal of Working Life Studies*, as well as in Danish journals and anthologies on new management discourses and related practices in the education area. At the moment, she is working on a new research project about the emergence and effects of new policy reforms within education.

Discussants

Chahrazad Abdallah is Associate Professor at École des sciences de la gestion, Université du Québec à Montréal (ESG UQAM) in Montréal, Canada. Her research interests include strategy as practice and management in the cultural and creative industries. Her current research focuses on strategy and creativity as ambiguous discursive practices. She works with qualitative methods using discourse analysis and ethnography. She has taught courses on strategy, organization theory, and qualitative research methods.

David M. Boje is Regents Professor and Wells Fargo Chair in the Management Department at New Mexico State University. He is an international and highly esteemed scholar in the areas of storytelling and antenarratives in organizations. He also holds an honorary doctorate from Aalborg University and is considered the godfather of their Material Storytelling Lab. He is founder of *Tamara: Journal of Critical Organization Inquiry*.

Barbara Gray is a Professor of Organizational Behavior and Director of the Center for Research in Conflict and Negotiation at Pennsylvania State University. Her research interests include interorganizational relations, multiparty collaborative alliances, organizational and environmental conflict, team conflict, and sensemaking.

Steven Griggs is Professor of Public Policy in the Department of Politics and Public Policy at De Montfort University, United Kingdom. His research focuses on poststructuralist policy analysis and its contribution to the critical explanation of policy practices, particularly in the fields of environmental policy and protest and local governance and collaboration. He is currently working on an eight-city comparative study into collaborative governance under conditions of austerity.

Dan Kärreman is Professor of Management and Organization Studies at Copenhagen Business School and Professor of Management at Royal Holloway, University of London. He is also affiliated with the Lumos group at Lund University. His research interests include critical management studies, knowledge work, identity in organizations, leadership, organizational control, and research methodology.

Davide Nicolini is Professor of Organization Studies at Warwick Business School. His recent research focuses on the development of a practice-based approach to the study of organizational phenomena and its implications for the understanding of knowing, collaboration, and change in organizations. Most of his current research is in health care, where he is studying the generation and circulation of safety knowledge, how top managers mobilize knowledge in their day-to-day work, and the process through which several ways of knowing are worked together.

Anne Reff Pedersen is Associate Professor at the Department of Organization at Copenhagen Business School. Her research field is organization studies with a particular interest in organization theory, ethnography, narratives, time, and the public policy field of health care. Currently, she is working on a research project about health-care innovation with a special interest in resistance and change practices.

Mike Rowe is Lecturer at the Management School at the University of Liverpool. His main areas of teaching and research are in public service and street-level bureaucracy. He is currently engaged in a long-term ethnographic study of police discretion, co-organizes the annual Ethnography Symposium at the University of Liverpool, and is co-editor of the *Journal of Organizational Ethnography*.

Danielle Zandee is a Professor of Sustainable Organizational Development at Nyenrode Business University. She is an organization theory scholar with a particular interest in change, innovation, sustainability, and action research within a variety of empirical settings—both national and international contexts. Currently, she studies organizational change processes that enable the emergence of sustainable enterprise.

1 Doing Organizational Ethnography

Anne Reff Pedersen and Didde Maria Humle

This book presents a new way of understanding organizational ethnography due to its strong emphasis on what the word *organizational* means in organizational ethnography. The concept of organizational ethnography can be defined in many ways, all dependent upon whether it is presented from the perspective of organizational studies or anthropology. From an anthropological perspective, the word *organization* means the empirical or organizational setting: the factory, the school, or the company where qualitative and descriptive ethnographic studies are conducted. From the perspective of organizational studies, the word *ethnography* is often translated into time-consuming field studies, where mixed techniques such as shadowing, writing, and interviewing are used to produce thick descriptions of organizational life and practices.

The purpose of this book is to draw attention to the meaning of the word *organization*, in organizational ethnography. Contemporary scholarly work in the field of ethnographic organizational studies has combined various theoretical perspectives with ethnographic methods and has demonstrated new insights into what organizations and organizing then becomes. These studies bring a renewed understanding of many organizational phenomena. Examples of such studies will be presented in this book.

In Search of the Meaning of Organizations and Organizing

In the past five years, a new enthusiasm has come to an old concept: organizational ethnography. Novel insights and reflections based on interesting methods and analysis-based field studies of organizations have been presented (Allbon, 2012; Brannan, Rowe, & Worthington, 2012; Herrmann, Barnhill, & Poole, 2013; Murthy, 2013). This contemporary development sheds light on some of the opportunities and challenges organizational ethnography offers. One of these challenges is the confusion that still remains as to the meaning of the word *organization* in organizational ethnography. This book describes the need for a stronger theoretical understanding of the concept of organization, presenting different possibilities of what *organizing* means in organizational ethnographic work.

We argue that the understanding and definition of organizing is influenced by the methods and analytical approaches used. In many ethnographic studies of organizations, there is a distance between the methods used and the understanding of organization. In some organizational ethnographic studies, descriptions of the organizational contexts, events and phenomena are placed in the methodological descriptions, and presented as the scene of the study rather than being related to the contribution. In this way the organizations are degenerated to the place or the space in which researchers explore new methods, tell exciting and exotic stories, and reflect on the value or difficulties of the new methods. We argue for the fruitfulness of including reflections on the effect of the methods on the understanding of organizing in doing organizational ethnographic studies. And for reflexive discussions on how the methods used and the theories adopted affects our analytical work and understanding of organizations and the phenomena studied.

In this book, we define organizing as an overall polyphonic, emerging, and processual concept (Kornberger, Clegg, & Carter, 2006; Humle & Pedersen, 2015) based on the multiple voices, discourses, frames, tensions, practices, interactions, and narratives of organizational life. Operating within the tradition of interpretative organizational research (Kostera, 2007; Ybema et al., 2009; Yanow, 2012), the book underpins the social constructivist assumption that organizational life emerges from places and temporal situations through the fragmented interaction of different voices and meanings between people, materials, and events. This shared definition of organizing provides the overall coherence necessary for systematic and profound theoretical and methodological reflections across the chapters.

Analytical Ambitions

First, we find that classical organizational ethnographic studies (Kostera, 2007; Neyland, 2007; Kunda, 2013) often favour specific methodological and ethnographic considerations and define organizations as empirical sites or contextual settings. We endeavor to add to these studies by expanding on them to encompass reflections on the effect of using specific theoretical perspectives and various ethnographic methods when analyzing certain organizational phenomena.

Our book links theoretically different social science perspectives to the analyses of organizations and organizational phenomenon to demonstrate how different theoretical perspectives imply or assume different modes of organizing. The main objective of the book is to offer students and scholars a profound understanding of organizational ethnography by presenting concrete examples, reflections, and discussions of how to conduct organizational ethnography and adequately conceptualize the meaning of the word organizing. This is done by analytically combining *organizational phenomena* (e.g., strategy making, policymaking) with *theoretical perspectives* (e.g., sensemaking, narratives), and *ethnographic methods* (e.g., observations, shadowing, interviews). Our ambition is that students and young researchers will use this knowledge as inspiration in their study of organizations.

All of the chapters in this book define organizational ethnography by combining theory, method, and organizational phenomenon. Some chapters emphasize method more strongly than theoretical perspective; other chapters place more emphasis on theoretical perspective compared to method. The book provides examples of the ways in which the combination and use of theory, method, and phenomenon are negotiated in each study. No standards of best practice can be recommended; instead, the book demonstrates a range of organizational ethnographic studies from more theoretical inspired studies to more method-driven studies, all with an emphasis on how researchers are crafting and applying organizational ethnography in research practice and how they are contributing to new understandings of organizing, and organizational phenomena.

In one example of how theory, method, and phenomenon are combined and intertwined, Chapter 3 describes strategy as the organizational phenomenon, using a performative theoretical perspective and interactive ethnographic methods. This enables a discussion of how to understand strategy as ongoing strategy talks and strategy work instead of understanding it as application, results, or effects of strategy.

Combining theoretical perspectives with descriptive and field-oriented points of departure can be viewed as an oxymoron. It can also be seen as a constructive obstruction that enhances a dialogical way of thinking, which makes it possible to revise and remake theoretical assumptions as well as methodological reflections. All of the chapters in this book present examples of how empirical work has led to adjustments and rephrasing of theoretical assumptions, as the empirical world is taken into consideration while doing research. One counterargument is that many organizational concepts, such as organizational context, are already included in theoretical assumptions regarding sensitivity towards empirical explanations. The studies in this book demonstrate how researchers' struggle to braid empirical findings into theoretical frameworks can create inspiring openings from which both theoretical assumptions and empirical observations are challenged.

The rationale behind the book is that our understanding of organization in organizational ethnography should include a stronger, more thorough, exploration of the meaning of organization for the benefit of research within both organizational studies and ethnographic studies. While there is a mounting literature on organizational theory and an abundance of literature on ethnographic methodology, few studies bring together both areas.

The Organizational Phenomena

This book demonstrates many different organizational phenomena and how organizing can be defined in many different ways when doing organizational ethnography. As Kärreman notes in his comment to Frandsen's chapter, we need concepts that are attached to findings and methods that provide findings. Findings that only reflect a straight story, hyper-specialized journal debates, or a theoretical concept often reveal very little. They only show the results and not the analytical work behind the results.

> *Chapter 4 is about internal branding in a call centre of a telecommunication organization. It takes its departure from the employee voice position and explores organizational branding with the use of critical organizational ethnography as a site of struggle over meaning, identity, values, and culture instead of an organization shaped and controlled by its overall corporate brand or strategy.*

All the chapters refer to organizing through specific organizational phenomena, not organizations as static, closed entities, but as fragmented networks or clusters of social interaction that occurs in specific times and spaces.

Theoretical Perspectives

Culture and identity are some of the theoretical and historical lenses that have defined the concept of organization in earlier organizational ethnography (Clifford & Marcus, 1986; Van Maanen, 1988; Deetz, 1994). Cunliffe (2009) divided organizational ethnographers into three research traditions: realist oriented studies, interpretative studies, and critical studies. Gray's comments to Mikkelsen's chapter call for a critical approach to gain richer understandings of the dynamics of everyday work and the combination of different theoretical approaches, such as sensemaking theory with discourse analysis, to enable a deeper exploration of the factors that shape organizational members' sensemaking. Common for the studies in this book is an understanding of organizing as based on social interaction, how people, together with artefacts, live their lives and make meanings through interaction, talk, and interpretation.

> *Chapter 5 is about consulting work and combines an antenarrative vocabulary with longitudinal ethnographic fieldwork to study the everyday work stories of consultants as a web of story performances, whereby meanings of work are negotiated.*

In their book on organizational ethnography, Ybema, Yannow, Wels, and Kamsteeg described how interpretivist organizational ethnography relates to meaning making, multivocality, and reflexivity (2009, 9). Nobody working within organizational ethnography can argue against this reasoning, or against a research aim of challenging taken-for-granted beliefs. But how are meanings, multiple voices, and reflexivity captured in concrete research processes, and how do theoretical definitions of e.g. practices, discourses, narratives, and sensemaking influence the findings. Nicolini argues in the chapter of Ernst that theory should work in a dynamic tension with the empirical material throughout the research process. He writes further that researchers have to remember the generative and constraining nature of theory in ethnographic research and of the necessity to establish a playful relationship between the two to remind us that concepts should always be used as sensitizing tools.

> *Chapter 2 explores everyday conflicts in a volunteer humanitarian aid organization. Instead of investing universal conflicts typologies, the use of a sensemaking perspective allows the study to situate conflicts as embedded in social relationships and different frames of sensemaking from management and employee perspectives.*

All the chapters relate contributions and findings to the use of theories, methods, and encounters with the field. Using different social science theories enables the investigation of how processes, social dynamics, interactions, and meaning making become central findings. In other words, working with organizational ethnography and different theories creates new ways for understanding organizational phenomena (e.g., strategy or conflict). This adds to and challenges the understandings of these phenomena that have been derived from traditional organizational theory (typology, structure, and internal thinking).

Ethnographic Methods and the Role of the Researcher

The ethnographic methods of organizational ethnography are historically derived from anthropology and have made their landmark in organizational studies. There are many methodological and reflective contributions in the studies of ethnography (Denzin, 2003; Angrosino, 2007; Hammersley & Atkinson, 2007; Davies, 2008) that focus on the methods used and the role of the researcher. The anthropologist has traditionally been the privileged pioneer in developing ethnographic methods, while organizational scholars have combined longer or shorter fieldwork with different theoretical social science perspectives. Today's scholars of organizational ethnography come from anthropology, psychology, business schools, public administration, political science, historical studies, and many other disciplines. The sharp distinction between organizational and anthropological studies can be considered outdated. Instead, organizational ethnography is a multidisciplinary field of research mixing multiple disciplines in different ways and providing new insights into the field of organizational studies.

Understanding organization from an anthropological perspective has, in classical terms, meant that organizing emerge after staying for a long time at the same place and observing and talking to people at that place (Bate, 1997). Czarniawska described how management and organizing occurs in a net of multiple, fragmented contexts and through a kaleidoscopic multitude of movements (2008, p. 6) that cannot always be captured by long observations of hours or even years in the same place. This is a new condition for scholars of organizational ethnography, who must decide what to follow, where to be, and when to follow.

> In Chapter 7, the organizational phenomenon described is patient involvement in quality development. The chapter illustrates how this kind of work is organized in different meetings and occurs in many places and processes. This condition demands of the researcher to understand organizing as complex and multi-sited.

Another strong trend in understanding ethnography from an anthropological tradition is the confessional description of "me as becoming an ethnographer" by taking a journey to explore and interpret organizational life. Gideon Kunda (2013) and John Van Maanen (1988) are two of the contemporary founders of this perspective. Part of the tradition is to define the organization by the stories, dramas, and interpretations of what is going on via different modes of writing—through dairies, autoethnography, and confessional stories. The aim of this approach is to avoid misguided equation with an institutionally enforced commitment to hegemonic theoretical discourses and authoritative answers, while continuing exploration and debate of data, interpretations, and reports (Kunda, 2013, pp. 21–22). In this book, the role of the researcher is discussed by all of the authors, with reflection on the problems and dilemmas of conducting fieldwork. The aim is to present reflections on interactions with the field. In this way, ethnographic work is not presented as a chronological description of the research process, or as continual 'travel' experiences, but instead researchers demonstrate all the unseen events in retrospective reflections.

Zandee writes in her commentary to Plotnikov, "Organizational ethnography is well positioned to also engage in research *with* rather than *on* actors involved in everyday meaning making actions". This position accentuates processes of co-creation of knowledge in doing organizational ethnography.

In Chapter 8, the researcher presents a new method of organizational mapping for understanding the collaborative discourses of public managers in the policy area of day care. To explore the social dynamics of these processes, new methods are needed, and the researcher describes the interplay between the role of the researcher with the informants and how the interaction created new types of data as well as new insight into discourse analysis.

All the chapters in the book use a combination of different methods and present reflections on the use of these methods. The aim is not to solely present new and exciting methods, but to show how the combination of different theories and methods lead to interesting analytical findings. To illustrate and clarify the combination of methods and various theoretical perspectives, each chapter presents one or two analytical vignettes. This is also meant as inspiration to other scholars doing organizational ethnography.

Contribution and Style

This book is an edited volume based on a variety of examples of qualitative research conducted as organizational ethnographies. Each chapter is based on organizational studies involving long-term fieldwork. At the end of each chapter, an experienced researcher in the field offers comments and discussion on the contributions of the chapter, providing reflections on the implications for research in the field to which they ascribe. Professor Boje, for example, discusses and comments on Humle's chapter about narrative ethnograhpic studies of everyday work stories in and around organizations. The combination of chapters comprising long-term fieldwork and reflections by senior, internationally respected scholars provides a basis for presenting new developments in the field of organizational ethnography and for demonstrating what organizing becomes in the different types of studies combining theory, method, and phenomenon.

Each chapter comprises a presentation of the organizational phenomenon studied, a short review of the theoretical perspectives employed, descriptions of the fieldwork methods, reflections on the role of the researchers, one or two vignettes illustrating data and analysis, and, finally, reflections on defining organizing. Collectively, the chapters provide students and researchers with a systematic, in-depth overview of the advantages and weaknesses of various approaches to organizational ethnography. The point is not to give readers a definitive explanation of how to understand organizing by organizational ethnography, but to enhance reflexive consideration of the complexities of what organizing is. In this way, we offer a contribution comprising a reflexive discussion of the organizational aspect of doing organizational ethnographies.

As a collective contribution, we have no intention of providing new ethnographic methods or theories. For the advanced scholar in organizational theory who is already working inclusively with ethnographic methods and practices, nothing new is probably added in this volume. Our attempt is more modest: to spread the understanding of what organizations and organizing become when working within a framework of organizational ethnography. All too many scholars are still working with old concepts and understandings of organizing, even when trying out new methods. We hope that this book will bolster the ways in which the combination of theories, empirical worlds, and methods can create new organizational understandings.

The conclusion of this book is that many young scholars are *doing* interesting organizational ethnographical work and by doing this, they also develop new understandings of what organizing becomes. Their contributions are to demonstrate how organizing becomes an emerging, relational, and polyphonic phenomena, which implies power relations and meaning making. Thus doing organizational ethnography is also about showing how methods, theories, and empirical worlds blend together in new ways.

Overview of the Book

Part I: Studies of Strategy, Conflict, and Branding in Nonprofit and Private Organizations

Chapter 2

EVERYDAY CONFLICT AT WORK: AN ORGANIZATIONAL SENSEMAKING ETHNOGRAPHY

This chapter is about everyday conflicts that occur at work and how meaning and action interact in processes of handling those organizational conflicts that arise naturally in daily life when people meet in social interactions. The phenomenon of conflict is approached by exploring those social processes of organizational sensemaking that arise when conflicts occur in a nonprofit organization. The chapter shows that sensemaking plays a critical role in the way staff and management experience and act out conflict. The empirical material derives from a two-year ethnographic field study of NGO Plus that involved observation of in-the-moment conflicts and listening to participants' own accounts of their experiences with conflict. An empirical vignette presents an episode of social interaction at NGO Plus, which both staff and management interpret as conflictual. The vignette is used to demonstrate how management and different groups of staff make sense of the same conflict episode in five different ways. They explain conflict interaction as rooted in deviating personalities, a culture clash between departments, status inequality between organizational groups, absent leadership, and external pressure. The chapter concludes with a discussion of how power relationships between individuals and organizational groups shape legitimacy in conflict sensemaking.

Chapter 3

DOING STRATEGY: A PERFORMATIVE ORGANIZATIONAL ETHNOGRAPHY

The organizational phenomenon under ethnographic investigation in this chapter is strategy. Whether justified or not, the concept of strategy has a prominent position in most organizations, and therefore if we want to know more about what organizations are like and how they become, strategy can be a very good place to look. The ethnographic fieldwork in the chapter involves strategy work in a multinational biotech company. The chapter employs a performativity-inspired organizational ethnographic approach. From this point of departure, organizations are considered to be "performed constructs" that are continually re-performed and re-negotiated through the words and actions of organizational actors. Adopting this epistemological stance signifies a radical departure from traditional strategy studies. During the fieldwork, the author assumed the role of participant observer in a corporate working group tasked with doing departmental strategy work. The analysis is based on field notes and interviews with other working group members. The empirical focus for the chapter is on how organizational actors use strategy work to establish their identities as strategists. The chapter concludes with a discussion of how a performative ethnographic approach can contribute to discussions of organising.

Chapter 4

EXAMINING BRANDING IN ORGANIZATIONS BY USING CRITICAL
ORGANIZATIONAL ETHNOGRAPHY

The chapter focuses on critical organizational ethnography and the implications of using an analytical approach derived from critical management studies. The *organizational phenomenon* is a culture change process propelled by implementation of a new corporate brand. *Empirically* an internal branding process is studied in a telecom corporation and focuses specifically on the brand as a mean of socio-ideological control targeting the call centre employees. The *critical analytical approach* highlights the power dynamics through a dialectical focus on identity regulation and resistance. *Vignettes* from the field demonstrate the employees' struggle to enact the new brand and problematizes how dominating control practices contradict each other and entrap the employees, giving rise to simultaneous engagement with and cynical distance from the brand values. On this basis, the commentary highlights the *power of findings* and suggests organizational ethnography as a route to give access to and insight in the messy, complex, and strange world of organizations.

Part II: Knowledge Organizations and Studies of Everyday Work

Chapter 5

A WEB OF WORK-LIFE STORIES: A NARRATIVE ORGANIZATIONAL ETHNOGRAPHY

This chapter uses a narrative organizational ethnographic approach to the study of everyday work stories of organizational members. The organizational phenomena studied are the work stories and the ongoing story work of organizational members.

The empirical material is from a two-year case study of a human resources (HR) consultancy that works with recruitment, HR services, and unemployment counselling. The theoretical/analytical perspective adopted is antenarrative and polyphonic focusing on the web of everyday story performances. The fieldwork involved a variety of ethnographic methods including interviews, observations, and a collection of different organizational documents such as PowerPoint presentations, intranet postings, and minutes from management meetings. Empirical analytical examples are presented, illustrating how members of this organization told both extremely positive work stories about being members of a fantastic company and making a genuine difference in the life of others while simultaneously telling critical counter stories about how exhausting work could be and describing the consultancy as a demanding place of work. The chapter concludes by discussing the insights provided by combining ethnographic methods with an antenarrative vocabulary in studying the ongoing story work of organizational members.

Chapter 6

THE LOGIC OF NURSING WORK: AN ORGANIZATIONAL ETHNOGRAPHY
OF PRACTICE

The chapter illustrates how combining ethnography with Bourdieu's practice theory offers a distinct analytical approach capable of providing rich and contextualized understanding of work and organization. The organizational setting is a hospital department where nursing practices have been standardized to a large degree as part of quality-leveraging initiatives. Based on ethnographic fieldwork, the manner in which the standards are handled in practice is examined, and Bourdieu's concepts of field and habitus are applied as an analytical framework. Theory and ethnographic methods are hence approached as interlaced and cooperating tools in research. The vignette of the chapter illustrates how the interaction between the practitioner and the researcher in the field impinges on the generated data and how Bourdieu's concept of logic in practice emerges as fertile for an understanding of standardized nursing. The vignette exemplifies how the researcher and the practitioner approach practice from different points of view. For the practitioner, logic is effortlessly created and sought restored in the ambiguous situations of work that emerge. The implications of the researcher's epistemic choices are discussed. The chapter concludes with the author's reflections on the assumptions that lie behind organizing through standards and what standards do to practice.

Chapter 7

CONTEXTING THE PATIENT: A MEETING ETHNOGRAPHY OF
PATIENT INVOLVEMENT IN QUALITY DEVELOPMENT

The organizational phenomenon explored ethnographically in the fieldwork grounding the chapter is patient involvement in quality development. The setting is an oncology clinic in a university hospital. The phenomenon turned out to be quite episodic in character since involving patients in quality development is not a fully consolidated and routinized part of the organization and clinic in question. Therefore, an ethnographic approach centred on meetings of different kinds turned out to be suitable in order to capture the object of study. Moreover, analytically, a work perspective was chosen. This approach makes it possible to notice that patient involvement is not a simple method-driven activity assuring the inclusion of 'the patient's voice' in quality development. A work perspective thus also brings to the fore the work going on outside the formal involvement methods. The analysis focuses on what is analyzed as the contexting work needed in order for it to be carried out. The first part of the analysis shows how what is taken to the table in the patient panel needs contexting—both before and after the meetings—in order for the professionals to attune it to, or disconnect it from, other practices and processes in the clinic. The second part of the analysis shows how the professionals also need contexting in order to create an understanding of what position the knowledge and experiences of the participating patients in quality development can take, since it does not have a 'natural' and consolidated position. The analysis thus points to some of the tacit work needed in order for patient involvement in quality development to be a doable endeavor.

Part III: Public Organization Studies of Management and Collaborative Innovation

Chapter 8

MEANING NEGOTIATIONS OF COLLABORATIVE GOVERNANCE:
A DISCOURSE-BASED ETHNOGRAPHY

This chapter explores the potential for developing organizational discourse approaches through ethnographic fieldwork in the context of collaborative governance: a procedure to involve stakeholders in public problem solving of, for example, policy and service innovation. In doing so, the researcher engages with recent debates about the complexity of such new governance forms, as well as discussions on the relationship between discourse and materiality and the calls made to develop multi-method approaches to study complex organizational phenomena. In effect, the chapter develops empirical and analytical approaches to unfold discourse-material aspects of the negotiations of meanings and matters of such new governance form in practice. The chapter provides examples based on ethnographic fieldwork in collaborations across actors from the welfare area of education. In conclusion, the author reflects on the potential of the discourse-based approach and its implications for engaging with, and understanding, the complex organizing of collaborative governance.

Chapter 9

LEADERSHIP OF COLLABORATIVE INNOVATION IN THE PUBLIC SECTOR:
AN ENGAGED-SCHOLARSHIP ETHNOGRAPHY

The organizational phenomenon studied in this chapter is leadership in collaborative innovation. Empirically, the chapter focuses on city planning in central administration in the capital municipality. In this empirical context, a cross-administrative policymaking process was initiated in a bottom-up fashion with the aim of targeting the problems disadvantaged neighbourhoods face. Theoretically, collaborative leadership is analyzed by means of a policy analysis of uncertainty. The field study was based on a three-year qualitative single-case study using field notes, observation studies, participant observations, interviews and document studies. Two examples are analyzed to demonstrate how city planners across organizations were forced to engage in different collaborative activities to overcome uncertainties. The first example clarifies how the emergent policy discourse provoked conflicts related to identity and the positioning of leadership and collaborators, which had implications for revision of the initial policy strategy. The second example sheds light on how leadership used sensemaking to overcome uncertainties and wicked problems, thus paving the way for approval of a cross-administrative policy. The chapter ends by describing the role of the abductive, engaged-scholarship research position applied towards theory building and the ethnographic case study approach. Finally, conclusions are drawn about the perspective this methodology generates on polyphonic ways of organizing in public organizations.

Chapter 10

MONTAGE ETHNOGRAPHY: EDITING AND CO-ANALYZING
VOICES FROM THE FIELD

The chapter presents a new ethnographic method where qualitative interviews are analyzed and edited into polyphonic sound montages. These can then be played for employees in an organization and facilitate reflection, discussion, and co-analysis. The chapter outlines the process of crafting the sound montages and discusses both the methodological and organizational implications of representing informants' perspectives in this way. The chapter investigates the organizational phenomenon of user involvement in a health-care setting. It explores how polyphonic sound montages can be used to capture and communicate patients' perspectives and experiences. What does this approach allow the researcher and the health-care staff to see, and what are some of the strengths and weaknesses of this approach? The chapter briefly discusses different approaches to user involvement in a health-care setting before describing the background and conditions for the health-care innovation project discussed in the chapter. The use of montage in ethnography is illustrated with a few examples. The chapter then goes on to discuss the concrete considerations and challenges of crafting polyphonic sound montages from ethnographic interviews. Finally, the chapter describes the process of co-analysis and gives some examples of the findings in the health-care innovation project while discussing the epistemological underpinnings of using sound montages in organizational ethnography.

References

Allbon, Caroline. (2012). Down the Rabbit Hole—'Curiouser and Curiouser': Using Autoethnography as a Mode of Writing to Re-call, Re-tell and Re-veal Bodily Embodiment as Self-reflexive Inquiry. *Journal of Organizational Ethnography*, 1 (1), 62–71.

Angrosino, Michael. (2007). *Doing Ethnographic and Observational Research*. London: Sage.

Bate, Paul S. (1997). Whatever Happened to Organizational Anthropology? A Review of the Field of Organizational Ethnography and Anthropological Studies. *Human Relations*, 50 (9), 1147–1175.

Brannan, Matthew, Rowe, Mike, & Worthington, Frank. (2012). Editorial for the Journal of Organizational Ethnography: Time for a New Journal, a Journal for New Times. *Journal of Organizational Ethnography*, 1 (1), 5–14.

Clifford, James., & Marcus, George E. (1986). *Writing Culture: The Poetics and Politics of Ethnography: A School of American Research Advanced Seminar.* Berkeley, CA: University of California Press.

Cunliffe, Ann. (2009). Retelling Tales of the Field: In Search of Organizational Ethnography 20 Years On. *Organizational Research Methods*, 13 (2), 224–239.

Czarniawska, Barbara. (2008). Organizing: How to Study It and How to Write about It. *Qualitative Research in Organizations and Management: An International Journal*, 3 (1), 4–20.

Davies, Charlotte A. (2008). *Reflexive Ethnography: A Guide to Researching Selves and Others.* London: Routledge.

Deetz, Stanley A. (1994). The Micro-Politics of Identity Formation in the Workplace: The Case of a Knowledge Intensive Firm. *Human Studies*, 17, 23–44.

Denzin, Norman K. (Ed.) (2003). *Performance Ethnography: Critical Pedagogy and the Politics of Culture.* London: Sage.

Hammersley, Martyn, & Atkinson, Paul. (2007). *Ethnography: Principles in Practice.* London: Routledge.

Humle, Didde M., & Pedersen, Anne R. (2015). Fragmented Work Stories: Developing an Antenarrative Approach by Discontinuity, Tensions and Editing. *Management Learning*, 46 (5), 582–597.

Kornberger, Martin, Clegg, Stewart R., & Carter, Chris. (2006). Rethinking the Polyphonic Organization: Managing as Discursive Practice. *Scandinavian Journal of Management*, 22 (1), 3–30.

Kostera, Monika. (2007). *Organizational Ethnography: Methods and Inspirations.* Lund: Lund University.

Kunda, Gideon. (2013). Reflections on Becoming an Ethnographer. *Journal of Organizational Ethnography*, 2 (1), 4–22.

Murthy, Dhiraj. (2013). Ethnographic Research 2.0: The Potentialities of Emergent Digital Technologies for Qualitative Organizational Research. *Journal of Organizational Ethnography*, 2 (1), 23–36.

Neyland, Daniel. (2007). *Organizational Ethnography.* London: Sage.

Van Maanen, John. (1988). *Tales of the Field: On Writing Ethnography.* Chicago: University of Chicago Press.

Yanow, Dvora. (2012). Organizational Ethnography between Toolbox and World-Making. *Journal of Organizational Ethnography*, 1 (1), 31–42.

Ybema, Sierk, Yanow, D., Wels, H., & Kamsteeg, F. H. (Eds.) (2009). *Organizational Ethnography: Studying the Complexity of Everyday Life.* London: Sage.

Part I

Studies of Strategy, Conflict, and Branding in Nonprofit and Private Organizations

2 Everyday Conflict at Work

An Organizational Sensemaking Ethnography

Elisabeth Naima Mikkelsen and discussant Barbara Gray

Introduction

This chapter is about everyday conflicts that occur at work and how mean-ing and action interact in processes of handling those organizational con-flicts that arise naturally in daily life when people meet in social interactions. I approach the phenomenon of conflict by exploring those social processes of organizational *sensemaking* that arise when conflicts occur in a nonprofit organization, which I will refer to by the pseudonym NGO Plus. I report from an ethnographic study undertaken to explore how sensemaking plays a critical role in the way staff and management experience and act out conflict at the collective level of the organization. I particularly investigate how staff and management at NGO Plus draw on particular perceptual frameworks to derive meaning in conflict and enact conflict dynamics. Over the course of a two-year ethnographic field study at NGO Plus, I observed in-the-moment conflicts and listened to participants' own accounts of their experiences with conflict. As shown in this chapter, I was able to capture, through observa-tions and interviewing, both overtly and covertly expressed forms of conflict.

The chapter is structured by the following parts: I begin with a synop-sis of relevant conflict research literature followed by a presentation of the organizational setting in which I undertook this ethnographic study. Then, drawing on Weick's theoretical framework of sensemaking, I argue for com-bining a sensemaking approach with an ethnographic fieldwork methodol-ogy, and I present the two key concepts of framework and enactment. I then reflect on my own role as a researcher in the process of doing ethnographic fieldwork at NGO Plus. I proceed to present an empirical vignette of a con-flict interaction and to demonstrate that management and different groups of staff make sense of the same conflict interaction in five different ways. I end the chapter by discussing what the combining of conflict, sensemaking, and ethnography can teach us about conflict at work.

Organizational Conflict

Many strands of research have contributed to the study of—and our knowl-edge of—organizational conflict. Two main, but separate, branches of research emerge from conflict research literature: one that is focused on the occurrence of interpersonal conflict and another that is focused on conflict management and resolution.

While early research on interpersonal conflict largely considered conflict to be a dysfunctional phenomenon, by regarding it as "altogether bad" (Fink, 1968, p. 445) and as "a breakdown in standard mechanisms of decision-making" (March & Simon, 1958, p. 112), at which conflict situations were best kept under control through elimination (Mack & Snyder, 1957), a paradigm shift from the 1970s to the 1990s began to distinguish between dysfunctional conflict and constructive conflict. This distinction between conflicts that are detrimental to organizational functioning and conflicts that are functional and beneficial for the organization led to the establishment of a conflict typology framework, identifying task and relationship conflict (Jehn, 1995; De Dreu, 1997). While task-related conflict concerns work procedures and the allocation of resources and is commonly associated with constructive conflict, relationship conflict involves values and interpersonal style and is often viewed to be detrimental for organizations (De Dreu & Beersma, 2005). The concepts of *task and relationship conflict* have become well-established concepts in conflict research literature, theorizing how to achieve the 'right' kind of conflict for goal achievement.

Research that is focused on conflict management and resolution is influenced either by a) Deutsch's theory of Cooperation and Competition (1949; 1973), which premises that conflict includes a blend of cooperative and competitive motives and takes a normative prescriptive approach to conflict, or b) grid theory, which has spurred the development of a two-dimensional measure of conflict management with "concern for self" versus "concern for others" as the two orthogonal dimensions constituting possible strategies for conflict management (Putnam & Wilson, 1982; Rahim, 1983). Today, the majority of research in conflict management is commonly characterized by numerous descriptions of disputants' management options, almost exclusively psychologically assessing their use of five specific *conflict management styles*: forcing/dominating, avoiding, accommodation/obliging, problem solving, and compromising.

Critics have, however, argued that the existing conflict typology frameworks of *task and relationship conflict* and *conflict management styles* reduce our understanding of conflict in organizations. Kolb and Putnam (1992), for example, argue that conflict "has its roots in the individual, social, organizational, and cultural relationships that overflow the existing descriptive and normative topologies" (p. 315). The authors subsequently contend that what is needed are different methods and theoretical frameworks to capture conflict dynamics in organizations. Moreover, we need to conduct studies of conflict at the centre of everyday experience of organizations if we want to further develop our understanding of conflict and from this deal with and potentially resolve conflict. Both Barley (1991) and Kolb and Putnam (1992) point toward ethnography as a method that has much to offer in moving the field of organizational conflict into new and promising directions; they call attention to an 'ethnography of disputing'.

Kolb and Putnam (1992) represent a particular strand of organizational conflict research which argues that the occurrence of conflict at work should not be studied separately from how conflict is handled. What is particularly important to our understanding of local strategies used in handling conflict are the social processes of how conflict is recognized and made sense of within the organizational system (Morrill, 1989; Barley, 1991; Kolb & Putnam, 1992; Van Maanen, 1992; Kusztal, 2002; Lewicki & Gray, 2003; Putnam, 2004; Kolb, 2008).

The study presented in this chapter about social processes of organizational sensemaking in conflict and how social meaning and action interact in processes of conflict handling builds on this particular strand of organizational conflict research. Applying a sensemaking perspective to the study of conflict emphasizes conflict as an inevitable part of everyday organizational life and aims to understand the dynamics of conflict in their particulars. In terms of wanting to change, or resolve conflict, there is much to learn from work concerned with understanding it. Thus, with a sensemaking perspective on organizational conflict, we gain insight into micro processes of ways that conflict, as a social phenomenon, plays out in organizational cultures and group dynamics and why conflicts take the form they do. However, before outlining this study's theoretical positioning of organizational sensemaking, I present the nonprofit organization NGO Plus.

The Organizational Setting

NGO Plus works with humanitarian aid and development to create social change for poor and marginalized groups in developing countries. From its foundation in 1970, it has had a highly moralized vision of a more egalitarian world, and its main purpose is to promote human rights and democracy by strengthening civil societies and encouraging them to participate in reforming authoritarian governments. NGO Plus employs 30 full-time staff members, including management, participated in the study. There are three departments at NGO Plus: the clerical department, the fundraising department, and the programme department. There is little diversity in staff and management; all are middle-class native Danes, the majority are women, and most have either undergraduate or graduate university degrees. Staff members with university degrees are termed academic workers, while staff members without university degrees are employed as, and termed, clerical workers.

Analytical Approach

Sensemaking is the process by which people give meaning to experience. Weick argues that "[t]he basic idea of sensemaking is that reality is an ongoing accomplishment that emerges from efforts to create order and make retrospective sense of what occurs" (Weick, 1993, p. 635). Organizational sensemaking often becomes more obvious in situations that emerge from a break in the routine, for example, when staff and management in organizations confront issues, events, and actions that are surprising or confusing (Weick, 1995). An evident approach to capture organizational sensemaking has therefore been to examine the social processes of sensemaking in contexts that are marked by extreme circumstances, such as crises, disasters, or major organizational changes (Weick, 1988; 1990; Gioia & Chittipeddi, 1991; Gephart, 1993; Weick, 1993)

However, as argued by Weick (2010), organizational sensemaking during extreme and turbulent contexts are not representative of ordinary processes of organizational sensemaking. Other students of sensemaking have additionally highlighted that the goal of a sensemaking perspective is to understand how everyday organizational life is possible in its particulars (Drazin, Glynn, & Kazanjian, 1999; Mills, 2010). Sensemaking processes can therefore advantageously be examined in ordinary everyday events rather than situations characterized by crisis and turbulence. Maitlis (2005), for example, focuses on everyday sensemaking processes in three British symphony orchestras to display how distinct forms of everyday sensemaking unfold, interact, and connect to different types of accounts and actions. And Patriotta (2003) studies the sensemaking activities through which organizational actors deal with everyday machinery disruptions at a Fiat auto plant in Italy to detect the human or non-human sources of technical breakdowns.

Similarly, I focus on the ways in which distinct forms of everyday sensemaking in processes of conflict handling are marked by being everyday organizational experiences rather than situations of crises. A sensemaking perspective on conflict emphasizes conflict as an inevitable part of everyday organizational life and allows insight into the dynamics of conflict: If we want insight into why people act and think the way they do in conflict and into what are meaningful ways for them to address conflict, then we must explore the conflict sensemaking that is constructed and enacted by particular organizational groups. With a sensemaking perspective on everyday conflict, we are able to explore the construction of meaning conveyed in organization members' talk about conflict.

Focusing only on talk and discourse is, however, insufficient. While we get insight into the construction of meaning when examining talk, we miss out on the tacit assumptions and cultural knowledge that are equally used in meaning constructions (Hansen, 2006; Gubrium & Holstein, 2009). I, therefore, combine my analytical approach of sensemaking with a methodology that is capable of capturing the tacit assumptions and cultural knowledge present in organizations. As Hansen (2006) writes, "If our focus is on the construction of meaning in organizations we must attend to the construction site, or context" (p. 1050). Both Maitlis (2005), in her study of British symphony orchestras, and Patriotta (2003) in his study at a Fiat auto plant, use the method of long-term fieldwork, combing interviewing and non-participant observations to explore micro-level processes of sensemaking among organization members. Combining a sensemaking approach with an ethnographic fieldwork methodology in the study of conflict affords insight into the context in which sensemaking and discourses are produced and, more importantly, the social order (Garfinkel, 1967) of the 'appropriate ways' for staff and management at NGO Plus to frame and act out conflict.

The concept of social order refers to a relatively persistent system of linked social structures, social institutions, and social practices which enforce and maintain 'normal' ways of relating and behaving (Garfinkel, 1967). The concept of social order emphasizes that people 'do' social life, and studying social order aims at documenting the mechanisms by which people construct and maintain social entities, thereby deeply implicating them in the production of social order. Social order is therefore not viewed as externally imposed by familiar social forces.

To explore how sensemaking plays a critical role in the way conflict is experienced and acted out, I apply two key analytical concepts: framework and enactment. I apply the analytical concept of framework because, as argued by Weick (1995, p. 108), our ability to understand the content of sensemaking is key when studying the role of agency in organizing. Weick conceptualizes the content of sensemaking as frames of reference or perceptual frameworks that "people 'draw on' to construct roles and interpret objects" (Weick, 1995, p. 109) in response to situations in the organizational environment. Accordingly, people draw upon perceptual frameworks to cue their understandings. Frameworks are pre-existing knowledge derived from past moments of socialization, and cues are the result of present moments of experience (1995). The way that these two settings of experience are connected forms the content of sensemaking. The idea in sensemaking theory that people draw on perceptual frameworks when they make sense of actions and situations is influenced by Goffman's (1974) theory of frame analysis. According to Goffman (1974), frameworks, or frames, constitute a repertoire for interpretation for members of a community, and this repertoire reflects a central element of that particular community's culture. Awareness of a community's repertoire of interpretation provides insight into that particular community's culture.

I, moreover, apply the analytical concept of enactment to emphasize that sensemaking is not only about cognitive processes but has agency at its core: "We make sense through acting", Maitlis and Sonenshein argue (2010, p. 574). The much-used phrase 'enacted sensemaking' shows how sensemaking is equally about action and cognition (Weick, Sutcliffe, & Obstfeld, 2005). With an enacted sensemaking perspective, the focus is on the development of meanings and how such meanings motivate engagements, actions, and practices. Hence sensemaking is not only about interpreting the world, but is equally concerned with creating the world around us by noticing and responding to cues in the environment. Daft and Weick even write, "The interpretation may shape the environment more than the environment shapes the interpretation" (1984, p. 287); it is through their actions and attempts to make sense of these actions that people generate the environment.

Before presenting the analysis of conflict and sensemaking frameworks at NGO Plus, I reflect on my own role as a researcher in the process of doing longitudinal ethnographic fieldwork at NGO Plus.

Ethnographic Fieldwork

I conducted ethnographic fieldwork at NGO Plus over a two-year period from 2008 to 2010. This included on-site participant observations (Bernard, 1994; Waddington, 2004), repeated open-ended qualitative interviews with staff and management (Kvale, 1996), and focus group interviews (Schensul, 1999). Over this two-year period, I gathered the empirical material in three periods of fieldwork, amounting to seven months of full-time fieldwork.

As with any research project, the story of this study begins with the decision to investigate a particular topic. My decision sprang from an interest in how conflict management training affected conflict in organizations: Could staff and management's participation in conflict management training change the ways that they dealt with conflict? And if so, how would these changes affect conflict at work? To answer these questions, the study employed a before-and-after research design which was longitudinally structured. However, throughout the longitudinal fieldwork, my attention was increasingly drawn to understanding the dynamics of conflict and conflict handling in their complexities and was not only focused on investigating training effects.[1]

My desire to understand the dynamics of conflict as they unfold at work was set off by how conflict was addressed in the empirical setting itself. During the early stages of fieldwork, I was told that conflict at NGO Plus was absent. People would praise the sense of community in the organization and emphasize their co-workers' support of each other. Practically everyone I talked to saw their job as a privilege, and it was repeatedly highlighted that working relationships among staff were comfortable and good. Although I did not ask any direct questions about conflict (at this point in the fieldwork), staff members talked about collaboration as being virtually "conflict-free". It was not that steps were taken to avoid conflict in this organization—conflict, I was told, just did not happen. On top of that, I was assured, more than once, that I had chosen the wrong organization as my research site if conflict was my object of study.

This denial of conflict was odd in two respects. First, if conflict was not a way to conceptualize social problems in the organization, why would they be interested in learning conflict management? Second, conflict played an important, albeit implicit role in the organization's mission for a more egalitarian world. NGO Plus works with aid and development in countries that are experiencing oppression, violence, and war. Its main purpose is to promote human rights and democracy by strengthening civil societies and encouraging them to participate in reforming authoritarian governments. Its exclusive deployment of bottom-up approaches reflects the organization's core belief in social change being attained from below. However, history has repeatedly shown that the process of enabling marginalized groups to challenge those in power is rarely accomplished without conflict. Hence the role of 'breathing the fire' constitutes an important implication of the organization's doings because the process of empowering marginalized groups to challenge those in power is often a conflict-ridden process that may worsen a country's instability, for a period at least. Given that conflict profoundly constitutes NGO Plus reason for being in the world, one would expect that an organization like this would deal with internal conflict in exemplary and role modelling ways. However, during formal and informal interviews, conflict within the organization was routinely denied, and many appeared to be ill at ease when I talked to them, as if they were afraid of what I would ask them.

These experiences made me aware that the subject of conflict was very sensitive in this organization. Conflict could even be interpreted as a taboo subject in the sense that its existence was denied and feared in the organization. I therefore had to build trust with staff and management before I could gain access to their knowledge and experiences with conflict at work. To build trust, I focused on the participant observations, which allowed me to engage in the mundane work activities at NGO Plus. Given that such research activities were not considered threatening by people in the organization, this approach took the edge off my role of conflict investigator and helped me establish relationships with staff and management that were based on trustworthiness and reliability. After a while, people in the organization began to talk to me about "problem situations" in the organization (although not calling them conflicts).

Besides helping me to build up trust in the organization, the participant observations revealed conflict as a pervasive aspect of the work that was carried out at NGO Plus, particularly related to how different departments and occupational groups interacted and how the organization's mission of social change was best brought to life. The longitudinal fieldwork and the many days and weeks when I was on site every day of the working week allowed observations which emphasized the everyday character of many conflicts at NGO Plus. However, as I will show in the remainder of this chapter, everyday conflicts and small dramas are as big, powerful, and dramatic as any other.

My ability to gain participants' trust before conducting interviews was crucial because I often used the interviews to get 'inside' people's heads (cf. Harris, 1976) by talking to them about their perspectives, intentions, and emotions involved in conflict interactions that I had either witnessed or heard about during fieldwork. In total, I conducted 56 interviews—that is, 52 individual interviews and four focus group interviews. I conducted the large number of interviews to obtain multiple perspectives on the same conflict situations. From this emerged the intriguing topic of staff and management's meaning making in conflict—not just because different groups in the organization interpreted the same conflicts differently, but because different groups' different sensemaking in the same conflicts appeared to be competing for legitimacy in what those conflicts were about and how they should be addressed and dealt with. In the next section, I present the analysis of how staff and management draw on five different frameworks to explain the emergence and dynamics of conflict interaction at NGO Plus.

Conflict and Sensemaking Frameworks

A number of different organizational rules and values shape the 'appropriate ways' to frame and act out conflict at NGO Plus. Staff and management draw on five different frameworks to explain conflict dynamics at NGO Plus: They explain conflict interaction as rooted in deviant personalities, culture clashes between departments, status inequality between occupational groups, absent leadership, and the external pressure to which NGO Plus is constantly subjected. To illustrate this, I provide an empirical vignette of a common episode of social interaction at NGO Plus, which both staff and management perceive as 'posing problems' by being conflictual. The vignette is constructed from observation notes and interview data.

Vignette

It is in the afternoon and Hilary is tired and her back keeps reminding her that she wants to leave today. She just wants to finish typing in a pile of new memberships into the database before she leaves. Hilary types fast. Her eyes scan computer screens quickly, checking everything but suddenly she is interrupted. Sarah, one of the fundraisers from upstairs, has just turned up in her office: "I need a printout of intake and costs of fundraising activities in the last quarter" she firmly says.

Given that all balance sheets are printed from a financial computer system, to which only staff from the clerical department have access, clerical staff members have to get involved every time someone needs a printout.

Sarah asks Jane, who is Hilary's office mate, to do the print, but Jane declines with a smile, explaining that she is in the middle of reporting the previous year's donations to the tax authorities. And with a deadline later this week, John, the clerical manager, has made this a high-priority task. Sarah then turns to Hilary, "Then you'll have to do it for me".

Hilary feels the frustration in her stomach. Can't she see that she is right in the middle of doing something? She sighs and then responds, "When do you need it for?" Hilary knows that she is going to do the print before she leaves today, whether she wants it or not.

Sarah senses the tension but ignores it and quickly replies, "Right away". Hilary mumbles something about having to leave early for her chiropractor appointment, but then says, without smiling or looking at Sarah, "Okay, I will do it now". But as soon as Sarah exits the office, Hilary bursts out loud, "Arh, why can't she do it herself!"

Jane sighs and shakes her head. "I know! Some people in this organization act as if we exist only to serve them".

In the following section, I use the vignette to demonstrate that staff and management apply one of five different frameworks to explain the emergence and dynamics of conflict interaction at NGO Plus depending on which dynamics they want to emphasize about a particular situation.

The Deviant Personality

Staff and management rarely talk about conflict at NGO Plus, but when they do, they label conflict situations 'frictions'. They commonly blame particular individuals who regularly get involved in frictitious situations because they cannot get along with everyone else in the organization. These individuals are therefore regarded as the black sheep in the organization, and it is the personalities of those black sheep that cause frictions. Accordingly, staff and management often draw on a framework of the deviant personality to explain conflict interaction.

Staff and managers talk about ongoing frictions at NGO Plus that "centre around the same three people and affect the job satisfaction of many others" one manager says. At NGO Plus, collectively shared meanings assert that Sarah, who is one of the fundraisers, is one of these black sheep. Sarah is particularly criticized for the way she communicates with other people in the organization when she needs them to do something for her. This, staff say, feels like she is ordering them to help her: In the empirical vignette, we see that Sarah approaches Jane and Hilary by stating nothing but her acute need and that she practically orders Hilary to help her as she realizes that Jane is busy. Jane explains, "It's particularly the way she always starts a sentence with 'I need' this or 'I need' that. She's really not very pleasant to talk to sometimes and many in here clash with her way of communicating".

Other staff members do not like how she often responds by saying no when they ask for her help: "She just said plain no and when I said that we couldn't move on before she had given her input she just said 'That's really not my problem!'" Helen, a programme worker, says. For these reasons, Sarah is someone with whom many have a strained relationship and many describe how they take a deep breath before approaching Sarah, almost as if they are afraid of her.

John, the clerical manager says, "Frictions in this place are ongoing and difficult to deal with because they often arise from high conflict personalities, like Sarah. Whenever she enters our department, everybody cringe". This explanation originates conflict effectively in Sarah's deviant personality because she virtually sparks conflict with her way of behaving, which clashes with the NGO Plus ethos of appropriate ways to communicate and relate to each other. Because of her rude way of communicating, she gets into conflict and alienates her co-workers. When staff and management explain frictions as arising because of Sarah's deviant personality, they draw on an institutionalized concept of individualism to diagnose frictions. Individualism leads to more blame-laden explanations in frictions and singles out and ascribes faults to certain individuals, such as Sarah, disregarding the systemic dimension of workplace behaviour and freeing others from responsibility.

Culture Clash

Conflict interaction at NGO Plus is also framed as intergroup conflict caused by clashing departmental subcultures. It is particularly the clerical manager and staff who use this framework to explain why they often experience conflict with the fundraisers. This framing of culture clash explains that, given that different staff groups undertake such different tasks, it is imperative that they have different skills and even different personalities. Accordingly, clashes happen because units at NGO Plus develop different, oftentimes divergent, subcultures. Stereotypical attributions and traits ascribed to the clerical workers contend that since their work is repetitive, requires meeting deadlines, and following fixed procedures, clerical workers have to be organized and punctual. By contrast, stereotypical attributions and traits ascribed to the fundraisers maintain that this group has to be good at getting and executing ideas and therefore has to be creative and impulsive. David from the clerical department neatly sums up the two group personalities: "We are the prudes of this organization and they [the fundraisers] are the creative staff".

It is John, the clerical manager who has constructed the framing of conflict as arising from clashing subcultures in an attempt to control and tone down the clerical workers' experience of conflict with the fundraisers. Grounded in the constructions of two divergent group personalities, this framing regards conflict as innate to the different organizational roles that clerical workers and fundraisers need to have: the roles of the organized prudes and the impulsive creatives, respectively. Due to these different roles, John argues, clerical workers and fundraisers see the world differently and sometimes act in opposing ways. In the empirical vignette, we see that while Hilary clearly resents Sarah's disruption of her work, Sarah appears aloof in wanting to wait for her acute wants and needs to be met.

John, moreover, argues that since NGO Plus needs both fundraisers and clerical staff, culture clashes should really be approached as a matter of organizational diversity: "What we are talking about is two different worlds, which both have to be here", John says. By emphasizing the value of the fundraisers being profoundly different from the clerical workers, John tries to exert his power to influence the sensemaking of his staff towards a preferred definition of reality: that the clerical workers' experience of conflict interaction with the fundraisers is really a matter of organizational diversity.

This framing of conflict interaction rationalizes that the fundraisers' behaviour of impulsiveness and 'right-this-minute' need fulfilment occur not because they are bad people but because they are so busy being creative and getting good ideas and therefore do not think about formalities such as procedures and rules outside their own domain. With this framing, John fosters collective indulgence among the clerical workers towards the fundraisers and in effect he manages to reduce conflict intensity. Enactment of organizational diversity in conflict interactions evokes NGO Plus's core ideology of egalitarianism. While egalitarianism founds the organization's vision of a more equal world, it also constitutes a common framework that staff and management actively apply to internal interpretive processes of relational enactments. This is illustrated by the common NGO Plus mantras that "we have a flat organizational structure", "everyone's contribution is equally important for NGO Plus", and "we're all paid the same".

Up to a point at least, the clerical workers buy into the culture clash framing of conflict interaction with the fundraisers. But as we will see in the next section, the clerical workers additionally frame conflict interaction as originating in status inequality between occupational groups.

Status Inequality

Conflict interaction at NGO Plus is also framed as emerging from status inequality between different occupational groups. It is the clerical workers who feel unequal to the academic workers at NGO Plus because they do not feel that this group respects them nor the work that is carried out in the clerical department. According to the clerical workers, there are two ways that status inequality is enacted. The first way has to do with *the way* the academic workers ask for clerical assistance. Alice, a clerical worker says, "I think that if they said it differently like 'Would it be possible to do this for me—I would really appreciate it if you could do it this afternoon', then I would lay down whatever I was doing even if it was urgent, and try to help them". The clerical workers feel that the way many academic workers communicate their needs for clerical assistance often signals a lack of respect for them and their work.

The second way of enacting status inequality is when the academic workers show up in the clerical department and expect to be served *instantaneously*. Jane explains, "Some always comes in and expect to be served right this minute". In the empirical vignette, we see that Sarah's expectation of instantaneous clerical assistance frustrates Hilary because she loses ground to decide what to spend her work time on, and due to Sarah's disruption, she might not even be able to finish her work for the day before she leaves. Compared to other groups at NGO Plus, the clerical workers generally feel that they are not in charge of their own work, which to them goes to show that their work is not as important as other types of work carried out in the organization. This dynamic is extremely frustrating to the clerical workers. Hilary explains, "We sometimes feel that some things they do only to annoy us. I mean, they don't seem to take in that they have to tell us in advance if they want our help. They could show a little more interest in our work".

Both ways of enacting status inequality position the clerical workers with an inferior status at NGO Plus: as a group that serves other groups. June explains, "I feel that some people in this organization take it for granted that we are at their disposal, and I don't think that's okay". The service provider position frustrates the clerical workers because they feel that this kind of work is invisible work that is not really recognized by the academic workers and therefore only takes time away from work activities that 'count'.

Interestingly, the clerical workers are not the only ones who frame conflict interaction as emerging from status inequality at NGO Plus. Joanne, one of the fundraisers, explains, "Generally the clerical department see themselves as the underdogs in this organization; they provide a service function that no one really values. This is a paradox because originally NGO Plus emerged from a very leftist university milieu and works for human rights". This framing of conflict interactions between the clerical workers and the rest of NGO Plus produces a paradox for the organization: It appears to be enmeshed internally in the same sort of conflict that it has been founded to deal with externally. On the one hand, organizational ideals of egalitarianism support the clerical workers' identification with NGO Plus that everyone is equal, but on the other hand, role expectations threaten their position as equal members of the organization, which shows organizational enactments of an invisible system (Gadlin, 1994) of hierarchical difference that contradicts the organization's strong ideology of egalitarianism. This sort of conflict in nonprofit organizations has been termed mission mirroring (Allyn, 2011). Given that egalitarianism at NGO Plus asserts that everyone and everyone's contribution is equal, conflict sensemaking drawing on status inequality is primarily covertly shared among the clerical workers.

Only a few academic workers frame conflict interaction as emerging from status inequality, emphasizing the invisibility of the hierarchical system at NGO Plus.

Absent Leadership

Virtually all staff members at NGO Plus agree that many conflict inter-actions essentially stem from absent leadership. Staff blame many conflict situations on management because it is not sufficiently visible and does not live up to its leadership role. Staff particularly criticize the absence of task coordination between departments and many feel frustrated because, "The departments are not collaborating but doing their separate thing", Frank, a programme worker, says. This absence of interdepartmental task coordina-tion becomes particularly visible when staff members from different depart-ments interact and try to work together:

> *Well, the management in that department is something of a problem. It is her job to coordinate and to make sure that everything works so that her staffs are able to do their job. But she doesn't do that and I feel that's missing when I collaborate with staff from that department.*
>
> (Laura, clerical worker).

Staff identify this lack of interdepartmental coordination as a major trigger of conflict interactions between staff members from different departments. In the empirical vignette, Sarah creates tensions by the way she talks to Hilary and Jane and because she insists on getting the printout right away. Staff members from all departments explained that such tensions originate in the absence of strong leadership at department level, specifically the lack of leaders who lead the staff and take an interest in task coordination across department lines. In interviews, Sarah explains that she has an extremely busy work schedule that involves joggling many different tasks and dead-lines: "A lot of the time my job is really about quickly settling tasks—getting them out of the way before the next ones come in. I know that I often come off as crude", Sarah says. She further explains that management is more focused on the needs of the organization than protecting the work situation of individual staff members: "For several periods of time, I have had to work the equivalent of two to three full-time jobs to make depart-ment ends meet because we really need more staff. Management knows this but they do nothing". Sarah knows that her behavioural style triggers people, but she has to speak very directly about what she needs and get them to do stuff for her if she is going to deliver what management expects of her.

What is interesting here is that the very same conflict interaction which may be constructed as a matter of deviant personalities, culture clash, and status inequality may also be constructed as originating in absent leadership, depending on whose sensemaking we access.

The External Pressure

The fifth framing of conflict interaction at NGO Plus comes solely from management. Management explains conflict interaction as emerging from the pressure that external donors, on which NGO Plus relies for funding, put on NGO Plus. The entering of neo-liberal political ideals in the funding system has established that NGOs have to raise a certain share of funding themselves to get access to funding from donors. Management at NGO Plus emphasizes that this external pressure has meant a significant shift in organizational practices: Doing well in humanitarian aid and development activities is no longer sufficient for the organization's survival; it also has to engage itself in fundraising, marketing, and branding.

Management explains tensions in the organizational social climate by emphasizing the external pressure emerging from changed regulations from donors. The external demands have taken its toll on the organization as it struggles with raising funds, branding, and marketing activities. NGO Plus now has to deliver on multiple fronts, which increases performance targets and creates more work for staff and management. Karen, the programme manager, says:

> Work pressures affect how people feel and create conflict when people are too busy. Basic conditions for us are that we're small, we've no money, and we're under severe pressure from the environment. We therefore want our staff to thrive better with the conditions that are given to us.

The effort to fulfil external demands creates more work for staff and management and produces irritation and stress among staff. These dynamics, management says, are particularly visible in the way people behave and talk to each other at work when they are under pressure.

Management explains the tensions described in the empirical vignette as arising out of the working conditions due to people having too much to do at work. This problem, management says, is evident given that a couple of staff members have been sick with stress during the last couple of years. The fundraising manager, Fran, explains the situation: "We are under severe pressure from the environment and we need tools to be able to cope with and effectively navigate in this pressure cooker of an organization". As illustrated by the quote, management's strategy for improving the working conditions is solely about providing the staff with tools to cope with the current work situation, not to try to change the external pressure. By contrast, the staff do not perceive the external pressure as a problem in itself; they see the struggle to fulfil external demands as tightly linked with the need for greater leadership at NGO Plus. Management's response to staff's continuous demand from leadership is that they—like the rest of the organization—have to deliver on multiple fronts and that the external pressure pushes the managerial practices away from prioritization of leadership of the staff.

In the last section, I discus implications for organizing when understanding everyday conflict through a sensemaking lens, and I reflect on what can be learned by combining a sensemaking approach with an ethnographic fieldwork methodology in the study of conflict.

Implications for Organizing and Reflections

Analyzing the empirical vignette of an episode of conflict interaction, I show that staff and management draw on five competing perceptual frameworks when explaining conflict interactions at NGO Plus. These five different frameworks act as lenses through which staff and management, from different areas of the organization, interpret conflict interaction, construct what it is about, and decide how it should be dealt with. My analysis of the different frameworks for making sense of conflict implies that some conflict sensemaking are more legitimate than others and that some have a greater impact than others. The deviant personality explanation was used widely and legitimately by all staff and management to explain why certain individuals, like Sarah, are difficult to work with. By contrast, the analysis also showed that the construction of conflict as arising out of status inequality between occupational groups appeared to be a marginalized and covertly expressed form of conflict at NGO Plus.

An important source of power, Weick (1995) argues, constitutes the control over which cues serve as the point of reference and get attention. Some individuals with more power may exert their power to influence the sensemaking of organizational members towards a preferred definition of reality. The analysis shows that the clerical manager's construction of conflict as culture clashes does the job of toning down the clerical workers' experience of conflict with the fundraisers. This framing accounts for a very appropriate interpretation of meaning at NGO Plus because it confirms the organization's self-image of being an egalitarian and democratic organization. Outwardly, toleration and avoidance constitute the clerical workers' way of dealing with conflict interactions across departments, and they appear to accept the culture clash framing of conflict interaction. However, underneath the surface of equality and diversity lurks another version of reality, which is about how the clerical workers view conflict interactions as expressions of hidden status inequality between them and the academic workers. Given that this is a very inappropriate sensemaking at NGO Plus, ensuing consequences for the clerical workers are that they continue to stay in a cycle of conflict tolerance and avoidance behaviour, never being able to openly express that they feel like "the underdogs".

While conflict may have indisputable manifestations in clashes and arguments, these are peaks in a process that is, most of the time, enacted in opposing, competing perceptual and verbal representations of what is going on. The other two frameworks competing in shaping the social reality of conflict sensemaking at NGO Plus are the framing of conflict as arising due to absent leadership or the external pressure, which displays that staff and management relate differently to power relations within the organization. While management has the formal power in the organization, it does not have much organizational power in terms of validity in its version of conflict at NGO Plus given that only members of management frame conflict as emerging due to the external pressure. By contrast, staff had sufficient organizational power to criticize management both covertly and overtly at meetings. The staff had taken on a very distinct role of being in opposition to management—the formal power at NGO Plus. They acted very critical of management, often blaming them for a range of problems, including conflict interactions between staff members. Interestingly, the role of being in opposition to those in power is a role that is central to the NGO Plus identity and mission of working for worldwide democracy by aiding marginalized groups to challenge powerful authoritarian governments. Due to the high value placed on this kind of behaviour, the staff's criticisms of management were often tolerated by management, as this only confirmed that the organization's 'flat hierarchical structure' really was flat!

As shown in this chapter (conflict), sensemaking should not be assumed to be a democratic process in which all voices are equally important because it may contain multiple, sometimes conflicting, accounts. I have shown that unequal power relationships among different groups at NGO Plus influence what kind of sense is being made of conflict interaction and its impact on organizational social practices, language, and experiences of which some become meaningful for individuals and groups, while others do not. Mills, Thurlow, and Mills (2010) suggest that the focus with a sensemaking perspective should be on how power and dominant assumptions privilege some identities over others. As we have seen, the importance of being an 'egalitarian organization' is privileged at NGO Plus through language and rules of behaviour that emphasize the characteristics of this identity. The construction of this identity maps out tacit and explicit rules for how staff and management should behave and relate to each other.

A sensemaking perspective allows a focus on the content of meaning and what frameworks people draw upon to construct reality. In the study of conflict, insight into the content of sensemaking is key to understanding why people act and think the way they do in conflict interactions. Insight into the content of meaning is also key to change conflict behaviours: "An important implication of sensemaking is that, to change a group, one must change what is says and what its words mean" (Weick, 1995, p. 108). However, conflict behaviours are not only about sensemaking frameworks; they are also about the cultural and structural context in which those sensemaking frameworks are constructed and enacted. By combining a sensemaking approach with an ethnographic fieldwork methodology, I was able to capture the situated content of talk in relation to local meaning making and explore the actual mechanisms by which the social order of how to address conflict at NGO Plus is accomplished in everyday conflict handling.

In this chapter, I have showed that local interpretations of issues and problems that make up a conflict are part of—and hence must be understood within—the organizational context of social relationships, rules, and values in which the conflict occurs. This study, therefore, contributes to the strand of conflict research that draws attention to meaning making in conflict in relation to how conflict unfolds, highlighting the role that social context and social process play in shaping the form and trajectory of a conflict (Barley, 1991; Bartunek et al., 1992; Kolb & Bartunek, 1992; Gadlin, 1994; Morrill, 1995; Putnam, 2004; Gray, Coleman, & Putnam, 2007).

A majority of conflict research explores conflict as an interpersonal phenomenon and assumes that this level of analysis represents all organizational conflict. Additionally, it works from the established categories of the conflict typologies and is directed towards the mantra of reducing those conflicts that are bad for the organization and stimulating those conflicts that benefit the organization. The analytical approach of combining sensemaking with ethnography to study conflict as an organizational phenomenon affords a particular perspective on conflict: It situates conflict contextually as a social, dynamic phenomenon, emphasizing conflict as embedded in the context of social relationships and the making of meaning that is attached to it rather than universal conflict typologies. By itself, conflict is meaningless; it is given shape and definition only when disputants take action.

As I described in the methodology section, my fieldwork involved difficult and unpredictable situations that forced me to consider how I could deal with the sensitivity surrounding conflict whilst researching it. As I gained access to the conceptual world of staff and management at NGO Plus, I managed to capture the multiplicity of conceptual structures in people's interpretations of conflict, including both overtly and covertly expressed forms of conflict. From my story of how I got access to information about conflict at NGO Plus, however, it becomes clear that I, in the role of a sensemaker, actively generated representations of what reality of conflict is. Such knowledge is a relational product because what goes on in the research context between my world of being the researcher and the worlds of the researched and the way that I organized and made sense of these research experiences shaped my construction of knowledge about conflict.

As I have showed in this chapter, conflict interactions at work are excellent occasions for the study of sensemaking through ethnographic methods. With this approach, however, focus is less on understanding how to reduce the level of conflict in the workplace than it is on understanding the processes through which individuals and organizations enact and make sense of conflict. Nevertheless, in terms of wanting to change, or resolve conflict,

I grant that there is much to learn from work concerned with understanding it. Although I do not provide specific steps for how to change and possibly resolve conflict, I lean towards Bartunek, Kolb, and Lewicki (1992), who argue that the broadening of our understanding of conflict and conflict handling in organizations may help practitioners to act from a more knowledgeable base.

Comment by Barbara Gray

This chapter offers us insight into everyday conflicts at work from the vantage point of participants in those conflicts, in particular, how they make sense of interactions that they label as conflicts. Drawing on ethnographic fieldwork and interviews and Weick's (1995) notion of sensemaking, Mikkelsen identifies five frameworks that members of NGO Plus enact to interpret workplace conflicts. Approaching workplace conflict in this way provides insights that a priori frameworks measuring conflict styles, distributive or integrative frames, or task versus relationship conflict cannot explore. It enables researchers to identify context-specific sensemaking about conflicts and to compare differences among organizational members. Still, as we shall discuss next, many of the sensemaking frameworks she uncovered at NGO Plus, while applicable to the specific setting, also transcend it to capture more generic bases for organizational disputes.

For example, as is typical in most organizations, Mikkelsen's workers explain conflicts as rooted in personalities. This type of attribution commonly masks other more structural bases for disputes by locating the source of the conflict in one or two "bad apples" (Trevino & Youngblood, 1990) instead of in misaligned roles or workloads, insufficient mechanisms for integration (Lawrence & Lorsch, 1967), systemic discrimination (e.g., racism or sexism), or power differences—all of which are more macro-level explanations. However, when organizational members interpret structural sources of conflict as personality problems, this often does generate relationship conflict that can erode performance (Jehn, 1995). Fortunately, Mikkelsen's research methodology also allowed her to discover that NGO Plus workers also attributed conflicts to other more systemic sources such as failed leadership, excessive workloads, and status inequalities. Thus her approach offers a more comprehensive and nuanced explanation for why employees at NGO Plus are at odds with one another than other approaches that single out only one source of conflict.

Mikkelsen's approach is also useful because it reveals that most organizational members (except management) seem to hold at least two or three different interpretations (frameworks) about the conflict. Also, and not surprisingly, she finds that interpretations of these conflicts differ by department and organizational level since these interfaces are the typical ones where conflicts tend to arise (Brown, 1983) and are perpetuated through ongoing network dynamics (Labianca, Brass, & Gray, 1998) if left unattended.

However, I was eager to learn more about how these sensemaking frameworks coexist. For example, are these interpretations compatible or in tension and what encourages employees to draw on one or the other in a given situation? Are they held in dynamic tension and how do organizational members select among them when choosing how to act? For example, fundraising staff perceive their work to be both important and overwhelming, while also holding that the organization's leadership is ineffective. In fact, they interpret their work to be so valuable that it entitles them (in their own minds, at least) to indiscriminately intrude on others' work. Meanwhile, administrative staff believe the funders are interpersonally rude but also that administrative work is demeaned by others. Additionally, the administrative staff are also encouraged by their supervisor to accept the interpretation that fundraising work is demanding and chaotic. It would be useful to know what makes one framework more salient than the other for these workers since their sensemaking implicates their ongoing actions, as I discuss next.

Consistent with Weick's notions of enacted sensemaking, organizational members' behaviour and responses to other members' sensemaking constructs the actions they take towards others. For example, fundraisers' interpretations of their plight appear to justify their interrupting the work of the administrative staff to press their requests for data on them—a clear violation of any norms of civility inspired by the espoused all-pervasive 'egalitarian' norm in this organization. Meanwhile, the administrative staff are caught between one interpretation based on personality conflict and another that the funders are under a lot of pressure to perform—presumably, interpretations would evoke different behavioural responses from the administrative staff. While the first would likely enkindle anger and resentment among the staff, embracing the second interpretation, urged by the administrative staff manager, could evoke more empathy towards the funders and tend to smooth over the conflict and dampen the anger. Teasing out the implications of sensemaking for actions with the organization, then, is an important area for extending this research.

Interestingly, the administrative staff also held a third interpretation: that they are victims of status inequality. The tension between feeling anger towards funders and excusing it because funders are overworked might very well foster this more subversive interpretation. This interpretation is consistent with recent work on both status conflict (Bendersky & Hays, 2012) and social-class differences within organizations (Gray & Kish-Gephart, 2013). Status conflict occurs when there are disputes over organizational members' relative status. A lack of respect is often at the heart of this kind of conflict, which tends to "have longer-term consequences, implicate other members more, and have more distributive outcomes" (Bendersky & Hays, 2012, p. 323).

Adopting a social-class lens goes further to suggest that status within organizations bestows certain entitlements or privileges on those in the higher echelons of organizations usually in contrast to and/or at the expense of those at lower levels. While status differences tend to capture interpersonal perceptions, social-class differences tend to be 'hardwired' into organizations because they are enacted through organizational arrangements, policies, and practices in addition to being enacted by individuals with differential status (i.e., both higher and lower-class members, Gray & Kish-Gephart, 2013). It is interesting that the administrative staff believe they have little discretion over their work. Through a social-class lens, lower-status members are rendered invisible, others are permitted to intrude on their space, and the needs of elites are elevated over the needs of others (Gray & Kish-Gephart, 2013). Enactment of social-class differences may also help explain Allyn's (2011) observations about mission mirroring in not-for-profit organizations, which Mikkelsen suggested may also be present at NGO Plus. This possibility deserves greater explication since it emphasizes the pervasive impact of social-class differences in organizations, even in those whose explicit mission is to eradicate inequality and oppression in the world. In my own work with an NGO riddled with conflict, we observed numerous oppressive dynamics, including racism and sexism within the organization, but these were roundly dismissed when we pointed them out in our feedback. Here psychodynamic studies of organizations can be of some use to help account for this dismissal. Like individuals, organizations can engage in repression and projection (Gray & Schruijer, 2010) attributing to others what is too reprehensible to acknowledge in their own behaviour. Psychodynamic studies help to explain why this occurs and the implications for individuals and organizations of disowning our own dark sides: namely, sensemaking that perpetuates status inequalities within organizations.

While status conflicts have been studied using conventional questionnaire methods, exploring social-class differences and psychodynamics may require more critical approaches such as critical discourse analysis (CDA) (Fairclough, 1995; Wodak & Meyer, 2009). CDA affords the possibility of "de-mystifying ideologies and power through the systematic and retroductable investigation of semiotic data (written, spoken or visual)" (Wodak & Meyer, 2009, p. 3). Coupling CDA with sensemaking approaches when such semiotic data are available may enable researchers to gain an even richer understanding of the dynamics of sensemaking about everyday conflict at work.

In summary, Mikkelsen's research has extolled the virtues of a sensemaking perspective for unlocking the frameworks that organizational members employ to enact their social-class positions within organizations and helps to explain the consequences of differences in members' sensemaking. Her work raises still unexplored questions about the consequences of competing interpretations for the ongoing enactment of conflicts and only hints at the role of structural power in shaping interpretation. To more deeply understand these issues, it will be useful to couple a sensemaking analysis with more critical theories and methodologies that enable deeper exploration of factors that may shape organizational members' sensemaking and explicate why it may result in persistent and, frequently, intractable conflicts.

Note

1. The findings of how conflict management training works have been reported elsewhere.

Discussant and Chapter References

Allyn, D. (2011). Mission Mirroring: Understanding Conflict in Nonprofit Organizations. *Nonprofit and Voluntary Sector Quarterly*, 40 (4), 762–769.

Barley, S. R. (1991). Contextualising conflict: Notes on the anthropology of disputes and negotiations. In R. J. Lewicki, B. H. Sheppard, & R. Bies (Eds.), *Research on Negotiation in Organizations: Handbook of Negotiation Research, Vol. 3*. US, Greenwich, CT: JAI Press Inc, 165–199.

Bartunek, J. M., Kolb, D. M., & Lewicki, R. J. (1992). Bringing conflict out from behind the scenes: Private, informal, and nonrational dimensions of conflict in organizations. In D. M. Kolb, & J. M. Bartunek (Eds.), *Hidden Conflict in Organizations: Uncovering Behind-the-Scenes Disputes*. US, Newbury Park, CA: Sage, 209–228.

Bendersky, C., & Hayes, N. (2012). Status Conflict in Groups. *Organization Science*, 23 (2), 323–340.

Bernard, R. H. (1994). *Research Methods in Anthropology*. UK, Oxford: AltaMira Press.

Brown, L. D. (1983). *Managing Conflict at Organizational Interfaces*. Reading, MA: Addison-Wesley.

Brown, A. D. (2005). Making sense of the collapse of Barings bank. *Human Relations*, 58 (12), 1579–1605.

Daft, R. L., & Weick, K. E. (1984). Toward a Model of Organizations as Interpretation Systems. *Academy of Management Review*, 9 (2), 284–295.

Deutsch, M. (1949). A Theory of Cooperation and Competition. *Human Relations*, 2, 129–151.

Deutsch, M. (1973). *The Resolution of Conflict: Constructive and Destructive Processes*. New Haven, CT: Yale University Press.

De Dreu, C. K. W. (1997). Productive conflict: The importance of conflict management and conflict issues. In C. K. W. De Dreu, & E. Van de Vliert (Eds.), *Using Conflict in Organizations*. London: Sage, 9–22.

De Dreu, C. K. W., & Beersma, B. (2005). Conflict in Organizations: Beyond Effectiveness and Performance. *European Journal of Work and Organizational Psychology*, 14 (2), 105–117.

Drazin, R., Glynn, M. A., & Kazanjian, R. K. (1999). Multilevel Theorizing about Creativity in Organizations: A Sensemaking Perspective. *Academy of Management Review*, 24 (2), 286–307.

Fairclough, N. (1995). *Critical Discourse Analysis*. London: Longman.

Fink, C. F. (1968). Some Conceptual Difficulties in the Theory of Social Conflict. *Journal of Conflict Resolution*, 12 (4), 412–460.

Gadlin, H. (1994). Conflict Resolution, Cultural Differences, and the Culture of Racism. *Negotiation Journal*, 10 (1), 33–47.

Garfinkel, H. (1967). *Studies in Ethnomethodology*. Evanston: Northwestern University Press.

Gephart, R. P. (1993). The textual approach: Risk and blame in disaster sensemaking. *Academy of Management Journal*, 36 (6), 1465–1514.

Gioia, D. A., & Chittipeddi, K. (1991). Sensemaking and Sensegiving in Strategic Change Initiation. *Strategic Management Journal*, 12, 433–448.

Goffman, E. (1974). *Frame Analysis: An Essay on the Organization of Experience.* New York: Harper & Row.

Gray, B., Coleman, P. T., & Putnam, L. L. (2007). Introduction: Intractable Conflict: New Perspectives on the Causes and Conditions for Change. *American Behavioral Scientist*, 50 (11), 1415–1429.

Gray, B., & Kish-Gephart, J. (2013). Encountering Social Class Differences at Work: How "Class Work" Perpetuates Inequality. *Academy of Management Review*, 38, 670–699.

Gray, B., & Schruijer, S. (2010). Integrating multiple voices: Working with collusion in multiparty collaborations. In C. Staeyert & B. Van Loy (Eds.), *Relational Practices: Participative Organizing.* Bingley, UK: Emerald, 121–135.

Gubrium, J. F., & Holstein, J. A. (2009). *Analyzing Narrative Reality.* Thousand Oaks, CA: Sage.

Hansen, H. (2006). The Ethnonarrative Approach. *Human Relations*, 59 (8), 1049–1075.

Harris, M. (1976). History and Significance of the Emic/Etic Distinction. *Annual Review of Anthropology*, 5, 329–350.

Jehn, K. A. (1995). A Multimethod Examination of the Benefits and Detriments of Intragroup Conflict. *Administrative Science Quarterly*, 40 (2), 256–282.

Kolb, D. M. (2008). Making sense of an elusive phenomenon. In C. K. W. De Dreu, & M. J. Gelfand (Eds.), *The Psychology of Conflict and Conflict Management in Organizations.* New York: Lawrence Erlbaum Associates, 425–433.

Kolb, D. M., & Bartunek, J. M. (1992). *Hidden Conflict in Organizations: Uncovering Behind-the-Scenes Disputes.* US, Newbury Park, CA: Sage.

Kolb, D. M., & Putnam, L. L. (1992). The Multiple Faces of Conflict in Organizations. *Journal of Organizational Behavior*, 13 (3), 311–324.

Kusztal, I. L. (2002). Discourses in the Use and Emergence of Organizational Conflict. *Conflict Resolution Quarterly*, 20 (2), 231–247.

Kvale, S. (1996). *Interviews: An Introduction to Qualitative Research Interviewing.* Thousand Oaks, CA: Sage Publications Ltd.

Labianca, G., Brass, D., & Gray, B. (1998). Social Networks and Perceptions of Intergroup Conflict: The Role of Negative Relationships and Third Parties. *Academy of Management Journal*, 41 (1), 55–67.

Lawrence, P., & Lorsch, J. (1967). "Differentiation and Integration in Complex Organizations." *Administrative Science Quarterly*, 12 (1), 1–47.

Lewicki, R. J., & Gray, B. (2003). Introduction. In R. J. Lewicki, B. Gray, & M. Elliott (Eds.), *Making Sense of Intractable Environmental Conflicts.* US, Washington, DC: Islands Press, 1–10.

Mack, R. W., & Snyder, R. C. (1957). The analysis of social conflict—toward an overview and synthesis. *Conflict Resolution*, 1 (2), 212–248.

Maitlis, S. (2005). The Social Processes of Organizational Sensemaking. *The Academy of Management Journal*, 48 (1), 21–49.

Maitlis, S., & Sonenshein, S. (2010). Sensemaking in Crisis and Change: Inspiration and Insights from Weick. *Journal of Management Studies*, 47 (3), 551–580.

March, J. G., & Simon, H. A. (1958). *Organizations.* London: Wiley.

Mills, J. H., Thurlow, A., & Mills, A. J. (2010). Making Sense of Sensemaking: The Critical Sensemaking Approach. *Qualitative Research in Organizations and Management: An International Journal*, 5 (2), 182–195.

Morrill, C. (1989). The Management of Managers: Disputing in an Executive Hierarchy. *Sociological Forum*, 4 (3), 387–407.

Morrill, C. (1995). *The executive way: Conflict management in corporations.* University of Chicago Press.

Patriotta, G. (2003). Sensemaking on the Shop Floor: Narratives of Knowledge in Organizations. *Journal of Management Studies*, 40 (2), 349–375.

Putnam, L. L. (2004). Dialectical Tensions and Rhetorical Tropes in Negotiations. *Organization Studies*, 25 (1), 35–53.

Putnam, L. L., & Wilson, C. (1982). Communicative strategies in organizational conflict: Reliability and validity of a measurement scale. In M. Burgoon (Ed.), *Communication Yearbook 6.* Newbury Park, CA: Sage, 629–652.

Rahim, M. A. (1983). A Measure of Styles of Handling Interpersonal Conflict. *Academy of Management Journal*, 26 (2), 368–376.

Schensul, J. J. (1999). Focused group interviews. In J. J. Schensul, H. M. D. LeCompte, B. B. K. Nastasi, & S. P. Borgatti (Eds.), *Enhanced Ethnographic Methods: Audiovisual Techniques, Focused Group Interviews, and Elicitation Techniques.* London: Altamira Press, 51–114.

Trevino, L. K., & Youngblood, S. A. (1990). Bad Apples in Bad Barrels: A Causal Analysis of Ethical Decision Making Behaviour. *Journal of Applied Psychology*, 75 (4), 378–385.

Van Maanen, J. (1992). Drinking our troubles away: Managing conflict in a British police agency. In D. M. Kolb, & J. M. Bartunek (Eds.), *Hidden Conflict in Organizations: Uncovering Behind-the-Scenes Disputes.* Newbury Park, CA: Sage, 32–62.

Waddington, D. (2004). Participant observation. In C. Cassel & G. Symon (Eds.), *Essential Guide to Qualitative Methods in Organizational Research.* London: Sage, 154–164.

Weick, K. E. (1988). Enacted Sensemaking in Crisis Situations. *Journal of Management Studies*, 25 (4), 305–317.

Weick, K. E. (1990). The Vulnerable System: An Analysis of the Tenerife Air Disaster. *Journal of Management*, 16 (3), 571–593.

Weick, K. E. (1993). The Collapse of Sensemaking in Organizations: The Mann Gulch Disaster. *Administrative Science Quarterly*, 38, 628–652.

Weick, K. E. (1995). *Sensemaking in Organizations.* London: Sage Publications.

Weick, K. E. (2010). Reflections on Enacted Sensemaking in the Bhopal Disaster. *Journal of Management Studies*, 47 (3), 537–550.

Weick, K. E., Sutcliffe, K. M., & Obstfeld, D. (2005). Organizing and the Process of Sensemaking. *Organization Science*, 16 (4), 409–421.

Wodak, R., & Meyer, M. (2009). *Methods of Critical Discourse Analysis, 2nd ed.* London: Sage.

3 Doing Strategy

A Performative Organizational Ethnography

Marie Mathiesen and discussant Chahrazad Abdallah

Organizational Phenomena and Setting

This ethnographic study is about strategy. Strategy barely needs an introduction—if you have worked in any setting, public or private, chances are that you have encountered and even worked with strategy. The concept of strategy has a prominent position in most organizations, and therefore if we want to know more about what organizations are like and how they become, strategy can be a very good place to look.

Having a strategy is to have a shared direction and a common clear vision for what needs to happen—and most modern organizations desire this kind of clarity. Strategy is a way to think collectively about where an organization is going, and (ideally) having a strategy formulated should make it easier for all organizational actors to make decisions, as they can look to the strategy for guidance on the decisions they need to make.

The definitions of strategy abound to a degree that makes it tempting to ask whether there is anything that *isn't* strategy. This chapter is not committed to a specific definition of strategy because the object of study for this ethnographic project is *strategy work*, which is defined as "that which people in organizations do when they say that they are doing strategy" (Mathiesen, 2013). Defining strategy work in this way is a deliberate choice of not focusing on finding a finite answer to the question of what strategy *is* but rather focusing on what happens when people engage in the topic and work with strategy. It is not the thing itself that is interesting; the focus of attention is on how people talk about it, make it happen, relate to and through it—the practices of strategy.

Perhaps strategy has won such prominence in recent years because we increasingly demand meaning and purpose from our work and from the organizations we belong to. And strategy is one way of scripting that purpose. In that sense, organizational strategy faces the paradox that it needs to set one clear unified direction while at the same time be able to accommodate our individually formulated meaning creation and identity work.

Strategy rolls out over organizations in cascades. In private corporations, it follows a fairly predictable path. There is usually one overarching strategy: the corporate strategy. And then each division has a strategy and below that each department also has a strategy, and below that each team can also have a strategy. This waterfall of strategy often has a certain logic where the first flow, the corporate strategy, is very high level and often accused of being 'fluffy', and then the formulation becomes increasingly specific as the strategy cascade pours downwards.

In this case, the strategy work under investigation covers the formulation of a departmental strategy in a multinational biotech company. The company is here called Bioforte, and at the time of the fieldwork, the company had around 2,500 employees globally. The department where the fieldwork takes place is here called the "Stakeholder Engagement Department". This department encompasses human resources (HR), communications, corporate social responsibility, and a process improvement team focused on implementing lean principles throughout the organization. In addition, Stakeholder Engagement also includes a HR service centre and facilities operations, which consist of the kitchen staff running the lunch canteen, as well as the groundskeepers and the mail staff at Bioforte.

Analytical Approach

Doing ethnography is all about working from your own experience in the field. Therefore when researchers work ethnographically, they are working through their own experience and through their own beliefs in a way such that the underlying epistemological stance of the researcher will necessarily inform the ethnographic approach. We cannot stand outside our experience. Because none of us are ever objective, it is crucial that the researcher is both aware of his or her own stance and willing to share where he or she came from. In my case, the philosophy behind the ethnographic work is a performativity-inspired and practice-oriented way of perceiving the world. From this point of departure, organizations are considered to be 'performed constructs' that are continually re-performed and re-negotiated through the words and actions of organizational actors.

The notion of performativity is used to describe the interplay between what we do (and say) and the reality we live in. Performativity was first explored as a linguistic concept and is most often attributed to the linguistic philosopher J. L. Austin and his concept of speech acts (Silverman & Torode, 2011 (1980)). Austin worked on developing a philosophy of ordinary language and argued for conceptualizing utterances, or speech, as action. His perhaps most well-known text is *How to Do Things with Words* (Austin, 1962). As can be deduced from the title, the main premise of performativity is that words and their performance 'do things'—they have effects. In a performative world view, our words, actions, and silences become constitutive of our reality.

The philosopher Judith Butler adopted performativity as a key element of her argument that gender is a cultural construct: "There is no gender identity behind the expressions of gender; that identity is performatively constituted by the very 'expressions' that are said to be its results" (Butler, 2006, p. 33). By way of Butler, performativity moved into feminist and queer theory and then onwards to become practically a mainstream social science concept (Callon, 2006; MacKenzie, 2006; Spicer, Alvesson, & Kärreman, 2009).

Performativty and practice theory are intertwined by the basic premise that we shape our reality through actions (practices). Andreas Reckwitz's discussion of Judith Butler's work terms her performative gender studies 'praxeological' because Butler is preoccupied with how doing gender is a social practice and with how the doing of gender at the same time is a way of reinforcing or altering that same practice (Reckwitz, 2002). In this sense, the most basic assumption of practice theoretical approaches, namely that concrete individual practices both make up, and are shaped by, social practice, *is* performative.

Straightforward cause and effect relationships are unsettled by performativity. Butler describes how across disciplines, performativity offers an "alternative to causal frameworks"; whereby she implies a rejection of realist or positivist ontology (Butler, 2010, p. 147). As a philosophical concept, performativity offers another causal relationship that is oriented towards both an effect→cause *and* a cause→effect mode of reasoning. In the case of strategy, a performative position questions the position that a strategy represents an already given reality. And instead argues the point that strategy as a concept only comes into existence through the doing of strategy. In the same vein, Michel Callon argues that a main benefit of performativity as a concept is the displacement of the "representational idiom" (Callon, 2006, p. 15); that is, the idea that science is supposed to represent reality. Callon also emphasizes that the performative power of a statement is not confined to the statement itself. The actions and the materiality surrounding that statement are also part of the constitutive effects (Callon, 2006).

The hopeful possibilities in peformativity enter because, although subjects are produced by their context, each doing or iteration will always be different, which means that each act, or word, contains the *inevitable possibility of difference*. It is in the repetition that possibilities (for resistance or affirmation) enter. This position also emerges in Michel de Certeau's work where he conceptualizes practices as performative—or, as he says, *sites of production* (de Certeau, 1984).

A common critique of performativity is the self-fulfilling prophecy argument, which states that through performativity language is granted too much power and that real political struggle is ignored in a cerebral linguistic philosophical discussion. Butler's response to this line of critique reiterates Austin's distinction between illocutionary and perlocutionary performatives:

> *The first characterize speech acts that bring about certain realities, as when judgments are pronounced by a court or federal increase rate changes are announced by the Federal Reserve chair in the US. The*

second characterizes those utterances from which effects follow only when certain other kinds of conditions are in place.

(Butler, 2010, p. 147)

The point of maintaining this distinction is to argue that actions are always situated in a specific time and place, and, depending on the context, they may work or they may fail. Performativity is not about ignoring the constraints and struggles of reality, but it is concerned with how those constraints and struggles were produced. With another parallel to practice theory, one could say that practices are not only producing reality, they are also produced by reality.

Martha B. Calás and Linda Smircich argue that the point of performativity is to view context as enabling and restraining specific actions:

Performativity is not a social constructivist or ethnomethodological account of what gender is or may be. Butler's ultimate concern is not how gender is "done" but examining the conditions of possibility for, and the consequences of such "doings" within norms that delimit acceptable and unacceptable expressions of gender.

(Calás & Smircich, 2008, p. 360)

This quote focuses on the *conditions of possibility* and the *consequences* as the real objects of importance in analysis. In this sense, performativity moves beyond self-fulfilling prophecy—it is a matter of interplay between context/structure/social practice and individual action and practice.

In the strategic management literature, the critical management–inspired strain of strategy scholars build their arguments on the premise that strategy is performative—that strategy creates the very problems it purports to solve (Knights & Morgan, 1991). This position contrasts to more traditional strategic management conceptions of strategy. Henry Mintzberg, who is one of the grand ol' men of strategy scholarship, dismisses performativity (although he calls it enactment) (Mintzberg, 1994). Rather than understanding performativity (or enactment) as a condition that conveys how our present reality is always both enabled and limited by a specific context, Mintzberg discusses it as the naïve idea that things will be 'as I say'. This is a simplified reading of performativity that relegates the concept to mean a self-fulfilling prophecy, and by adopting that view, Mintzberg joins the common and also, as I hope the previous section demonstrated, misguided critique of performativity.

The key question, however, is not so much whether Mintzberg has misunderstood enactment/performativity, but rather what happens if you do not care about investigating the conditions of the possibility for, and consequences of, strategy. The answer to this becomes that the engagement with strategy is thus 'un-critical' in that it is uninterested in examining the normative aspects of the concept.

Working ethnographically from a performativity and practice-oriented point of departure presents a whole host of challenges because instead of a 'solid' object to study, the ethnographer focuses on practices, which are shifty, ephemeral, temporary, contradictory, individual, collective, contradictory, enigmatic, specific, and more. As an ethnographic researcher working in this way, you are denied a stable external property to observe and analyze; instead, you study something that comes into being through doing. And then it disappears again. In other words, studying practices means that there is no stable external property to pin down; rather, all we have is something that comes into being through doing. And that something then shapes and directs that same doing. From this point of view, strategy is always an ongoing accomplishment that is likely to slip away at any moment.

In the context of an ethnographic study of strategy work, Michel de Certeau's *The Practice of Everyday Life* can be an inspirational guide. The book is a loose and fabulating treatise dedicated to 'the ordinary man'. The main argument, grossly simplified, is that everyday practices such as reading, walking, and cooking are sites of production and should therefore be analyzed as such (de Certeau, 1984). Social activity—culture and meaning—happens *in and through* everyday life, which is why a theory of practice is necessary. This shifts the analytical focus away from individuals, and also away from structures, to practices: de Certeau states that his goal is to enable a discussion of practices and that this goal will be achieved if, "everyday practices 'ways of operating' or doing things, no longer appear as merely the obscure background of social activity, and if a body of theoretical questions, methods, categories, and perspectives, by penetrating this obscurity, make it possible to articulate them" (1984, p. xi). De Certeau places his own approach as an extension of ethnomethodology and also points out that the anthropological studies he builds on have been conducted 'away from home', while his explicit ambition is to study the everyday life that is around him. This chapter embodies a similar ambition in the study of the organizational strategy work that I participated in at Bioforte.

The Role of the Researcher

As is often the case with ethnographic work, serendipity did have a role to play in strategy becoming the main focus of this study. Originally I was interested in the concept of corporate social responsibility and that topic was also my entry to Bioforte. However, once I began discussions with the company and started to hear about what they had going on, it became obvious that the strategy process was more exciting to follow and more timely as it coincided with the period I was available to do fieldwork. Given that ethnography is the study of stuff as it happens, I speculate that this kind of evolution of topic is quite common. You can never know exactly what will happen when and what process or project will turn out to be the most interesting to study or simply accessible to you, so you need to have some flexibility and be open towards shifting your focus as the field beckons.

Prior to being an academic researcher, I worked as a consultant within the field of strategy. This previous work experience as a consultant, and to some extent, I suspect, my identity as a researcher from a university, was the entry ticket that granted me access. I was allowed to be a part of the strategy process and to use the process as empirical material.

This agreement meant that on the one hand I was expected to make myself useful by acting as a sort of consultant and on the other hand I was at Bioforte to observe and gather field material. This dual position is inherent to the participant observer role, but that does not mean that it does not present a set of challenges (Moeran, 2009). In my case, I navigated the tensions between my role as the pragmatic strategy practitioner and the critical strategy scholar. I had both of those roles in my fieldwork, and at times, the first would be censored by the second. In order to not be completely paralyzed, I developed some strategies for navigating this. First of all, I made an agreement with the head of the Stakeholder Engagement department that I would not lead the strategy work. Instead, I would be a resource to the team and support them—in concrete terms this meant, for example, conducting interviews and feeding the inputs back to the working team and designing meetings based on input from the teams. The tensions that I experienced are widely described in the ethnographic field when the concept of 'participant observer' is discussed, and I do believe it is a condition of doing ethnography; however, in practice, it can be very difficult because as a person you are always *in* a situation at the same time as you are analyzing that same situation, including your own participation in a given situation (Watson, 2011, p. 206). You could argue that as cognizant humans, this is a fact of life—it may even be the distinguishing feature of humans: We do things and think about the things we do, plus we are then able to discuss this doing and thinking with others. Still, this double layer of constantly participating and observing is in practice both what makes ethnography possible and what makes it hard.

An additional occupational hazard of the participant observer role is that the ethnographer often ends up in the middle of things and that can be difficult: You might be told secrets and be expected to keep them; you might overhear, or otherwise come into possession of sensitive information and thus be obliged to treat such information sensibly. Navigating these kinds of situations successfully requires an ethical compass and a sound sense of judgment, just like in life.

The Identity Work of Strategy Work

In the modern Western society that Bioforte inhabits, work has become intimately related to personal identity. We demand meaning, purpose, and fulfilment from work. In this aspect of our work lives, strategy takes on a special role because strategy has not only permeated all layers of organizations but also become a privileged site of making meaning.

There is a sense that strategy provides spiritual nourishment in organizational life. With strategy we can talk about dreams and hopes. It is about mission and vision and about articulating how the work makes sense. This kind of articulation is invariably wound up with our personal sense of self and meaning. Strategy is a discussion about who we truly are and who we want to become. Strategy becomes the answer when we ask: How are we to find meaning in our organizational lives?

In this way, strategy work also organizes the selves of those working with strategy.

The following is an excerpt from an interview with one of the members of the strategy working group and myself:[1]

Marie asks Monika if it's important to be part of making strategy.

MONIKA LAUGHS A BIT AND EXPLAINS: There's a perception that it is. You notice that your colleagues look at you a bit, perhaps interested or with a tilt. I'm not sure what it is. They notice that you're part of some strategy work. That then means you're somehow at a certain level. Where things happen. Then you're part of deciding the future, right? I think that's how people think.

MARIE: Yeah and their future too.

MONIKA: Yes and then it creates a sense of insecurity also actually, and that's probably why one gets a second look. But what, are we doing something . . . [uuuUU sucks air in between her teeth] What about my competences? [uuuUU sucks air in between her teeth] Are they sufficient in the new? And that kind of thing, right? I mean, those are the kind of things that play into it. And to that I would say that I've been lucky to often be involved in those processes and not because I especially have signed up for it, but probably because I've shown somehow that I think it would be really fun. Although I didn't do that in this case, because I've been so incredibly busy, but earlier, right.

Working on strategy is to be "where things happen" and Monika's first response to Marie's question is to laugh. In this laughter is a signal that there is something between the lines with this business of making strategy. There are some kinds of assumptions that are not easily made explicit. In this realm, it will not do to state reasons and facts; rather, Monika describes how people look at her and what this look might mean.

Monika's use of the words 'lucky' and 'fun' conveys a sense that strategy work is special. On the outside of strategy work, there can be insecurity about how what you have to offer will fit into the future that is created and shaped through the strategy work. In this sense, making strategy is also a way to work yourself, and what you have to offer, into the organization going forward, to make sure that what you bring will be valued and needed. There is no doubt that it is better to be making strategy than to be on the receiving end of a strategy that others have made.

When strategy emerges as a story about why work matters, it also becomes a vehicle to find personal fulfilment through work and in that sense, to connect the work to the private sphere. Strategy becomes important in the organization as influential and powerful, but it also becomes important to the identity of people in the organization—we make strategy, therefore I am. The strategy work structures (organizes) the individual in the sense that making strategy turns you into a person who makes strategy. Doing strategy shapes and influences who you are.

The following field note and interview section describes how Marie interviewed the communications manager, Elizabeth, about her decision to take part in the strategy work while on maternity leave. She would bring her baby, Eric, into the office so that she could participate in key meetings.

To accommodate Elizabeth's life as a new mom, Marie drives from Bioforte to Elizabeth's house to interview her there. She lives in an affluent suburb of Copenhagen. There's a brand new SUV in the driveway. From the open kitchen, Marie hears the slight hum of a dishwasher. There's a large glass wall out to the secluded garden. Elizabeth and her husband bought the house from a couple of architects who thoughtfully renovated the place. Marie arranges herself and her belly[2] in a comfortable position on Elizabeth's cream-colored couch. There's no coffee table, so Marie holds the tape recorder in her lap; she's a bit worried that it will pick up the noise from the dishwasher. Eric is awake and lying on a blanket by the window.

MARIE: Does it mean something to be someone who makes strategy? I mean, if John had not invited you to be part of it?

ELIZABETH: I would've been really sad then.

MARIE: Why?

ELIZABETH: For several reasons, I mean because we have, both when we were put together under John in this Stakeholder Engagement Department and before, John and I have worked very closely together. Before, John and I and communication and HR, if you will, had some joint assignments. So I had discovered that it makes a lot of sense; so to not be included, I would think was 100 steps backwards. And from a professional standpoint as a communications person, I don't think that it would make sense to not include communications. Personally, since I'm passionate about it and think it's important, and I want to make it happen. It isn't because I can't operate according to strategies defined by others. We do that with the corporate strategy and that I'm not part of making, but it's definitely a piece of work that I like a lot, think is crucial and which I also think I can contribute to and at the same time learn from.

That's also the reason I'm not just on maternity leave.

MARIE: Well, yes.

ELIZABETH: It's a very obvious sign that I'd like to be part of it. I could just have said, and I had the full freedom to say, I'll step in and see where you are in January after my leave.

MARIE: Does it work? To roll the pram into the boss's office?

ELIZABETH: It's pretty amazing. Pretty amazing. The openness and acceptance that's there. And maybe it wouldn't have been this way if we hadn't had good collaboration up until this point. I mean, first of all, John is very informal in this way, which I think is fantastic. I mean, he's pretty, without bringing the pram into the picture, he's pretty untraditional in his methods and approaches at times, which I appreciate a lot. I think it's nice when people aren't, I mean, when someone once in a while does things a little differently than is normally done. But also from my colleagues, it's amazing how they just accept the pram and me. I think that's great.

MARIE: How do you get it to work?

ELIZABETH: Well, I'm at work, if you want to call it that, to the extent that I feel like it, also here at home and in between, because I think about it. I reflect. I did that before too. I mean, it's perhaps the way I work. For example, now there's this new book *When the Business Communicates*, which I showed you. As soon as I see that in the newspaper, I think that I'd like to read that, because I know the author a bit, and I know what he represents. So I read that because I want to while I'm at home on maternity leave. It isn't because anyone has said to me that I need to do this, or anything like that, but I just want to. I found some ideas and have taken some notes for when we go more operational on our strategy within communications. I've taken notes for ideas, tips and tricks, some of it we can use and some of it we can't because we're past that stage, but I do it to the extent that I think it's fun and that I feel like it. I mean, it isn't something that I feel obliged to do. I mean, I feel that, and this is also thanks to my colleagues and John, that if I didn't feel like it and if I said, I just can't manage to participate because I didn't sleep all night or he's been screaming or something, well, then I'd feel that that was fully acceptable.

MARIE: But you'd lose something else?

ELIZABETH: I'd lose something else, right?! I mean, I do it because I think it's super interesting, and I can feel that it gives me something. It also gives me more energy to be on maternity leave. I don't necessarily get more energy from, as people tell you, lying on the couch. I'm not very good at that. I can get more energy from, even if I can be tired because I've been running around with him on my arm a whole day at Bioforte, then mentally it's like an energy injection to be part of the work.

MARIE: Did John ask you?

ELIZABETH: We talked, I mean, we've talked about the strategy process, and we've talked about how actually we should do it later when I'll be back, but then the opportunity came, among other things with you and you have a natural deadline too, and on top of that, it probably made sense to get started already now. So John said that we started now, and then he asked me to think about what I thought. And then I said, well, I'd like to join, and then John said, "You should only do it if you feel like it. I mean, there are no requirements from this end and you have the full right to hold your maternity leave and I understand". For my part I feel that there's been full understanding for both things. John does know me well enough by now that he knows that I'm not that good at staying at home and being on leave, but the fact that there's an openness and acceptance towards the pram and bringing the baby to work and openness and acceptance towards if, I mean it hasn't been necessary yet, but if one day, I need to say, today he's so whiney, so I'm not coming today. Then I'm also sure that would be accepted fully.

Strategy work *allows* a narrative about personal fulfilment, growth, and meaning to be constructed around work. And at the same time, it *requires* this kind of narrative as well: Strategy demands that you find meaning in your work. As a consequence of this dually benevolent and demanding characteristic of strategy, it becomes framed as an essential task that only you can do. Elizabeth clearly does find personal fulfilment in the strategy work. Probably also in other kinds of work, but it is not random that she chooses to go through the extra effort to be part of strategy work during her maternity leave. It is because it is more important than other kinds of work to her. Strategy gives people in organizations a way to inscribe themselves into the work. It is about shaping the mission and vision of the work, which connect to deeply personal beliefs of how and why things matter. Therefore, strategy is not just a task that you can let others handle because that would mean handing over the power over your own future to someone else. Strategy is about how it all makes sense and what story we tell about ourselves at work; letting someone else tell your story is not very appealing. Likewise, you cannot refuse to tell the story, as that merely means that some other story, over which you have no control, will be told.

Elizabeth also expresses that her colleagues and her boss at Bioforte accept her both as a co-worker and as a new mother. They accept the premises that come with being the mother of an infant and still wanting to go to work sometimes: Elizabeth brings Eric and the pram with her; she needs to step out of meetings sometimes to comfort and feed her baby; she cannot make ironclad promises about when she will be there. The circumstances of her work and private life shape her as a specific kind of strategy maker: The ambitious working mom who balances her obligations and makes it all work.

Reflections

This study turns the attention to the other kinds of work that are also happening when people do strategy work. One could call this a preoccupation with the second-order consequences. For example, as in the fieldwork excerpts presented here, identity work happens through strategy work.

Working with a performative lens means that instead of asking what strategy is, I ask, "What does strategy do?" This is a rebellious way to study strategy because the vast majority of studies of strategy that are in the traditional strategic management tradition are nonreflexive. Few studies of strategy are ethnographic, even fewer use performativity in their theoretical discussions of strategy—the irony is that practitioners, in my experience, are very aware of the performative nature of their work and navigate the tensions that come with that on a daily basis. And given that strategy in organizations is often an attempt at shaping the future by setting forth a collective intention, you could argue that strategy and performativity are actually made for each other—the performative preoccupation with the conditions and consequences of a given act link up extraordinarily well with strategy work.

Hopefully this study with the performativity-inspired and practice-oriented ethnographic lens contributes with an organizational study that demonstrates how our lives in organizations are lived and shaped through the strategy work that we do. In that sense, strategy can never be an innocent bystander but is rather a central player in our modern organizational lives.

In order for an ethnographic study to do anything, it has to work, and while it is not up to me to decide if it works, I would like to propose the three concepts of *trustworthiness*, *beauty*, and *use* as preconditions for a story working. The first, *trustworthiness*, I poach from a discussion of organizational ethnography by Peregrine Schwartz-Shea and Dvora Yanow (2009). The latter two, *beauty* and *use*, are proposed by Czarniawska (1998; 2008) as more helpful than validity and reliability when it comes to evaluating social science.

In terms of the first criterion, *trustworthiness*, the key is that it is not about perfection, but rather about the research being taken seriously: "What is most notable about trustworthiness as a standard for assessment is that it places scientific research squarely in a social context, recognizing the interdependence of researcher and readers as contextually embedded, sense-making actors" (Schwartz-Shea & Yanow, 2009, p. 63). This idea of the centrality of social context for research is in tune with describing research as a more-or-less believable story. In that sense, trust is the precondition for research even being accepted as research. In the organizational ethnography tradition, trustworthiness is usually achieved through the researcher providing a credible and detailed account of the circumstances of the study, as I have also attempted to do here.

In terms of *beauty* as an assessment criterion, there is not much more to say than it matters because form and function are interrelated, and we humans are aesthetic creatures. Additionally, beauty is not singular; a study can be beautiful in many ways. Nor is beauty universal; it depends strongly on context and on the audience. In this sense, beauty and use are intertwined.

The third criterion of *use* for research is possibly the most reader-dependent of the three. Shifting from case to story in the question, "What is a case story useful for?" allows imagining better and more open answers. Good stories work in different ways for different people, and stories that tell you what they are good for are rarely any good. Similarly, Law and Mol argue that cases are not representative, but that they are "able to do all kinds of other work" (Law & Mol, 2002, p. 15). In terms of other work, they suggest that a case can be useful by working to sensitize and seduce, suggesting ways of thinking, condensing or symbolizing, acting as an irritant, destabilizing expectations, and working allegorically. To that list we can add other workings such as inspire, confuse, critique, or remind. Which kind of work a given case can do depends on the reader's specific situatedness because when you read you interweave your experience, your needs, your inclinations, and your position in time and space in order to put the text to use. This is how reading becomes a site of production as de Certeau says (1984).

Comment by Chahrazad Abdallah

Mathiesen's work is not about strategy; it is about what strategy does, how it is made, how it is talked about, how it is constructed, how it is created, how it is shaped, and how, in turns, it makes, constructs, builds, creates, and shapes the world around it. In her study, Mathiesen addresses *strategy work* which is broader than strategy making because it stretches to "that which people in organizations do when they say that they are doing strategy" (Mathiesen, 2013).[3] Strategy work happens through people's engagement with the process and the identity work that accompanies it. That strategy is not just strategy but a much broader concept that mobilizes a variety of dimensions such as identity, meaning making, and responsibility is one of the important findings of this study. There are two important ideas in Mathiesen's chapter: The first is that strategy is far bigger than itself and that it can only be understood in light of what it continuously *becomes* (what it *performs* as it is 'performed' or brought to life), and the second is that one can only grasp that 'ongoingness' of strategy work by studying it ethnographically.

By addressing the performative nature of strategy and strategy making, Mathiesen tackles an ever-growing interest in organization studies for the performative dimension of strategy, i.e., for what strategy *does* in and through practice(s). As Mathiesen clearly argues, performativity is an alternative framework to understand a concept that has been successively and sometimes simultaneously conceived of as a plan, a position, a way to use resources, a process, a discourse, and a practice. Mathiesen's work is a great addition to the body of knowledge on strategy as it widens the focus towards the conditions, effects, and consequences of strategy work on broader issues such as meaning making and identity. The 'conditions of possibility' of strategy work in their complexity and intricateness are a drive of Mathiesen's work and shed a remarkable new light on a complex endeavor enabling a—thus far, sorely needed—subtler conceptualization of strategy in organizations.

To do that, Mathiesen relied on ethnography, which, as a method, but more broadly as an epistemology, offers the most relevant way of understanding, what 'goes on' when people 'make' strategy. The study of strategy practices in organizations has been increasingly calling for and, to an extent, relying on the use of ethnographic approaches in the last few years.[4] The recent calls for new ways of collecting and writing ethnographic data such as video or virtual ethnographies and the need for more convincing forms of writing ethnographic texts (Jarzabkowski, Bednarek, & Le, 2014; Vesa & Vaara, 2014) are welcome additions to the hitherto underexplored methodological subfield of studying practices. Sadly, studies that focus on the intricate links between fieldwork, headwork, and textwork in strategy practice research are still rare. Despite the encouraging positive 'move' towards ethnography and a recent call for it, research on strategy as a social practice is still very much based on a focus on ethnography as a method and not as an exercise in understanding and vividly conveying the "lives of others". Happily, however, Mathiesen's study is an enlightening answer to that call and enables a broader understanding of strategy through a close examination of what people 'do' when they 'do' strategy.

After years of studying strategy from a content or process perspective, the strategy-as-practice research field has been suggesting a view of strategy as a social practice that should be addressed from the point of view of what people do in organizations. Therefore, the question became, following Pettigrew, "What if we were to place human values, ambitions, and imperfections squarely at the core of the strategy formation process, rather than being peripheral to it?" Mathiesen's work addresses exactly that question by tackling the issues of identity work and meaning making in organizations and by focusing on not

> *finding a finite answer to the question of what strategy is but rather focusing on what happens when people engage in the topic and work with strategy. It is not the thing itself that is interesting; the focus of attention is on how people talk about it, make it happen, relate to and through it—on the practices of strategy.*
>
> (p.1)

Strategy research is strengthened by such a study that ultimately seeks to "explore artfully the human condition" (Brown & Thompson, 2013, p. 1155). In so doing, the scope of strategy—which has been an object of discussion and contention in strategy research—is itself broadened to "take into account not just the practices of those tasked with strategizing, but also those of a much wider population of organizational members" (Sminia & de Rond, 2012, p. 1347).

An obvious argument for the use of strong ethnographic approaches in the strategy practice research field is that it is difficult to say much about practice without looking at what people do and how they interact. Indeed, and as mentioned previously, strategy as practice "calls for an examination of how practitioners act, what work they do, with whom they interact, and what practical reasoning they apply in their own *localized experience* of strategy" (Jarzabkowski, 2005, p. 9). An additional argument can be drawn from the need for this research to focus more on how to convey a sense of what people do using day-to-day, mundane, detailed accounts of what happens within organizations. If the aim is to get a subtler, more precise sense of what strategy 'performs' (willingly and unintentionally) then ethnographic approaches are much needed. It is only through immersing herself in the field that the researcher stops seeing it as a 'context' and starts treating it as the magma of actions, practices, activities, emotions, relations, and discourses that shape how people make sense of their lives within organizations. More traditional research approaches are not always the most appropriate to get a grasp of the other types of 'work' that accompany strategy work in organizations.

Marie Mathiesen's chapter does not only open the proverbial 'black box' of strategy making but also *looks* at it and explores its contours to determine what it is made of and, more specifically, what happens when it is opened. Immersing oneself in the day-to-day entanglements of organizational life is the only way of getting a sense of what these entanglements are and what they mean to the people who deal with them every day. Beauty, as one of the criteria advocated by Mathiesen to make ethnography 'work' is not only in the ethnographic exploration of the complex phenomenon of strategy making but can also be found in strategy making itself. How to convey a sense of it is a challenge that Mathiesen's work has successfully overcome.

Notes

1. The field note and interview sections used in this chapter also appear in my PhD thesis *Making Strategy Work* (Mathiesen, 2013). Some of the arguments unfolded in this chapter also appear in the thesis, although as a whole, the thesis has a much broader scope.
2. Marie is pregnant and in the third trimester.
3. This commentary is based on the previous chapter, but also on Mathiesen (2013).
4. For a comprehensive review, see Cunliffe (2015).

Discussant References

Brown, A. D., & Thompson, E. R. (2013). A Narrative Approach to Strategy-as-Practice. *Business History*, 55 (7), 1143–1167.

Cunliffe, A. L. (2015). *Using Ethnography in Strategy as Practice Research: Handbook of Strategy as Practice Research, 2nd ed.* Cambridge: Cambridge University Press.

Jarzabkowski, P. (2005). Strategy as Practice: An Activity Based Approach. London: Sage.

Jarzabkowski, P., Bednarek, R., & Le, J. (2014). Producing Persuasive Findings: Demystifying Ethnographic Textwork in Strategy and Organization Research. *Strategic Organization*, 12 (4), 274–287.

Mathiesen, M. (2013). *Making Strategy Work-an Organizational Ethnography*. Doctoral School of Organisation and Management Studies, Copenhagen Business School, Frederiksberg.

Sminia, H., & de Rond, M. (2012). Context and Action in the Transformation of Strategy Scholarship. *Journal of Management Studies*, 49 (7), 1329–1349.

Vesa, M., & Vaara, E. (2014). Strategic Ethnography 2.0: Four Methods for Advancing Strategy Process and Practice Research. *Strategic Organization*, 12 (4), 288–298.

Chapter References

Austin, J. L. (1962). *How to Do Things with Words, Vol. 88*. London: Oxford University Press.

Butler, Judith. (2006). *Gender Trouble: Feminism and the Subversion of Identity, Routledge Classics*. New York: Routledge.

Butler, Judith. (2010). Performative Agency. *Journal of Cultural Economy*, 3 (2), 147–161.

Calás, Marta B., & Smircich, Linda. (2008). Feminist theorizing. In D. Barry, & H. Hansen (Eds.), *The Sage Handbook of New Approaches in Management and Organization*. London: Sage, Chapter 60.

Callon, Michel. (2006). What does it mean to say that economics is performative? In D. MacKenzie, F. Muniesa, & L. Siu (Eds.), *Do Economists Make Markets? On the Performativity of Economics*. Princeton, NJ and Oxford: Princeton University Press.

Czarniawska, Barbara. (1998). *A Narrative Approach to Organization Studies, Qualitative Research Methods*. London: Sage.

Czarniawska, Barbara. (2008). *A Theory of Organizing*. Cheltenham: Edward Elgar.

de Certeau, Michel. (1984). *The Practice of Everyday Life*. Translated by S. Rendall. Berkeley, CA: University of California Press.

Knights, David, & Morgan, Glenn. (1991). Corporate Strategy, Organizations, and Subjectivity: A Critique. *Organization Studies*, 12 (2), 251–273.

Law, John, & Mol, Annemarie. (2002). Complexities: An introduction. In J. Law, & A. Mol (Eds.), *Complexities Social Studies of Knowledge Practices*. Durham: Duke University Press, 1–22.

MacKenzie, Donald. (2006). *An Engine, Not a Camera: How Financial Models Shape Markets*. Cambridge, MA: MIT Press.

Mathiesen, Marie. (2013). *Making Strategy Work-an Organizational Ethnography*. Doctoral School of Organisation and Management Studies, Copenhagen Business School, Frederiksberg.

Mintzberg, Henry. (1994). *The Rise and Fall of Strategic Planning*. Hertfordshire: Prentice Hall International.

Moeran, Brian. (2009). From participant observation to observant participation. In S. Ybema, D. Yanow, H. Wels, & F. Kamsteeg (Eds.), *Organizational Ethnography: Studying the Complexity of Everyday Life*. London: Sage, 139–155.

Reckwitz, Andreas. (2002). Toward a Theory of Social Practices. *European Journal of Social Theory*, 5 (2), 243–263.

Schwartz-Shea, Peregrine, & Yanow, Dvora. (2009). Reading and writing as method: In search of trustworthy texts. In S. Ybema, D. Yanow, H. Wels, & F. Kamsteeg

(Eds.), *Organizational Ethnography: Studying the Complexity of Everyday Life*. London: Sage, 56–82.

Silverman, David, & Torode, Brian. (2011) [1980]. *The Material World: Some Theories of Language and Its Limits*. New York: Routledge.

Spicer, Andre, Alvesson, Mats, & Kärreman, Dan. (2009). Critical Performativity: The Unfinished Business of Critical Management Studies. *Human Relations*, 62 (4), 537–560.

Watson, Tony J. (2011). Ethnography, Reality, and Truth: The Vital Need for Studies of 'How Things Work' in Organizations and Management. *Journal of Management Studies*, 48 (1), 202–217.

4 Examining Branding in Organizations by Using Critical Organizational Ethnography

Sanne Frandsen and discussant Dan Kärreman

Introduction

> *We need ethnography more than ever to build up an alternative to this mass manufacturing of control technologies that we experience today. We do not need it in order to build better control technologies. In fact a main business of ethnography is critique [. . .] of the control technologies imposed on people. Perhaps we only need it in order to confirm that there is life and meaning beyond the rationalities that we encounter every day in the business of organization and management.*
>
> (Jørgensen, Henriksen, & Dembek, 2015, p. 2)

Kornberger (2010) argues that the world today is increasingly being taken over by a 'brand logic'. While early literature on branding was focused primarily on the customer, from its first conception as a physical mark on a product as a certification of standard and quality (Willmott, 2010), today branding has also become "management's weapon of choice to structure the *internal* functioning of organization" (italics in original) (Kornberger, 2010, p. 10). These observations occur after the rise of a new body of so-called integrated branding literature (Schultz & Chernatony, 2002; Hatch & Schultz, 2003; Schultz, Antorini, & Csaba, 2005) stipulating the importance of alignment between the externally and strategically communicated brand promise and the organizational behaviours in the 'moments of truth' between the organization and its environment. The simple fact that customers often have to interact with employees as part of their purchase of (and ongoing relationship with) a company's product or service has led branding experts to ask: How can we ensure that employees "internalize brand values" and "live the brand" (Ind, 2001)? As a result of this shift, the marketing field has become increasingly engaged in theories and practices of management to control not only the 'hands' of employees, but also their 'hearts' (Hochschild, 1983).

This systematic shift in contemporary employment relations has been highlighted by the increase in aesthetic, emotional, and identity work, particularly prominent in the context of interactive service work (Brannan,

Parsons, & Priola, 2013). Value is extracted from employees not only through the exchange of wages for physical labour but also work performed in and through employees' thoughts, feelings, manners, and physical appearance. Many of the qualities and attributes that makes us 'human'—the way we think, feel, speak, and look—are now turned into a 'tradable' asset in the name of the brand. However, the voice and experience of the organizational agents in question, the employees, are largely overheard in the existing research and to date the literature on branding has yet to link branding practices targeting and involving employees with the analysis of the forms of domination, control, and exploitation that are well-established in critical management studies (Alvesson & Deetz, 2000; Alvesson & Willmott, 2002).

Spicer (2010) argued that serious investigation should be made into "how brands work as new form of power in the workplace and how they are resisted" (p. 1740). This chapter responds to this call, in that I advocate for the use of critical organizational ethnography as a way to illuminate tensions, struggles, and ambivalences that emerge when lofty ideals of branding meet the reality of the day-to-day working life of service employees. Critical ethnography is a certain genre that seeks to "describe, analyze, and open to scrutiny otherwise hidden agendas, power centers, and assumptions that inhibit, repress and constrain" (Thomas, 1993, p. 3). A critical organizational ethnography of branding thus contributes to the existing functionalistic and interpretive literature on internal branding by giving voice to the employees and paints a more diversified portrait of implications of internal branding practices as a form of managerial control from the employees' point of view.

Empirically, I study an internal brand process in a telecom corporation and the fieldwork is based on observations, shadowing, and interviews conducted during the planning process of a new corporate brand and the 'implementation' phase, with specific attention to the reactions of service employees in the company's call centre. Vignettes from the study demonstrate the employees' struggle to enact the new brand and problematizes how internal branding as a dominating control practice conflicts with the technocratic forms of control and bureaucratic systems of work-organization, leaving the employees entrapped between contradictory logics. The chapter comes to a close by summarizing the implications of a critical perspective in ethnographic research on branding before discussing the role of ethnographic research in the emancipating project of critical management studies.

The Organizational Phenomenon Under Study: Branding

Despite the widespread agreement that employees play a vital role in successful corporate branding (Harris & Chernatony, 2001; Ind, 2001; de Chernatony & Segal-Horn, 2003; Hatch & Schultz, 2003; Olins, 2003, Schultz, Antorini, & Csaba, 2005), there is a striking absence of employees' voice in both the marketing and organizational studies literature on branding. Thus we have little knowledge about the intra-organizational effects of corporate branding from employees' point of view. The marketing literature produce a 'romantic' discourse of employees who are eager to be part of their employer's branding activities and who long to "live the brand" (Ind, 2001; Olins, 2003). Ind (2001), for instance, argues that

> *People need an outlet for their passion and their intellect. One outlet can, and indeed should be, the world of work. Brands can come to life if organizations engage with people's deeper needs and if they help to fill the vacuum that has emerged within the lives of many.*
>
> *(Ind, 2001, p. 27)*

Yet this 'romantic' discourse seems to leave in the dark the everyday power struggle of enacting, embracing, refusing, or resisting the brand logic. Therefore, there appear to be good reasons for taking an 'up-close' look at the internal branding practices and the implications of these practices from the employees' perspective.

Internal branding practices are designed to facilitate brand value internalization among employees by enhancing employees' awareness, knowledge, understanding, involvement, commitment, and identification with the brand values (Ind, 2001; de Chernatony, 2002; Hatch & Schultz, 2003) in order to generate 'on-brand' behaviour (Barlow & Steward, 2006). The marketing literatures' descriptive focus centres on a plethora of examples and advice of how to produce this 'on-brand' behaviour. The more traditional means of external marketing—persuasion, imagery, emotional arousal—is utilized to target an internal audience (Kelemen & Papasolomou, 2007), high-frequency brand messages using multiple channels is used to inform employees about the brand (Bergstrom, Blumenthal, & Crothers, 2002), and various HRM practices are put in place to enable the firm to attract, retain, train, and motivate employees based on-brand values (Lings, 2004).

Internal branding is also proposed to align the corporate culture, identity, symbols, and stories with the desired brand values in order to ensure that employees "live the brand" and "enact the brand" as "brand evangelists" (Ind, 2001; de Chernatony, 2002; Olins, 2003). As a result, key concepts from organization studies—culture, symbols, stories—along with a 'fantasy' of managerial control of organizational processes linked to identity formation (Christensen & Cornelissen, 2010) has entered the corporate branding vocabulary and transformed corporate branding from a marketing- and campaign-orientated set of activities towards customers to an organizational phenomenon with wide-ranging implications internal to the organization.

Interestingly, the internally focused perspectives approach to branding emerged as a counter-perspective to the very descriptive, rational, functionalist traditions of the marketing literature (Schultz et al., 2005). Yet while the 'integrated' approach highlighted the need to study organizational processes and meaning making inside the organization to ensure aligned behaviours with the externally communicated branding practice, this literature tends to use empirical material of case studies (Hatch & Schultz, 2003), anecdotes (Ind, 2001; Olins, 2003), or interviews with consultants (de Chernatony & Segal-Horn, 2003) that lacks the ethnographic depth, diversity, and polyphony. Instead this tradition reproduces 'the romantic' discourse of the employees who willingly engage in the organizations' brand work without attention to the tensions, struggles, and ambivalences of service employees expected to enact the brand. The ethnographic methodology is capable of uncovering these micro-level issues, by observing and documenting people's actions and accounts in their everyday contexts (Hammersley & Atkinson, 2007). Jørgensen, Henriksen, and Dembek (2015) argue that ethnographic approaches to study cultural management such as internal branding is demanded to provide organizational subjects with a voice and to discover a different type of meaning with organizational life than proposed in 'logics' of branding, lean, total quality management, etc. (See the quote opening this chapter.).

The current literature does hold a few exceptions of ethnographic studies of internal branding practices, yet they all focus primarily on prestigious, highly skilled, professional, or 'knowledge' work such as Kärreman and Rylander's (2008) study of an IT/management consultancy firm, Kelemen and Papasolomou's (2007) study of bankers, Andriopoulos and Gotsi's (2001) study of corporate identity consultants and product designers, and Brannan, Parsons, and Priola (2015) study of graduates doing call centre work in a highly prestigious IT consultancy corporation. In all these studies, the branding is seen as a form of socio-ideological control, which has taken over—or works in tandem with—more traditional forms of technocratic control and work-organization (Alvesson & Kärreman, 2004) and which positively infuses the sometimes meaningless work with positive (branded) meaning embraced by the employees. Yet at present we have little insight in the implications of the brand logic in the context of low-prestige, low-skilled, low-paid service work, where the work-organization may be bureaucratically structured and work against socio-ideological messages of, for example, empowerment and quality in service.

The Case

Call centres represent a 'critical case' for exploring such questions because they have been identified as the modern day electronic 'sweatshops' exhibiting some of the most extreme forms of (electronic) control and surveillance systems (Taylor & Bain, 2003). Technocratic forms of control based on standardization and Tayloristic principles ensuring streamlined labour processes and limited personal involvement in the work dominate the call centre environment, despite concurrent pressures to also grow employees' 'on-brand' service mindset through empowerment, internalization, and personification of the brand values (see also Frandsen, 2015a). To employees, this means that they are expected to simultaneously step forward as subjects to personify the brand, while also stepping back and in machine-like fashion follow official scripts, procedures, and guidelines to ensure a streamlined, consistent brand experience. Ethnographic research showing how employees respond in various ways to such contradictory technocratic and socio-ideological forms of control in the "customer-oriented bureaucracies" (Korczynski, 2001), is, however, still scarce—particular in the context of internal branding practices.

The empirical setting of my study was MGP (pseudonym), a European-based telecommunication provider with approximately 2.5 million customers spread over a variety of telecom services. In October 2009, a new corporate brand was launched after MGP had experienced years of battling a stigmatized brand. According to the marketing director, MGP, as a former state-owned telecommunication corporation, was perceived by customers to be bureaucratic, old-fashioned, clunky, and arrogant. A new brand was to change that. The new slogan was "Us with MGP". The idea was to break down the negative associations of MGP and instead build up new associations of MGP as a cooperative community embracing all customers with MGP subscriptions, hence the new slogan. In order to deliver on this brand promise, several initiatives were taken to change the culture of the organizational frontline, the call centre, for employees to act more in line with the new brand. The critical ethnographic study of this chapter examines how the brand was implemented and assesses its implications for the call centre employees. Before engaging more with the empirics, I introduce the critical analytical framework, which guided the generation and analysis of the empirical material.

The Analytical Framework: A Critical Approach

In this chapter, I argue for a critical approach to understand the implications of internal branding among service employees in a call centre context. By attending to the 'dark sides' of internal branding and challenging the 'romantic' taken-for-granted discourse about employees' engagement with the brand, I follow the footpath of other scholars within critical management studies who have previously engaged in critique of 'culture management' in its various forms within literature on organizations, labour processes, and organizational communication. Critical management studies emerged in the late 1970s in light of emerging globalization, increases in the size and power of corporations, implementation of information technology, widespread ecological problems, and turbulent markets, which together significantly changed the mode of managerial control, the nature of the work, and the professionalism of the workforce (Alvesson & Deetz, 2000). *In Search of Excellence* by Peters and Waterman (1982) marked a new era where organizational culture was seen not only as a route to corporate success but also as something that could be engineered, managed, amended, and adjusted to serve the interest of the corporate elite. Critical organizational ethnographies surfaced to shed light on the dark side of culture management and its implications for low-skilled, low-prestige workers on the shop floor, those in call centres, and those doing other service jobs, for example, flight attendants (Hochschild, 1983; Collinson, 1992; Fleming, 2005), as well as knowledge workers (Alvesson & Kärreman, 2004; Kunda, 2006; Costas, 2012).

I was initially drawn towards critical management studies because it provided a vocabulary with which I could illuminate the tensions, struggles, and ambivalences I experienced when observing brand implementation among the call centre employees. Having observed how the 'romantic' discourse of employees were repeated by MGP's directors of the marketing communication and corporate communication departments in their planning of the new brand, I was surprised to observe how the lofty ideals of branding clashed with the reality of the day-to-day working life of the service employees. The attention to various forms of control and resistance—and to identity regulation and negotiation—became cardinal for me to make sense of and give sense to the empirical mysteries I encountered. In the following, I briefly introduce some of the central terms of critical management studies along with examples of other critical organizational ethnographies that have trampled the path before me.

Socio-Ideological Control

Critical management studies sees the organization as socially constructed through processes of power and control (Mumby, 2013). While there may be many different forms of control, critical management studies is, in particular, preoccupied with the more hidden forms of socio-ideological or normative control forms, including themes of organizational identity, quality management, service management, and management orientation towards leadership, soul, charisma, and corporate religion (Alvesson & Deetz, 2000). Socio-ideological control targets the mind, emotions, beliefs, values, and self-image of employees in contrast to technocratic forms of control, which are used to guide the output or conduct of employees (Alvesson & Kärreman, 2004). Such socio-ideological forms of control are often celebrated as easing the technocratic forms of control and thus empowering employees and ensuring a more democratic workplace—similar to the 'romantic' discourse of the employees in the branding literature (Ind, 2001). Critical management studies, nevertheless, unpack or deconstruct such popular 'buzzwords' of recent leadership styles to expose the implications of the more symbolic forms of control over employees' cultures, identities, and values. The ethnography by Kunda (2006) serves as a prime example. Kunda examines normative control and its consequences among knowledge workers in a high-tech corporation. He illustrates how, on the one hand, top management attempts to 'engineer' a high-commitment organizational culture around keywords and strong images of the organization, which serves—through repetition and rituals—to manage the meaning of who *we* are. On the other hand, Kunda also uses ethnography to demonstrate the micro-emancipatory efforts taken by the members of the organization to resist, to distance themselves, and to escape the corporate colonization.

Identity Regulation

Critical management studies also see organizations as important sites for creation of human identity (Alvesson & Willmott, 2002). The more fluent boundaries between time at work and off work and increased demand to invest personality and authenticity while aligning 'personal' values and identity with that of the organization make employees' subjectivity the new locus of control in the managerial 'search for excellence'. The concept of identity regulation is often used among critical management scholars to understand how management's socio-ideological or technocratic forms of control produce a subject position of the 'appropriate' employee, which seeks to regulate employee subjectivity by celebrating the appropriate mindset and behaviour, while punishing those who deviate (in material or symbolic ways). For example, Costas and Kärreman (2013) demonstrate how the management of two consulting firms use CRS as a specific type of aspirational control aimed at producing an appropriate 'ethical' employee subjectivity. The critical ethnographic study is also illustrative of the variety of responses ranging from believers to straddlers to cynics. In addition, Thomas and Davies (2005) study, at a micro-level, the identity regulating practices of new public management and how these are resisted by four individuals: a civilian manager of the police, a uniformed police officer, a social worker, and a head teacher. In sum, the critical management perspective draws attention to the struggles inherent in the management's identity regulating activities when individuals resist and evade their organization-defined identities.

Resistance

Much of the research on resistance with a critical orientation does not view resistance as an ineffective reaction to organizational change or as a psychological defect of employees, but rather as a natural part of the power relations in any organization. In fact, Fleming and Spicer (2003) argue that cynicism, as a form of resistance, is not only a typical reaction to socio-ideological forms of control but also one that inevitably sustains the power asymmetry. With the ambition of challenging the status quo and supporting silenced or marginal voices, critical organizational ethnographies have increased our attendance to organizational resistance, dissent, cynicism, and counter-narratives on behalf of the oppressed, namely employees. For example, Collinson's (1992) ethnographic work of shop floor workers is illustrative of the various forms of resistance to managerial domination. Also an appreciation of the local understandings and lived experiences of employees play a significant role to van Maanen (1991) in illustrating 'mental numbness' of employees in the 'smile factory' of Disney Land. Similarly, Costas and Fleming (2009) seek to understand consultants' self-alienation as a result of the intense work pressure caused by long working days, the failed search for authenticity outside work, and the managerial neo-normative control system targeting employees' 'real self'. Resistance here is portrayed as employees' subtle strategies to protect a 'real self' from a management-designed 'fake self' through surface acting (Hochschild, 1983) and/or cynical distancing in the form of limited psychological investment and involvement in their jobs (Fleming & Spicer, 2003).

In the following section, I use the critical approach to ethnography to attend to the creative forms of resistance through which work identities may be embraced, negotiated, or resisted by the employees' in the context of internal branding.

The Critical Organizational Ethnography

As is evident in the previous section, a critical orientation is characterized by a questioning of the dominating logics, ideologies, discourses, and narratives to examine how these constrain or suppress human beings' (in an organizational context often employees') freedom, autonomy, values, identities, and cultures. One can say that critical social science is a discourse of suspicion (Mumby, 2013), because focus is on the asymmetry in power relations and taken-for-granted assumptions about the world. The critical orientation is, in other words, preoccupied with breaking up or opening up established traditions and conventions to expose and critique the underlying structures of repression. Ethnographies play a vital role in this quest; for example, van Maanen (1988) defines ethnographies as "portraits of diversity in an increasingly homogenous world. They display the intricate ways individuals and groups understand, accommodate, and resist a presumably shared order" (p. xiv). The intention is to expose power asymmetry and leave it open for critique and change in order to emancipate the oppressed. As such, the critical orientation is motivated not only by theory development or empirical investigations but also by a political purpose of achieving a better world marked by democracy, empowerment, participation, and freedom.

The critical approach has certain implications to conventional ethnography. The critical ethnography draws upon the same qualitative methods as conventional ethnography in terms of both data collection and grounded theory analysis (Glaser & Strauss, 1967). What distinguishes conventional and critical ethnography are their political purpose and the pre-existing assumption that our world is dominated by broader structures of social power and control (Thomas, 1993). Conducting critical organizational ethnography may in various ways be more difficult than conventional ethnography given its ambition to reveal the at-first-glance unnoticeable and unsettle the taken-for-granted 'truth' by bringing to light the underlying, hidden and obscure processes of power and control. Madison (2005) argues that this means that the critical ethnographer must "use the resources, skills and privileges available to her to make accessible—to penetrate the borders and break through the confines in defence of—the voices and experiences of subjects whose stories are otherwise restrained and out of reach" (p. 5).

Methods and the Role of the Researcher

In the following, I briefly introduce my research design before turning to two sets of dilemmas that I faced as a critical ethnographer doing fieldwork at MGP.

Research Design

I was engaged with MGP as an in-house ethnographer for 25 months, which was roughly divided into three phases based on the acute concerns of the corporation in 2008, 2009, and 2010. In Phase 1, MGP's organizational image was under siege, and the company experienced a reputational free fall. In Phase 2, the management attempted to deal with this reputational free fall by designing a new corporate brand. In Phase 3, the new corporate brand was 'implemented' in the organization with a particular focus on the call centres. The remainder of the chapter focuses specifically on the fieldwork and analysis based on the latter phase (for more information on the entire project, consult Frandsen, 2011).

The fieldwork centered on a team of 13 newly hired employees, and it started on the first day of employment at MGP (see also Frandsen, 2015a). First, participant observation was used during the full-time training sessions of weeks 1–3 to document and examine how the corporate brand was presented to the newcomers and if it was perceived and adopted—or perhaps even embraced—by them. Second, interviews were conducted in weeks 2–3 in order to explore participants' motivation to and expectations of their new jobs. Third, I individually shadowed five of the new staff members for three days. I shadowed participant number 1 on Mondays of weeks 5, 10, and 13 of his employment, participant number 2 on Tuesdays of weeks 5, 10, and 13, and so on. During the three months, I also collected training material, newsletters from senior management, and emails sent via the teams' distribution list.

The role as a *critical* ethnographer created some challenges, and I continuously found myself in dilemmas centred on conflicting expectations of producing corporate-useful versus academic-useful research, as well as balancing between the inductive, ethnographic research approach and the 'deductive' approach of critical management studies.

Corporate-Useful Versus Academic-Useful Research

The role as a critical ethnographer calls for some consideration of 'usefulness', and my experience is that, particularly for critical researchers, the question of corporate- versus academic-useful research is a delicate one (for an additional case, see Frandsen, 2015b). Often the discourse on usefulness in a corporate setting means that research has to pay-off in terms of increasing the company's productivity or revenue. To do so requires the delivery of simple, tested, comparative, and absolute results (Staunæs & Søndergaard, 2005). This discourse clashes with the critical, academic discourse on 'usefulness' or 'relevance', in which simple, tested, comparative, and absolute results would be seen as useless in an increasingly complex and diverse corporate world. In critical management research, the germ for useful knowledge lies in the ambiguities, mysteries, struggles, and micro-emancipations (Spicer, Alvesson & Kärreman, 2009).

In MGP, the corporate discourse was naturally dominant. At the beginning, I was asked to produce business cases based on my research. The usefulness of my research was evaluated based on its abilities to produce an 'employer-branding balanced scorecard', to develop employer-branding concepts and activities to increase the number of applicants to the management trainee programme, to improve MGP's rankings in various reports, and even (ironically) to 'grow' MGP ambassadors among managers and employees.

At the same time, my own perception of usefulness began to move in the direction of the critical, academic traditions. While I was still motivated to investigate problems that were of acute concern to the organization (and possibly of relevance to other organizations), I wanted to use my privileged access to MGP to examine critically the brand logic and the ways in which employees responded to this logic. Thus I became increasingly interested in what was taken for granted—the 'truth' about branding among MGP managers and employees—as I believed that the underlying assumptions about employees' roles in the corporate branding process may have prevented the organization from succeeding in its previous branding attempts. However, this interest was difficult to express as arguments of usefulness in the logic of MGP.

Therefore, I tried to be useful in other ways, such as by examining areas that were known to be problematic but where the complexity of the situation was not well understood (such as motivation and retention of call centre employees). In this regard, my ethnographic approach could provide a more comprehensive picture of the issues and problems from different angles. Furthermore, in my feedback to the organization, I tried to be useful by challenging the basic assumptions made about employees, management, and control, which I had come across in my interviews and observations. There were some indications that this approach worked. After finishing my fieldwork, I presented the results to the call centre director. We discussed my findings, and he asked me to conduct a new action research study in the call centres. He wanted to hire a new team of call centre employees to be exclusively trained and managed based on my recommendations and separated from the rest of the organization. The idea was to evaluate whether this experimental team would perform better or worse than the ordinary teams

I had observed. Although this was a compelling offer, it came only five days prior to my planned research stay abroad and thus I could not accommodate his wishes. I did, however, view this offer as an indication of the usefulness of my research results for MGP's call centre.

The Inductive Ethnographer Versus the 'Deductive' Critical Researcher

A different set of tensions emerged as a result of the inductive approach of the ethnographic work and the 'deductive' approach of the critical orientation. The analytical process was guided by an inductive approach, moving from the empirical observations towards more theoretical abstractions and contributions. As such, I was in search of a theoretical vocabulary, which could inform my empirical observation and bring forward what has previously been unexplored or unchallenged in the previous research on branding within organization studies as well as marketing. However, with the theoretical vocabulary of the critical management studies also comes a certain political, epistemological, and ontological perspective (as described earlier), which may on one hand 'illuminate' empirical findings, while on the other holding the potential risks of 'taking over' the empirical findings.

By focusing on control-resistance dynamics, for example, there is a danger of *only* examining 'control-resistance dynamics' in an almost deductive fashion and thus missing important insight to understand the processes studied in the empirical field. Thus in the attempt to counter the dominant ideals and understandings, the ongoing challenge of a critical approach is to strike a balance between a critical orientation informed by theoretical and political ideas on the one hand and remaining open and sensitive to the empirical phenomena brought about in the empirical work on the other (Alvesson & Deetz, 2000). To avoid a 'self-fulfilling' approach to the empirical field and phenomenon under study, reflexivity is imperative as a critical ethnographer, entailing "an interpretive, open, language-sensitive, identity-conscious, historical, political, local, non-authoritative and textually aware understanding of the subject matter" (Alvesson & Deetz, 2000, p. 113). In reflecting on this balancing act, Watson (2001) writes in this critical ethnographic study of managers that his critique of contemporary managerial work is "a critique which emerges from my dialogues with organizational managers, rather than one imposed on the world by a holier-than-thou radical or critical sociologist" (p. 7). Similarly, I found that my own critical orientation emerged when making sense of the lived experiences of the call centre service employees, not from a pre-existing theoretical position.

In my own ethnographic work, I found that the critical perspective was valuable for challenging the 'romantic' discourse of employees prevailing in the branding literature and highlighting the negative implications of the internal branding practices, which were otherwise celebrated as empowering and engaging. Giving voice to the employees became important. Yet the voice given did not only 'speak' in terms of repression and resistance but also produced a passion for customer service and embracement of the brand. Such ambivalences and the positive, self-enhancing dimensions of dominant branding discourse challenged the usual focus on the resistance, cynicism, and self-alienation of critical management studies. This will be elaborated more in the following empirical insights, but first I provide an introduction to the control mechanisms dominating the service employees' of the call centre when the new internal brand practices were 'implemented'.

Vignettes From the Field

Producing Efficient Identities

The call centre work environment at MGP is designed to produce efficient employees, who focus on the time and quantity of service encounters. Traditional technocratic means of control are used to 'encourage' employees to adopt this efficiency path. Employees are measured and rewarded according to no fewer than nine different parameters including time logged on the phone, consistent punctuality, use of freeze[1] (standby), number of customers handled, average handling time, number of redirections, customer service index, and first-call resolutions.

All these criteria and the individual's performances are listed in a 'coach report' on which a biweekly 'performance dialogue' between team leader and employees is based. Some of the parameters are also directly observed by managers and coaches, while time on freeze is managed by a tone, which sounds every few seconds if a customer is waiting. In terms of the number of customers being served, a screen in the middle of the room displays the number of employees on the phone, the number of customers waiting, and the average waiting time. The numbers update in real time every second or so. The individual performance statistics are sent to the team leader daily, and she or her coaches[2] put them on the whiteboards for everyone to see. Some are part of the team provision, so everybody seemingly has an interest in high numbers for these targets. The exact targets to be met are sent out every month by email by the team manager. The email usually also contains sales targets. If employees fail to meet the performance targets, this could result in a subtraction of their salary, while exceeding expectations may lead to an additional bonus. A further bonus can also be achieved by selling products to customers; the more premium the product, the bigger the cash bonus.

Producing 'On-Brand' Identities

The new 'community' brand 'Us with MGP' is launched internally through a 'culture change programme', Take Responsibility for the Customer (TRC), initiated to ensure 'on-brand' behaviour among the service employees. The CEO himself emphasizes the importance of the culture change programmes associated with the new corporate brand. The monthly nomination and celebration of 'The TRC employee', who has done something extraordinary to "take responsibility for the customers" becomes an organizational ritual demarcating for both employees and visitors (as the TRC employees' photos are framed and put in the lobby) the managements' and employees' dedication to the new values called 'rules to live by'; 'customer first', 'cooperation' and 'simplicity'. The new employees are naturally unaware of this when they first begin their jobs at MGP's call centre; however, in the call centre job ad, the socio-ideological messages sketch the path of appropriate employees to potential employees (even before entering the organization). The MGP call centre job ad contains clear messages of the importance of the required customer-oriented mindset:

> *The goal is to give the customer a superior experience with focus on individual counseling and identification of needs. This requires ambitious employees, who are eager to reach their goals—and show happiness when you succeed.*

The appropriate employee is furthermore described as ambitious, eager, happy and successful. More of these adjectives follow in the ad, positioning the employee as "positive", "full of initiative", "self-driven" and with "a desire to reach individual and team goals".

In the training sessions for the newcomers, they are presented to video material of *Pike Fish Market*, which illustrates the 'fun spirit' of selling fish at the Seattle Pike Market, and how the employees there are allegedly enthusiastic and passionate about providing superior customer service. Also the New Age film *The Secret* is used to convince the employees that by thinking positively (about work, the customers, the calls), they will change their (work) lives to entail positive work experiences, positive customers, and positive conversations on the phone. As such, they are made individually responsible for their own success and the outcomes of the interactions with the customers.

The socio-ideological identity regulation focusing on 'serving customers' and 'selling' manifests itself in several ways in the daily routines of MGP's call centre. Each employee's sales results and service performance are listed and updated every day on the whiteboards next to the efficiency statistics. Daily rituals of sales competitions propel the employees to compete against each other to improve sales. As described in Frandsen (2015b), the atmosphere is intense during such competitions and the room filled with human noise. A small reception bell is located next to the boards, and every time a team member manages to sell, he/she rings the bell, and the rest of the team will loudly applaud and cheer for him/her, while still being on the phone with customers.

In sum, employees' 'on-brand' identities are regulated by promoting the brand values and 'rules to live by', by making the employees' individually responsible for a positive spirit and 'tone' towards the customers, by applying rituals of celebrating appropriate brand behaviours, by a persuasive brand discourse, and by reports, checklists, and direct surveillance. Yet the 'brand' is not truly imbedded into the actual work process of the call centre that is set up to produce 'efficient' employees. In the following, I will draw an ethnographic portrait (Frandsen, 2015a) of Marianne to illustrate the ambivalent nature of the responses to the 'on-brand' identity in the time-efficient work environment and also the development of responses during the three months.

The Responses to the 'On-Brand' Identity

The newly hired call centre employees were surprisingly positive towards their new jobs. The interviews revealed that for many the brand of MGP had influenced their decision to take the job, and they narrated themselves as highly motivated to make a difference to customers and improve the brand through their service. Marianne was 20 years old and one of the most customer-service-oriented newcomers. She was known to take pride in making even the most 'angry' customer happy. The performance monitoring data showed a high customer service index for Marianne, which presumably reflected her customer-oriented behaviour. Marianne appeared to be the perfect case of a 'brand ambassador'. The story of Marianne shows an initial positive embracement of the brand values of 'taking responsibility of the customer' in spite of the technocratic forms of control which limited the brand value enactment through the job design and work-organization. In the beginning of the observation she states,

> I like the challenge, and it may take a little while, because you have to handle all sorts of problems. You need to help the customer, right, and I like being a peoples' person. You need to talk to him. To solve the customers problem and establish a strong connection. And then I really like the variations of situations to handle. They are just as varied as the people, right. Plus, you should also try to make a sale. There are many levels in this job, which makes it challenging, exciting and fun.

During the three months of observation, I did, however, experience a decrease in the team's enthusiasm as a cynical distance developed. One of the members of the team left, while others had sick leave or went on holiday; an apathetic and resistant attitude was detected among the once positive newcomers. I became increasing curious about why this development took place. Taking a closer look at the customer interactions revealed how these often were experienced as stressful.

Extract: Marianne: Is Everything Under Control?

"The customer (an elderly lady) is interested in a mobile broadband subscription, but she is unsure if there are enough signals in her summer cabin. Marianne is unable to answer the question, so she calls 'technical support' who tells her that the customer can use a mobile broadband because there is 3G coverage, although she may experience problems with her mobile phone if it only runs on 2G. Marianne calls the customer back and repeats the message she got from 'technical support.' The elderly lady asks if Marianne can send her an offer on a mobile broadband and also for a new mobile phone that has 3G. Marianne asks for the lady's email, but she does not have an email account.

MARIANNE: Maybe you can ask in one of our shops then? We usually only send out offers by email.
CUSTOMER: Can't you just send it to me by post?
MARIANNE: I don't think so but I will ask.

Marianne again puts the customer on hold and asks her coach if it is possible. She returns to her desk and explains to the researcher:

MARIANNE: Oh no, I have to find the [standard] email and print it out myself; it is not good for my freeze time.

Marianne explains to the customer that she will receive the offers by post within a few days, and she ends the call. While taking off her headset, she exclaims:

MARIANNE: We can put them [the headsets] down now; we will not need them for a while. This is shit! And I have a break in five minutes. Maybe I can just finish beforehand.

Marianne locates the standard emails and starts reading them. She corrects them and adds, "Visit us in our store". She then looks up prices on a mobile handset and finds a cheap one. She adds its details to the letter. Marianne finds more details on the mobile broadband connection, adjusts the information to suit the elderly lady's needs, and then, finally, she starts printing. At this point in time, Marianne is red in the face, working fast, and almost running to the printer. Time is ticking. The printer is located in another room, and when she arrives, she discovers it is not working. She returns to her desk and tries again. This time she has more success. Now she tries to find an envelope, so she is walking about in the office room. While putting the papers into the envelope, she is interrupted by the coach:

COACH: Marianne, is everything under control?
MARIANNE: I had to send something to a customer.
COACH: [upset, irritated voice] Next time you should log out. You have been on "freeze" for 20 minutes. It is bad for our average handling time.

Marianne posts the letter, rushes to the desk, and immediately starts answering calls. She does not take her break that day." (Frandsen, 2015a, p. 6)

During my fieldwork, I observed many interactions similar to Marianne's, when the employee seemed torn between competing expectations and a cynical distance emerged.

Cynical Distance: A Response to Conflicting Identities

Comparing the 'on-brand' identity and 'efficient' identity produced by the management through both socio-ideological and technocratic forms of control shows that they not only stand in contrast to each other but that they are also mutually exclusive. It is impossible to be both 'on brand' and 'time efficient'. Indeed, the conflicting character of the appropriate organizational identities seems to create vast challenges for employees. While Marianne in the aforementioned example provides good customer service and takes responsibility for the customer's problem, she is aware from the very beginning that this is not good for her quantitative performance measurement documenting her success as a 'time-efficient' employee. She is stressed and, in the end, she decides to suggest a handset that does not match the customer's needs. She also suggests that the customer should visit one of the company stores. By doing so, she avoids a negative impact on her first-call resolution statistic, even though she will not be able to log the call as a sale. Perhaps Marianne in this case expects that a new encounter with this customer will cost her more on the performance targets than on her sales account. The fact that she follows through on the customer's request to print the offer (and thereby overlook the standard procedures) shows that Marianne is committed to the brand values of 'serving customers' and wants to take responsibility for the customer. She uses her own judgment to adjust the letter so that the information is relevant to the customer, and she agrees to post it, as the customer has no email account. In the end, however, she is not rewarded for embracing 'serving customers' as a value. Instead, she is punished by the management.

The consequences of the conflicting identities promoted by management are already evident within the first three months of employment, as described at the beginning of this section. In one case, an employee quits her job, as she feels trapped between conflicting messages and she, therefore, cannot live up to her own expectations of 'serving customers'. Others keep going, and cynical distancing seems to be the preferred coping strategy when they are not rewarded for embracing the 'on-brand' identity because it inherently involves disengagement with the 'efficient' identity. Lars dryly states to me,

> They [the management] say we are MGP's face to the outside world, but really we still get a low base salary and I have to go through sales pitches and three systems before I can get [0,4 Euro] for the sale of a simple subscription. I might as well not do it.

What is significant in this study is that the resistance did not arise because employees did not identify with the brand values, or because they sought to protect their 'real self' from the intrusions of a managerially designed 'fake self' as found in previous studies (ex. Hochschild, 1983). Nor did the employees seem bored or apathetic about their jobs, nor did they have an instrumental orientation towards their work (Ogbonna & Wilkinson, 1990; van Maanen, 1991). Most had a keen sense of passion and pride about their work. Rather, cynicisms emerged precisely because they genuinely wanted to 'live the brand' and provide good customer service and were frustrated by the technocratic control that worked against it. Positive self-images were nurtured through providing good customer service and gaining appraisal from customers. Thus, instead of 'resisting' the brand values as such, they simply 'twisted' them in a manner that worked for them rather than for management. The employees would actively and knowingly 'bend the rules', such as by issuing credits or refunds to satisfy unhappy customers. The internal branding programme was thereby 'turned on its head' and used to legitimize their subtle resistance.

Contributions

At the present time, we have little empirical knowledge on what kind of organization the corporate branding logic creates. Theoretically, the literature focusing on the internal aspects of corporate branding offers a logic under which management is able to define and communicate an idealized organizational identity to close gaps between the internal and external perceptions of 'who we are' and to align organizational behaviour with the brand promise. The 'organization' we find in the corporate branding literature is, thus, "an organization defined, shaped, and controlled by its overall corporate message" (Christensen & Cornelissen, 2010, p. 12). From a critical perspective, the 'organization' is seen as the site of struggle over meaning, identity, value, and culture. The brand domination lies in its discursive, narrative, and mythic characteristics, which attempt to control the hopes, desires, longings, and aspirations of both consumers and employees (Kärreman & Spicer, 2010). Here I advocate that we need to focus on brands as powerful carriers of meaning that regulate the identity of not only consumers but also employees working on the frontline in order to challenge the 'romantic' discourse of employees' longing for and embracing the brand, which is dominating the branding literature. We need not only insight to how management actively uses branding as a way to manage meaning but also its implication for employees in order to gain new knowledge on the intra-organizational consequences of the corporate branding logic. In particular, we need to understand the brand logic from the perspective of employees who, despite their centrality in corporate branding efforts, are largely overlooked in the literature.

The chapter contributes in multiple regards. First, the chapter demonstrate how the brand functions as a socio-ideological form of control internal to the organization, yet only on a discursive and symbolic level, while the work-organization is dominated by more technocratic forms of control to ensure efficiency. The contradictory logics at play leaves the employees entrapped. Kärreman and Rylander's (2008) ethnographic work among knowledge workers shows that the brand—as socio-ideological control—is seemingly supplementing and even substituting the more technocratic forms of control and thus deeply inserting the brand logic into the organization. The case of MGP, however, presents a different situation of co-existing yet clashing forms of control. It is a case that contributes to the academic conversations of the ambiguous organizational implications of branding. Here branding—as a socio-ideological form of control—is decoupled from the technocratic forms of control put in place to propel a standardized and efficient working call centre. As such, it demonstrates the implications of the brand logic for employees in a situation of contrasting logics by highlighting the cynical distancing, but also engagement, that arise in response.

Second, in critical management studies, branding may also be considered to be 'the new kid on the block' in regard to the various forms of 'culture management' previously investigated. The 'living-the-brand' construct is conceived within the branding literature as empowering employees and liberating them from technocratic forms of control (Ind, 2001; Chernatony, 2002; Olins, 2003). The present study demonstrates, alongside Brannan, Parsons, and Priola (2015), that the brand *is* a powerful discourse, which informs and directs employees' organizational identification. The employees' are initially willing to 'live the brand' and embrace the discourse of 'taking responsibility for the customer'. As such, the case of corporate branding at MGP also highlights that the implications for employees may not be rightly understood if only examining employees' resistance and dissent towards the dominating brand logic, as is common in critical management studies. The edited volume by Brannan et al. (2013) shows that employees' relationship with the brand of their organization may be far more ambivalent and complex—even positive— as it is seen to provide meaning in otherwise mundane types of work, which was also the case in the Marianne example presented in this chapter. The critical ethnographic approach, therefore, holds potential to further explore the multiple and diverse forms of responses to corporate branding.

Third, this chapter draws attention to the necessity and opportunities of using critical ethnography to explore the implications of the corporate brand. The chapter highlights the need to hear employees' voices, which have largely been overheard in the typical functionalist and even interpretative studies of branding. Such voices gives us insight to the dynamics of organizational control and varied forms of resistance, ambivalence, and identification, as well as any shades in between in contemporary corporate life, which has been taken over by a brand logic. I concur with the quote opening the chapter that we need ethnographic research to confirm that there is life and different types of meaning in organizations and work beyond the rationalities prescribed in mainstream marketing and management literature on branding.

On a final note, it is appropriate to draw attention to one of Brookfield's (1987) characteristics of the critical social science researcher and the obligation to "imaging and exploring extraordinary alternatives, ones that may disrupt routines and established orders" (cited in Alvesson & Deetz, 2000, p. 8). The political ambition of doing critical ethnography entails a preoccupation with giving a voice to the marginalized and silenced and to contributing to their emancipation by imaging and exploring extraordinary alternatives. Yet, critics of critical management studies have pointed out that critical management studies often fails on this ambitious promise (Foster & Wiebe, 2010; Klikauer, 2015). This chapter points out the difficulties, dilemmas, and paradoxes one may encounter as an ethnographer and their implications for the emancipatory vision. In my case, I continuously found myself in a double role of both critiquing internal branding and adding to the development of the very same practices. While I aimed to give voice to employees and successfully convinced management of the problems with their current branding strategies, management instead asked me to take over the initiative of producing employees that were even more 'on brand'. On this basis, I propose that future research engages more in the ethical dilemmas of critical approaches to organizational ethnography.

Comment by Dan Kärreman: The Power of Findings

One of the biggest irritations with contemporary organization and management studies is the way we are encouraged—indeed, forced—to chop, slice, and mix our empirical findings in ways that support an abstract argument: the holy contribution. It is rare to find someone, anyone, who tells a straight story. It is even rarer to find someone who speaks out and supports the telling of stories from the field in the name of finding out about social phenomenon.

Suffice to say, we can't avoid abstractions all together. After all, our job is to speak to larger issues, as well as reporting our findings. However, at this moment in time, the larger issues are (mis-)interpreted in ways that clearly overwhelm the reporting of findings. Today we think of larger meaning as more abstract and specialized meaning, as almost devoid of broad meaning and consequence, and as a product for the consumption of a hyper-specialized tribe with its own language, beliefs, and rituals.

It is unusual to find a study that ponders the importance of the object under study on its own merits, in contrast to endless jockeying for positions in various hyper-specialized debates. The question hanging over the researcher in organization and management studies is rarely "What is going on here?" but rather "How can I make this contribute to contemporary micro-debates and nano-controversies in institutional theory, critical management studies, identity theory, entrepreneurship, innovation studies, gender at work, leadership", and so on, as if social reality neatly reflects today's division of labour in academic work.

Ethnography, of course, sits uneasily with the hyper-specialization of academic work. It forces the researcher to 'follow the animal': to pay attention to local meanings and behaviour. It is not often clear how ethnographic data will speak to the latest vexations in organization and management studies. In fact, when doing organizational ethnography, most intra-academic debates and controversies seem baffling and absurd. The addition of yet another state of identity work, leadership fad, and mode of isomorphism seems pointless and misleading when contrasted to what is going on in the organization, where these abstractions supposedly are playing out. That makes ethnography a poor fit for pursuing the average academic career. It takes too long to do well, and the data is never going to have a good fit for wherever the intra-academic hemline is at any moment in time.

However, ethnography does make a good fit if you are in for understanding organizations and for revealing findings about organizational life. Sanne Frandsen's chapter is a strong reminder of the value of findings. I want to focus particular attention on how Frandsen uses ethnographic data to show rather than tell. The key passage is the thick description of Marianne's struggle with, on one hand, the new branding initiative's call for customer care and, on the other, the mechanics of an instrumentalized workplace. We can intuitively understand the tension that this would entail, and we can perhaps also guess the various responses different employees would engage in. We are, however, at a loss without the ethnographic account to understand the meaning of this struggle and how it affects an individual and the workplace on the level of lived experiences.

Frandsen's account makes it possible for us to understand Marianne's wish to help the elderly customer and the consequences of actually acting out the imperatives of customer care. It also makes us understand exactly why it is so costly in terms of the instrumental imperatives of the workplace. Marianne's heeding of the call for superior customer care is costly for her, for her managers, and her co-workers. We feel her pain, and theirs. We now have an understanding of what it means to live the brand without the necessary support. We now are in a better position to understand why individuals cynically distance themselves, why they feel unsupported, and why they burn out.

Showing this, rather than telling it, is the true advantage of a compelling finding. In this sense, a finding compels because it is specific and concrete rather than abstract and general. A finding speaks of larger issues not because it provides a hyper-specialized abstraction but because it gives insight to the moment and meaning of actual social reality. It speaks to larger issues not because it reveals mechanisms and patterns but because it shows the layered minutiae of interactions and dynamics in everyday settings. A finding speaks to larger issues not only because it can be used to fire academic controversies—although it certainly is capable of doing that—but, more importantly, because it can put them to rest.

I think it is clear that we focus far too much on contributions rather than findings in organization and management studies. This is not to say that contributions, in the form of abstract concepts, vocabularies, and theories, are bad or useless. On the contrary, we need them to do our jobs. We always should try to trade in poor concepts and theories for better ones.

However, for now, we are preoccupied with creating concepts that cover less and less and reveal almost nothing. We need to move out of this dead end. We need concepts that are attached to findings. We need methods and techniques that provide findings. This is why I find hope in the work Frandsen and other organizational ethnographers are doing. It is my belief that organizational ethnography is well positioned to provide findings—findings that can give access to and insight in the strange world of organizations.

Notes

1. 'Freeze' means that an employee is logged onto the system but his/her calls are directed to other colleagues.
2. Coaches are experienced employees who have privileged responsibilities and act as the team leader's deputy.

Chapter References

Alvesson, M., & Deetz, S. (2000). *Doing Critical Management Research*. London, Thousand Oaks and New Delhi: Sage Publications.

Alvesson, M., & Kärreman, D. (2004). Interfaces of Control: Technocratic and Socio-Ideological Control in a Global Management Consultancy Firm. *Accounting, Organizations and Society*, 29 (3), 423–444.

Alvesson, M., & Willmott, H. (2002). Identity Regulation as Organizational Control: Producing the Appropriate Individual. *Journal of Management Studies*, 39, 619–644.

Andriopoulos, C., & Gotsi, M. (2001). 'Living' the Corporate Identity: Case Studies from the Creative Industry. *Corporate Reputation Review*, 4 (2), 144–154.

Barlow, J., & Steward, P. (2006). *Branded Customer Service*. Oakland, CA: Berrett-Koehler.

Bergstrom, A., Blumenthal, D., & Crothers, S. (2002). Why Internal Branding Matters. The Case of Saab. *Corporate Reputation Review*, 5 (273), 133–142.

Brannan, M. J., Parsons, E., & Priola, V. (Eds.) (2013). *Branded Lives: The Production and Consumption of Meaning at Work*. Cheltenham: Edward Elgar Publishing Ltd.

Brannan, M. J., Parsons, E., & Priola, V. (2015). Brands at Work: The Search for Meaning in Mundane Work. *Organization Studies*, 36 (1), 29–53.

Brookfield, S. D. (1987). *Developing Critical Thinkers: Challenging Adults to Explore Alternative Ways of Thinking and Acting*. San Francisco: Jossey-Bass.

Christensen, L. T., & Cornelissen, J. (2010). "Bridging Corporate and Organizational Communication: Review, Development and a Look to the Future". *Management Communication Quarterly*, 25 (3), 383–414. doi:0893318910390194

Collinson, D. L. (1992). *Managing the Shopfloor: Subjectivity, Masculinity and Workplace Culture*. Berlin and New York: de Gruyter.

Costas, J. (2012). ""We Are All Friends Here": Reinforcing Paradox of Normative Control in a Culture of Friendship". *Journal of Management Inquiry*, 21 (4), 377–395. doi:101177/1056492612439104

Costas, J., & Fleming, P. (2009). "Beyond Dis-Identification: A Discursive Approach to Self-Alienation in Contemporary Organizations". *Human Relations*, 62 (3), 353–378.

Costas, J., & Kärreman, D. (2013). "Conscience as Control- Managing Employees through CSR". *Organization*, 20 (3), 394–415.

De Chernatony, L. (2002). Would a Brand Smell any Sweeter by a Corporate Name. *Corporate Reputation Review*, 5 (2/3), 114–132.

De Chernatony, L., & Segal-Horn, S. (2003). The Criteria for Successful Service Brands. *European Journal of Marketing*, 37 (7/8), 1095–1118.

Fleming, P. (2005). Worker's Playtime? Boundaries and Cynicism in a "Culture of Fun" Program. *Journal of Applied Behavioural Science*, 42 (3), 285–303.

Fleming, P., & Spicer, A. (2003). Implications for Power, Subjectivity and Resistance. *Organization*, 10 (1), 157–179.

Foster, M. W., & Wiebe, E. (2010). Praxis Makes Perfect: Recovering the Ethical Promise of Critical Management Studies. *Journal of Business Ethics*, 94 (2), 271–283.

Frandsen, S. (2011). *Productive Incoherence: A Case of Study of Branding and Identity Struggles in a Low-Prestige Organization*. PhD thesis. Frederiksberg: Copenhagen Business School.

Frandsen, S. (2015a). Portraits of Call Centre Employees: Understanding Control and Identity Work. *Tamara Journal for Critical Organization Inquiry*, 13 (3), 5–19.

Frandsen, S. (2015b). Doing Ethnography in a Paranoid Organization: An Autoethnographic Account. *Journal of Organizational Ethnography*, 4 (2), 162–176.

Glaser, B. D., & Strauss, A. L. (1967). *The Discovery of Grounded Theory: Strategies for Qualitative Research*. Chicago: Aldine.

Hammersley, M., & Atkinson, P. (2007). *Ethnography: Principles in Practice*. London: Routledge.

Harris, F., & de Chernatony, L. (2001). Corporate Branding and Corporate Brand Performance. *European Journal of Marketing*, 35 (3/4), 441–456.

Hatch, M. J., & Schultz, M. (2003). Bringing the Corporation into Corporate Branding. *European Journal of Marketing*, 37 (7/8), 1041–1064.

Hochschild, A. (1983). *The Managed Heart*. London: University of California Press.

Ind, N. (2001). *Living the Brand*. London and Philadelphia: Kogan Page.

Jørgensen, K. M., Henriksen, L. B., & Dembek, A. (2015). Doing Organizational Ethnography: Movement, Relations and Agency. *Tamara Journal of Critical Organization Inquiry*, 13 (3), 1–4.

Kärreman, D., & Alvesson, M. (2004). Cages in Tandem: Management Control, Social Identity, and Identification in a Knowledge-Intensive Firm. *Organization*, 11 (1), 149–175.

Kärreman, D., & Rylander, A. (2008). Managing Meaning through Branding: The Case of a Consulting Firm. *Organization Studies*, 29 (1), 103–125.

Kärreman, D., & Spicer, A. (2010). *Brands, Branding and the Branded. Towards a Critical Theory*. Paper presented at EGOS, July 2010, Lisbon.

Kelemen, M., & Papasolomou, I. (2007). Internal Marketing: A Qualitative Study of Culture Change in the UK Banking Sector. *Journal of Marketing Management*, 23 (7–8), 745–767.

Klikauer, T. (2015). Critical Management Studies and Critical Theory: A Review. *Capital & Class*, 39 (2), 197–220.

Korczynski, M. (2001). The Contradictions of Service Work: Call Centre as Customer-Oriented Bureaucracy. In Sturdy, A., Grugulis, I., & Willmott, H. (Eds.). *Customer Service: Empowerment and Entrapment*. New York: Palgrave Macmillan, 79–101.

Kornberger, M. (2010). *Brand Society*. Cambridge, UK: Cambridge University Press.

Kunda, G. (2006). *Engineering Culture. Control and Commitment in a High-Tech Corporation*. Philadelphia, PA: Temple University Press.

Lings, I. A. (2004). Internal Market Orientation: Construct and Consequences. *Journal of Business Research*, 57 (4), 405–413.

Madison, D. S. (2005). *Critical Ethnography: Methods, Ethics and Performance*. London, Thousand Oaks and New Delhi: Sage Publications.

Mumby, D. (2013). *Organizational Communication: A Critical Approach*. Los Angeles, London, New Delhi, Singapore and Washington, DC: Sage Publications.

Ogbonna, E., & Wilkinson, B. (1990). Corporate Strategy and Corporate Culture: The View from the Checkout. *Personnel Review*, 19 (4), 9–15.

Olins, W. (2003). *On Brands*. London: Thames & Hudson.

Peters, Tom J., & Waterman, Robert H. (1982). *In Search of Excellence—Lessons from America's Best-Run Companies*. London: HarperCollins Publishers.

Schultz, M., Antorini, Y. M., & Csaba, F. F. (2005). *Corporate Branding. Purpose/People/Process*. Denmark: Copenhagen Business School Press.

Schultz, M., & De Chernatony, L. (2002). "The Challenges of Corporate Branding". *Corporate Reputation Review*, 5 (2/3), 105–113.

Spicer, A. (2010). Branded Life: A Review of Key Works on Brands. *Organization Studies*, 31 (12), 1735–1740.

Spicer, A., Alvesson, M., & Kärreman, D. (2009). Critical Performativity: The Unfinished Business of Critical Management Studies. *Human Relations*, 62 (4), 537–560.

Staunæs, D., & Søndergaard, D. M. (2005). Interview i en tangotid. In M. Järvinen, & N. Mik-Meyer (Eds.), *Kvalitative metoder i et interaktionistisk perspektiv*. Copenhagen: Hans Rietzel Forlag, 49–72.

Taylor, P., & Bain, P. (2003). 'Subterranean Worksick Blues': Humour as Subversion in Two Call Centres. *Organization Studies*, 24 (9), 1458–1509.

Thomas, J. (1993). *Doing Critical Ethnography*. Newsbury Park, London and New Delhi: Sage Publications.

Thomas, R., & Davies, A. (2005). Theorizing the Micro-Politics of Resistance: New Public Management and Managerial Identities in the UK Public Service. *Organization Studies*, 26 (5), 683–706.

Van Maanen, J. (1988). *Tales of the Field: On Writing Ethnography*. Chicago: Chicago Guides to Writing, Editing, and Publishing.

Van Maanen, J. (1991). "The Smile Factory: Work at Disneyland", in P.J. Frost, L.F. Moore, M.R. Louis, C.C. Lundberg and J. Martin (eds) *Reframing Organizations*, Newbury Park, CA: Sage, 58–76.

Watson, T. J. (2001). *In Search of Management: Culture, Chaos and Control in Managerial Work*. London: Cengage Learning EMEA.

Willmott, H. (2010). Creating 'Value' Beyond the Point of Production: Branding, Financialization and Market Capitalization. *Organization*, 17 (5), 517–542.

Part II

Knowledge Organizations and Studies of Everyday Work

5 A Web of Work-Life Stories
A Narrative Organizational Ethnography

Didde Maria Humle and discussant
David M. Boje

Introduction

This chapter uses a narrative organizational ethnographic approach to the study of everyday work stories of organizational members. The organizational phenomena studied are the work stories and the ongoing story work of organizational members. The empirical material is from a two-year case study of an HR consultancy that works with recruitment, HR services, and unemployment counselling. The theoretical/analytical perspective adopted is antenarrative and polyphonic focusing on the web of everyday story performances. These story performances are not necessarily full-blown retrospective BME (beginning, middle, and end) narratives (Boje, 2008) but instead consist of many possible and intertwined storylines about work and the organization. The fieldwork involved a variety of ethnographic methods, including interviews and observations, as well as a collection of different organizational documents such as PowerPoint presentations, intranet postings, and minutes from management meetings. Empirical analytical examples are presented, illustrating how members of this organization told both extremely positive work stories about being members of a fantastic company and of making a genuine difference in the lives of others, while simultaneously telling critical counter stories about how exhausting work could be and describing the consultancy as a demanding place of work. The chapter concludes by discussing the insights provided by combining ethnographic methods with an antenarrative vocabulary in studying the ongoing story work of organizational members as they make sense of their work-life experiences by performing and negotiating a plethora of potential plotlines and possible constructions of self, work, and organization.

The Organizational Phenomena: Everyday Work Stories of Self, Work, and the Organization

The organizational phenomena studied in this chapter are everyday work stories of self, work, and the organization performed by organizational members as they go about their everyday work while collectively, through different storytelling practices, perform and negotiate different notions of themselves, their work, and the organization as a work community. This was, however, not the initial subject of interest as the research project was initiated. Instead, the original focus was on the retention of employees, and the case organization was interested in research collaboration because they, as many other companies at this particular point in time, had trouble retaining their employees. One obvious cause of the problem was the economic boom. At that time, the employment rates were high and many companies had trouble finding enough qualified employees. At the case organization, the employees were considered to be the most important resource and contributor to the success of the company. Further, the consultancy employed many knowledge workers, a group of employees in high demand, and when these workers left, they took with them important knowledge, expertise, and customer relationships. Thus the work of retaining and developing employees was a top priority for the company. More generally, particularly in times of a positive economic climate, retention is considered to be an important topic among practitioners and considered crucial to the success of both private and public organizations. Studying retention as an object of research, however, turned out to be more complicated than expected, requiring researchers to pose difficult-to-answer questions such as "When is an employee retained?" and "How can we see if somebody is retained".

In addition, the data gathered through interviews with consultants about the world of practice and everyday life at the case organization was confusing. Interviews with consultants were conducted posing questions of how they felt about their jobs and the company as a place of work. The first interview, with a female consultant employed by the company for many years, was very long and critical. The consultant gave many explanations of what was 'wrong' with the company, and a plethora of possible reasons for employees leaving the company were introduced. More interviews were conducted and more time was spent in the company; however, the result was not clarification but confusion. The stories of self, work, and the organization changed and conflicted. Standing-at-the-water-cooler stories of time pressure and lack of quality were shared, and moments later contradicting storylines of success and the joy of work were performed on the company intranet, during interviews, or over lunch. There were no simple answers to how the consultants felt about their work or the organization and no simple ways to assess if the consultants were retained or not. Consultants expressing work joy and enthusiasm one moment, handed in their notices the next and left while praising both the organization and everyday work in their farewell emails. Others, having shared their frustrations and ambivalent emotions towards the company, stayed on for years and simultaneously shared stories of success on the company intranet.

The literature on job retention, consisting mainly of quantitative studies, was not helpful either. This body of research focuses on measuring variables of satisfaction and perceived possibilities of finding employment elsewhere. According to Mitchell, Holtom, and Lee (2001) these two parameters, even in the most extensive studies, explain only 25 percent of the variance of voluntary resignations among employees. Finding no help in the retention literature to conceptualize or explain the confusing experiences of everyday life at the case organization, I looked instead for inspiration from ethnographic studies focusing on everyday work (e.g., Orr, 1996; Evans, Kunda, & Barley, 2004), storytelling practices in and around organizations (e.g., Boje, 1991a; 1991b), and narrative organizational research on sensemaking and identity construction processes in relations to organizational life and work (e.g., Mishler, 1999; Linde, 2001; 2009; Humphreys & Brown, 2002; Thisted, 2003; Pedersen, 2008; Driver, 2009; Belova, 2010; Cunliffe & Coupland, 2012). Thus the focus of the research changed and the organizational phenomena became everyday work stories of self, work, and the organization, not as individually 'owned' identity stories but as storytelling performances connected in webs of dynamic organizational storytelling practices.

An Antenarrative and Polyphonic Analytical Approach

As the earlier description of the organizational phenomenon indicates, the study was conducted using a dialogical process of going back and forth between theory, method, and the field (Thisted, 2003; Renemark, 2007). Early on, the primary theoretical inspiration was derived from narrative identity research. This is a huge field consisting of many different branches (e.g., within sociology, anthropology, social psychology, psychology, organizational and management studies) departing from a mutual understanding that narratives are important elements in individual, collective, and organizational identity construction processes. Some of these studies take as their departure a relational and dynamic understanding of identity and accentuate the intertwined nature of the relationship between individual, collective, and organizational identity construction processes. This body of literature can roughly be divided into two groups, one consisting of studies with individual identity construction as their primary focus (Mishler, 1999; Thisted, 2003; Pedersen, 2008; Driver, 2009; Belova, 2010; Cunliffe & Coupland, 2012; Mallett & Wapshott, 2012) and the other focusing on organizational or institutional identity (Linde, 2001; 2009; Humphreys & Brown, 2002; Coupland & Brown, 2004; Brown, 2006; Kornberger & Brown, 2007).

However, the work of David Boje (1991a; 1991b; 2001; 2005; 2006; 2008; 2011) on the interaction of stories and story fragments, the multivoiced, dynamic nature of organizational storytelling, and the concept of antenarrative storytelling became a great inspiration in unfolding, understanding, and analyzing the storytelling practices of the case organization. Conceptualizing the everyday work stories of organizational members of the consultancy as a dynamic web of story performances intertextually related across time and space made it possible to describe and understand how organizational members were able to pursue more than one and sometimes even contradictory storylines at the same time.

The case organization had a strong tradition of sharing positive stories of success and of portraying the organization as a fun and rewarding work community. After spending some time at the company, other kinds of stories became visible. As I will illustrate in the analytical section of this chapter, these stories or story fragments were less positive and often described or hinted at the difficulties of everyday work and the less positive elements of being employed by the organization, e.g., a strong managerial focus on making money. The work of Boje on antenarrative storytelling helped me analyze this not as 'true' or 'false' storytelling but as different organizational dialogues going on simultaneously. Further, it helped me to describe how the story work of the organizational members is antenarrative in the sense that it is never finished or concluded in narrative retrospection. The organization is not a monolithic unit; there is not one 'true' story to tell about any organization but a multiplicity of stories and storylines being created and performed across time and space.

To conceptualize the dynamic, fragmented nature of the storytelling that goes on in daily life, Boje (2001) proposed the term antenarrative and defined it as "the fragmented, non-linear, incoherent, collective, unplotted, and pre-narrative speculation, a bet, a proper narrative that can be constituted" (Boje, 2001, p. 1). Antenarrative storytelling stresses the unfinished nature of storytelling in and around organizations:

A story can begin as an impulse in the middle; a story can emerge in widely distributed fragments without endings, without being assembled into a coherent-singular-performance, in simultaneous partial tellings people can twist and turn bits every which way, and people in separate offices, walking hallways, in vehicles, and in some restaurant can be referencing some unfolding story quite differently.

(Boje, 2006, p. 34).

The antenarrative perspective has in recent years received some attention and has been used to study a variety of topics, e.g., the work life of the chronically ill (Vickers, 2005), management and gender in the US Coast Guard (Eriksen, 2006), graffiti artists (Sliwa & Cairns, 2007), corporate identity (Johansen, 2010; Humle, 2014), collaborative innovation in the health-care system (Pedersen & Johansen, 2012), and fragmented work stories (Humle & Pedersen, 2015).

An antenarrative vocabulary is helpful in conceptualizing how we in our everyday organizational life are constantly engaged in making and negotiating sense through stories. The meaning of antenarrative is elaborated by Boje (2001) and can be described as having five dimensions (2001, pp. 3–5). 1) Antenarrative is before "(. . .) whatever narratology as a method and theory supplements, frames and imposes onto story" (2001, p. 3). Ante has the double connotation of being before narrative and a bet that there is a story to be told. 2) Antenarrative makes room for the speculative nature of making sense and our constant posing of the question; "What is going on here?" 3: Antenarrative directs our analytical attention towards "the flow of storytelling" by focusing on how storytelling unfolds in organizational contexts through disrupted and unfinished story performances. 4) In an organizational context, there is always more than one narrator telling the same story and always multiple storylines being shared simultaneously. 5) Antenarrative is, according to Boje, the collective memory, characterized by being a continuous process never finished because people are always chasing and telling several storylines at the same time.

An important aspect of antenarrative organizational storytelling is intertextuality. Storytelling episodes and storylines are connected and interrelated, forming webs of stories. One way to describe this is by the notion of "living story networking" (2011, p. 14) insinuating how "a person's story denotes or implies (between the lines) relationships to other stories" (2011, p. 14). In this way, antenarrative storytelling episodes form dynamic clusters of shared meanings. Further, as described earlier, people are always chasing multiple storylines simultaneously and relating their stories to the past, present, and future: to what has happened, to what is happening now, and to what we anticipate, desire, or fear will happen in the future. Thus an antenarrative vocabulary and the metaphor of Tamara-land (which I will return to shortly) allow us to work with multiple pasts, presents, and futures at the same time (Jørgensen in Boje, 2011). When sharing stories in and around organizations, there are always elements of retrospective, here and now, and prospective sensemaking involved. We are not only constructing ourselves, others, work, and the organization in relation to what has happened, but we are also occupied with creating positive or meaningful self-representations of the moment and into the future.

By applying these concepts, attention is given to both the organizational polyphony (Boje, 1991; 2006; Hazen, 1993; Humphreys & Brown, 2002; Belova, King, & Sliwa, 2008), referring to the many voices and conversations going on across time and space in and around organizations, and personal polyphony (Belova, 2010; Pedersen & Johansen, 2012; Humle, 2013, 2014), referring to the work of performing and constructing different creative stories of self, work, and the organization (Driver, 2009) as an ongoing process of navigating a plethora of possible potential organizational storylines. In this way, there is room for storytelling that is fragmented, polyphonic, and emerging (Vickers, 2012), as well as full of contradictions and contrasts:

> *The crisis of narrative in modernity is what to do with non-linear storytelling, with fragmented and polyphonic (many voiced) stories, the Tamara of collective story production and everyday storyteller*

immersed in fragmentation. Stories are antenarrative and everywhere in organizations, and are somewhat difficult to analyze. People are always in the middle of living and tracing their storied lives.

(Boje, 2001, p. 5).

Inspired by Boje (1995; 2001; 2006; 2008), I use Tamara as a metaphor for organizations to describe how organizational storytelling is situated in many different 'rooms' in and around organizations at the same time. This image is inspired by a play called Tamara, where actors are playing out many different scenes at the same time in different rooms while the audience moves from room to room without being able to follow all that is going on at the same time. Similarly,

(. . .) there are people in any given organization, narrating and storing, but situated in different rooms. Not being God, it is impossible for someone to be in all the rooms at once. In this simultaneous situation, people must choose which rooms to be in each day, stitching together a path of sensemaking

(Boje, 2008, p. 15).

The particular analysis presented in this chapter draws our attention to the fact that organizational life does not only consist of voices, stories, and words. There are also technologies, concepts, artefacts, human bodies, etc. Thus the antenarrative vocabulary is fruitfully combined with the notion of sociomateriality defined as "the constitutive entanglement of the social and the material in everyday organizational life" (Orlikowski, 2007, p. 1438) to explore how "(. . .) human bodies, spatial arrangements, physical objects, and technologies are entangled with language, interaction, and practices in the doing of activities" (Bruni, Oinch, & Schubert, 2013, pp. 57–58). In the analysis presented in this chapter, the company intranet is an example of a technical device that is intertwined with the storytelling practices of the organization as it facilitated a certain kind of storytelling and enhanced the positive storytelling tradition of the organization. In addition, documents (e.g., PowerPoint presentations and strategy documents) and the spatial separation of employees in different offices and conceptual artefacts (e.g., ideas, theories, and idiosyncratic organizational terms such as 108 percent) also affected practices, interactions, and stories constituting everyday life and the storytelling practices of organizational members and external stakeholders.

Methods and the Role of the Researcher

In 1993, Hazen argued that a polyphonic approach to the study of organizational life makes room for not only the loud and articulate voices but also the "(. . .) humming of groups of people organized to do their work" (Hazen, 1993, p. 23). Hazen's article can be said to be one of the markings of the polyphonic turn of narrative organizational studies where increased attention is paid to the negotiation of meaning and collaborative sensemaking in relation to everyday work and interactions in different work contexts. With this increased focus on the polyphonic nature of organizations and everyday organizational life, the use of ethnographic methods has gained considerable acceptance as an important and fruitful way of doing fieldwork. Many interesting studies have been conducted adopting a narrative and ethnographic approach to capturing the many voices in and around organizations (e.g., Boje, 1991a; 1991b; Orr, 1996; Barley & Kunda, 2001; Linde, 2001; 2009; Humphreys & Brown, 2002; Rhodes & Brown, 2005; Chreim, 2007; Pedersen & Johansen, 2012).

In this chapter, the empirical material used to illustrate and exemplify the work of doing narrative organizational ethnography comes from an ethnographic study of a middle-sized (100–150 employees situated at ten to twelve offices) private consultancy house working with recruitment, HR services, and counselling for the unemployed. During the time I conducted the fieldwork, the company was experiencing rapid change. It underwent multiple organizational restructurings and rounds of firing and relocation of employees due to changing markets and circumstances. During a two-year period, I had the unique opportunity to follow the everyday life of organizational members, engage with managers and employees, and attend all types of organizational activities, e.g., staff meetings and gatherings, and thus to "(. . .) share first hand environment, problems, background, language, rituals, and social relations of a more-or-less bounded and specified group of people" (Van Maanen, 1988, p. 3).

The empirical material is a combination of narrative interviews (Czarniawska, 2004) and ethnographic (Van Maanen, 1988; Czarniawska, 2007) studies of everyday organizational life. This combination proved to be very useful in the study of stories told by employees about their everyday work. Thirty-two narrative interviews were conducted with job consultants working with unemployed jobseekers and personnel consultants working with recruitment of permanent and temporary workers and HR services. The interviews were semi-structured and lasted one to two hours. In the interviews, the consultants were encouraged to talk about their work-life experiences and aspirations and to share stories of everyday work practices. This latter activity was inspired by the Critical Incident Technique (CIT) (Flanagan, 1954; Czarniawska, 2004) and included questions such as "Can you tell me what you did yesterday?" or "Can you tell me about a situation where you felt you did your job well?" Further, I attended professional and social gatherings and followed consultants in their everyday work-life activities such as visiting customers, interviewing candidates, meetings, and teaching. Also included in the analysis were a variety of different organizational documents, e.g., posts from the company intranet, group emails, minutes from management meetings, PowerPoint presentations, and commercial material.

This close, longitudinal affiliation with the company gave me extensive access to everyday organizational life and the opportunity to study both everyday work practices and the sharing of work stories. I attempted to listen open-mindedly to all members of the organization, and as time passed, I learned to resist the urge to add narrative closure to the stories of self, work, and the organization as they constantly emerged and changed across time and space. In this process, the antenarrative vocabulary and Tamaraland as an organizational metaphor helped me to handle the multiplicity of voices and storylines. The combination of ethnographic longitudinal fieldwork and the antenarrative vocabulary proved the ability to shed light on an organizational phenomenon without simplifying it. Spending time at the company and talking to a variety of organizational members made it difficult to draw simplistic conclusions, e.g., on the positive storytelling traditions of the organization as creating a 'fake' management-initiated community to exploit employees as much as possible and to facilitate a certain kind of employee as the ideal consultant or salesman. Instead, as I will elaborate on later, the positive storytelling traditions served many functions. One function was to create a sense of community and coherency among geographically separated employees doing different types of work. Further, the more critical counter stories of employees were not immediately visible or accessible to an outsider, and it was only after spending some time at the company that I was able to hear these more critical voices. Also, in everyday conversations and interviews with consultants, I began to recognize all the small, often implied, hints that there were different critical organizational dialogs, e.g., about the lack of quality due to a pressure in time and scarce resources. In this way, consultants often shared fragments of critical stories and made statements far beyond the specific storytelling episode. Sometimes these hints related to other storytelling performances and sometimes they related to, e.g., strategic documents or CEO blogs on the company intranet. None of these interrelationships nor the inherent severity in some of the statements would have been visible had the research been conducted only using, e.g., interviews or surveys and not combined with ethnographic observations of everyday life.

Empirical Vignettes: Examples of Analysis

The analysis of the empirical material showed how members of the organization gathered around different parallel storylines that apparently contradicted each other, however, co-existed and continually performed on different storytelling occasions across time and space (Humle, 2014b). In the organization, there was a strong tradition of sharing work stories that praised work and the organization. These stories described the organization as a unique and fantastic place to work, one where employees felt successful, enjoyed their work, and felt they were making a difference in the lives of others. Simultaneously, there were stories critical of the organization, of how demanding everyday work could be, and how focused management was on making money, which for employees sometimes led to a lack of work quality and resources. This section is divided into three parts. The first part explores the web of positive storytelling episodes praising everyday work and the organization. The next part describes the more critical voices, and in the final part, I illustrate how everyday work stories are antenarrative in the sense that organizational members are able to handle and navigate a plethora of different, sometimes contradicting, storylines at the same time.

Examples of Positive Storytelling Practices

> *This is clearly the greatest place I've ever worked. And for several reasons. First, it's because of what we do is, is so incredibly enriching. Just last Friday we were at a get-together with friends and while hanging out, people asked what I do and I can still get excited when I tell them about what I do and what this company does. And that's cool (. . .) What we do for our customers, find them employees, help them when an employee is let go, filling temporary positions, what our job consultants do when helping the unemployed. It's like that, like that all the way around, including the courses we do; we're on a par with pharmaceutical companies when it comes to helping others. We do something for others; there's no doubt about that and that's an incredibly great feeling that I've never experienced before in other places.*

> (Senior personal consultant)

In this quote from an interview with a senior consultant, the consultancy house is described as an extremely meaningful place of work providing qualified products and services to customers, candidates, and collaborators and consultants making a genuine difference through their everyday work. Positive stories about work and the organization were performed on many different storytelling occasions across time and space and in different rooms of the Tamara of organizational storytelling, such as interviews, comments made during lunches, meetings, and parties, and posts on the company intranet.

The analysis shows how organizational members often performed two intertwined positive storylines that are both present in the vignette of the consultant presented above. The first storyline portrays the everyday work of being a consultant as meaningful and rewarding:

> *A story like that about a man who looks like he is about to die, and now he is well and happy to be working, that is amazing and it carries its own reward.*

> (Consultant)

> *If I can make a difference by posing the right questions, then I think that I am good at my job. And then there is nothing that could give me a greater sense of success.*

> (Consultant)

A good day is a day where you feel like you have made a difference, and people are happy about what you have done for them. Luckily a lot of people say that they are. And that is what we are here for actually. There are a lot of rules that we need to convey to and we do, but you also get a sense of really making a difference in the life of others.

(Consultant)

The other storyline describes the organization as a meaningful, rewarding, and fun place to be employed at and work in.

CONSULTANT: I feel pretty good about where I am working at the moment. I would actually go as far as to say that this is the best place I have ever worked. I know it sounds stupid to say this as a job consultant where you every day tell people you should have a plan for the next 5–10 years and then not have one yourself. Right now this is what I want to do and in this company. I think that it is an amazing company to be employed by. My former place of work was also amazing but this is just 100 times better.

INTERVIEWER: How is that?

CONSULTANT: There is just a sense of joy, you can feel it all around, when you meet people (. . .) everybody greets you with a big smile. It is simply a cool company; you can just feel that people are happy.

These stories describing work as rewarding and meaningful and the organization as a great place of work were numerous and appeared as a central part of how organizational members strove to create and sustain a sense of community and coherence across time and space. Performing stories of success and quality was an important part of the everyday storytelling practices of the organization not only in relation to customers, collaborators, and candidates but also internally among organizational members. This was reflected in the daily storytelling practices, where stories of success, collaboration, fun, and commitment were shared during lunch, meetings, and social and professional gatherings.

Turning attention towards the material facilitation and manifestation the company intranet, introduced in the beginning of the fieldwork, proved to be a strong facilitator of positive storytelling performances by organizational members. Employees separated in different locations and doing different types of work were now connected on a more daily basis than the company gatherings. At first, not many employees visited the company intranet, but after a while, it became a rich site for storytelling. Managers gave praise to employees and departments for performing well, and employees shared stories of success and collaboration and reflected on why they were happy to be part of the company:

A great story from a new client. Yesterday I was called by a new client. She needed a temporary employee on Monday, so off I went to a client meeting straight away. We defined the task and the employee she needed. Along the way, I asked her about her own background and she told me that she had once been on a team of temporary employees at Agency X (a temp agency competitor) for many years but had found permanent employment. She had been interviewed by someone from the company once a long time ago and was treated so well at the time that she felt like calling us rather than the agency that had given her jobs for many years. Agency X had not taken any interest in her when she was doing her temporary work, but we did just that during the interview, which is why she chose us. I was completely elated by that client meeting; it's fantastic and it bears witness that 108% is part of the company :-).

(Consultant, company intranet)

We had a job-seeking candidate trained in day care who was ill due to stress and who had been sent to the company by the municipality for evaluation. The job consultant, Anders, had various contacts at day care centers and could have easily found an internship in a kindergarten; however, the candidate did not want this. Instead of pressuring her, Anders collaborated with the candidate, thought innovatively and found an internship in a shop instead. Thus, there was not only a sense of mutual respect for the candidate but also the creation of results beneficial to the customer (the municipality), the candidate and, internally, to the company and Anders.

(Book of Values)

Examples of Critical Storytelling Practices

After spending some time at the company, I began to see a different type of story work. These were less positive stories describing how exhausting working with people could sometimes be and how everyday work was *not* always rewarding, meaningful or fun:

What surprises me is how exhausting it is to deal with many people during the day; how exhausting it can be (. . .) it surprises me how hard it actually is (. . .) I become tired; this has meant that I've been tired when I come home. And that has affected my family. In that way it's been hard on me. In that way I think that this type of job makes me use a lot of energy.

(Consultant)

I have a hard time letting go and I get too involved. Sometimes I meet candidates who are incredibly hopeless and that's too bad for them, but just I find it difficult to help them move on from where they are because they are so hopeless. I also disappoint a lot of people and that gets me down, also when the candidates, for example, back out. And all those things get to me a lot, also all the things that you can't really explain.

It depends on what you're like as a person. Of course I realize that when ten people apply for a job, nine of them will get turned down, but I never imagined it would be as hard on me as it is.

(Consultant)

And there were also stories critical towards management and the organization, which accentuated how this was not always a positive work community and criticized the strong managerial focus on making money.

There aren't enough people—if that changed, things could become better. Then there would be time to get them [the candidates] out. I don't have time to escort the candidates. It seems as if we have to become worn out (. . .) we say it every day, and we have done so for months, but nobody comes, it's getting to be too much now.

(Consultant)

I demand a lot of myself. That creates stress; I make myself stressed. But also because I'm in a company that says: results, results and results, otherwise my job is gone.

(Consultant)

The critical work stories did not appear on the company intranet, customer meetings, or official gatherings but were reserved for more intimate storytelling occasions such as hallway conversations, smaller meetings, and appraisal interviews. These fora allowed the sharing of critical counter stories of how this organization was not always a fun place to work and that everyday work was not always rewarding, meaningful, or successful. These stories were often more fragmented and personal; however, they proved to form a large and persistently performed web of critical counter stories, or noisy silences (Linde, 2001; 2009).

Antenarrative Work Stories

The analysis shows how both the positive and the critical storytelling episodes were related in dynamic webs of stories and created shared meanings. Further, the analysis shows that both organizational dialogs were important in explaining how organizational members worked to negotiate different understandings of the organization and everyday work and that they affected the story work of organizational members, e.g., the constant organizational focus on success, collaborations and fun facilitated by company gatherings, and the company intranet made the critical stories more personalized and fragmented. Further, a negative or indifferent presentation of work or the organization became an excluding statement in the sense that it meant breaking with a work community everyone loved to be a part of.

The presentation of the webs of positive and negative storytelling practices, however, does not fully explain the story work of organizational members as they perform and negotiate different notions of themselves, their work, and the organization. The study also shows how members of the organization in their everyday story work were able to handle and navigate different, sometimes contradicting, storylines simultaneously and sometimes even in the same storytelling episode, allowing the consultants to present many different constructions of self, work, and the organization. They were able to present work as being both satisfying and rewarding but also potentially stressful and overly demanding.

Many different considerations and possible storylines are present all the time in the story work of consultants. There is a negotiation of many different work conditions, demands, expectations, ambitions, and considerations. In conceptualizing this, the antenarrative vocabulary proved useful in making room for the discontinuity and tensions reflected in these everyday work stories. By not focusing on how stories of work create coherence and causality, I was able to study how consultants handle contradictions and tensions by balancing several potential storylines simultaneously, e.g., between being satisfied and dissatisfied, between personal achievements and failures, and between dreams, ambitions, and the 'reality' of everyday work. A single story performance often expressed both potentially positive and potentially negative aspects of being a consultant employed by this organization:

> As long as the company has values and is willing to live by them, then I can live with it (the focus on financial results). And I do think it is a place where there is a certain kind of openness. I have been very surprised by the spirit of the company. In the beginning I thought oh my god is this some kind of newly religious sect I have become part of. What is this? Because it seemed very overwhelming and a little exaggerated and definitely too much selling.
>
> (Consultant)

These story performances and the ethnographic fieldwork point to the antenarrative and the ongoing and often fragmented nature of making sense in relation to work and the organization when sharing everyday work stories. The stories of self, work, and the organization are never finished in retrospective narrative closure, e.g., work is at the same time both potentially fantastic and hard.

Conclusion: Implications for Organizing and Reflections

The analysis of the tensions between positive and negative storytelling practices of the case organization draws attention towards several interesting aspects of how we as individuals, groups, and organizations work to make sense of our everyday experiences and construct different possible notions of 'who we are' and 'what we do'. First of all, the analysis shows how the web of positive storytelling episodes is a powerful excluding factor in the sense that it does not leave much room for the expression of ambivalent or negative emotions or opinions on official storytelling fora or occasions.

The analysis shows how the intranet enhanced the web of positive story-telling practices by forming a meeting place connecting the geographically separated employees on a daily basis. The intranet did not facilitate critical 'neutral' or ambivalent voices. However, it had both the 'positive' effect of enhancing the sense of being part of a meaningful and important work community and the 'negative' effect of individualizing failure and ambivalence. Another important contribution is the concept of antenarrative story work to conceptualize how the construction of our self in relation to work and the organization is constituted in ongoing processes of collective story work related to a multiplicity of story performances taking place across time and space in the Tamara-land of organizational storytelling. The stories of self, work, and the organization are never finished or completed in retrospective narratives, and a multiplicity of possible storylines and considerations are always present and must be creatively handled and navigated.

The dialogical approach proved useful in embracing the multiple perspectives within the case organization and allowed me to do research from the point of view of the participants rather than seeking a detached Olympian perspective (Smircich & Stubbart, 1985). The reflexivity created by going back and forth between practice, theory, and empirical work of others allowed the empirical context to take centre stage and made possible a bottom-up construction of categories in the sense that there were no predefined stages or categories. The advantage of this explorative process is that insights are not gained from testing theory or from the empirical material, but from applying theory to the material in different creative and meaningful ways (Cunliffe & Coupland, 2012; Humle, 2014a). Further, adopting an antenarrative and polyphonic approach proved useful in exploring the experience of being an employee of the organization and being a part of the organizational life as it is enacted in the midst of an infinite number of ever-changing and entangled individual and collective stories (Hazen, 1993). Combining ethnographic methods with an antenarrative vocabulary created an interesting analytical perspective, allowing me to study the complex organizational negotiations of what it means to be an employee of this organization, to do your job well, to be a success, and to show pride in the 'product' of this company, which is considered unique compared to that of other companies in the industry.

Further, it facilitated nuanced understandings of the specific organizational context and phenomenon, i.e., to resist the temptation to conclude that the positive storytelling community and the image of the 'ideal' consultant as hardworking and extremely engaged was created by monolithic and repressive management voices in a deliberate attempt to push the employees to perform as much as possible. The most obvious conclusion would have been that the positive storytelling community was 'fake' in the sense that it was initiated and maintained by and for management or as impression management of employees demonstrating their commitment and willingness to work hard. While the critical counter stories, on the other hand, may seem to be the more 'genuine' stories of the organization, revealing the true nature of the organization and the work performed. I claim that this conclusion would be an oversimplification of how organizational members navigated and made sense of their everyday experiences. The longitudinal ethnographic fieldwork, the close affiliation with the organization, and the application of an antenarrative and polyphonic analytical approach allowed for a more complex and nuanced understanding of the everyday story work of organizational members as they struggled to make sense of their experiences and negotiate different notions of who they were and the nature of the work performed.

Comment by David M. Boje

A critical encounter between consultancy and the ongoing organization's storytelling as Humle tells us is a time of performing and renegotiating a plethora of potential plotlines and character constructions. It restories the organization strategy, the identity, the work itself, and the relations to the community and ecology. In short, "the stories of self, work, and the organization changed and conflicted" with the consultation work.

I appreciated the dialectic understanding of the interplay of more formed stories and story fragments, monological and polylogical accounts, and the retrospective and prospective aspects of unfolding sensemaking.

The case portrays the sharing of more positive stories with the less positive stories. The antenarrative analysis of the before (fore-having of sense), the beneath (fore-concepts needed to make sense), the between (fore-structuring requisites of spacetimemattering of sense), the bets on the future (fore-telling of possible futures arriving for sensing), and the becoming (fore-care of the entire storytelling dialectic). For more on antenarrative analysis see Boje, Svane, and Gergerich (2015). With the strong managerial focus on making money, the becoming (fore-care) develops in the organizational dialog encounters in the moments when the monological (monolithic) official story meets its antithesis (negations of the one story in the plurality of polyphonic storylines in spacetimemattering). The living story networking comes into the foreground in the antenarrative analysis. This sets the stage for creating more positive, more realistic, and more meaningful self-conscious reflections of being-for-self in relation to being-for-others.

It also brings consultancy into the Tamara-land of simultaneous storytelling in different rooms (floors, buildings, etc.) and the movement of people networking between these spaces in paths of sensemaking. Thus the entanglement of social material in the *spacetimemattering* (Boje & Henderson, 2014; Henderson & Boje, 2015) of storytelling attempts to overcome the spatial, temporal, and mattering separations of organizational storytelling.

Can the CIT (used by Humle as inspiration in conducting interviews) reconstruct the spacetimemattering of Tamara-land? Certainly as the author insists, the retrospective sensemaking by members must have a longitudinal involvement with the consultants and moments of dialectic and/or dialogic encounter. Otherwise the 'fake' and 'pretending' of a positive spin by a dominant narrator will substitute for reflexivity by the members, thereby missing the antenarrative undercurrents of storytelling (Saylors, Boje, & Mueller, 2014).

The empirical material presents samples of different storytelling occasions across spacetimemattering. The underlying image is a web of storytelling episodes with an antenarrative underbelly of untold stories (Hitchin, 2015). I am not sure Tamara-land is a metaphor, as Humle proposes, as it seems to describe the actual circumstance and contingency of storytelling entanglements as multiple storytelling occurs simultaneously in a multitude of locations in most any organization. Perhaps the metaphor we need to challenge is the efficacy of the solitary CEO making sense of it all in some linear and simple narrative. The vignettes testify that there are genuine differences in storytelling by the customers, consultants, CEO, and many other organizational members.

It is exciting to see the critical challenges to the profit motive, an opening to a more dialectic understanding of how important people and planet are to organization survivance. The problem, of course, is that when profit is the only measureable outcome, people and planet get restoried through the only bottom line that matters quantitatively, leaving the qualitative in the dust. It is therefore important in consultancy for the critical dialectic work to take place, to get at the noisy silence (Linde, 2001; 2009), to balance the webs of positive with the webs of negative storytelling practices, and to show their co-existence.

In sum, this chapter, and its analysis, has many important implications for storytelling consulting. It accentuates, as I have also suggested, a dialectic approach to balancing the more monological storytelling with the polylogical, the positive with the negative, and the negation of the negations (Varra, Sonenshein, & Boje, 2015). Further, the antenarrative in relation to Tamara-land brings out what Linda Hitchin (2015) calls the *untold stories in organizations*. Spacetimemattering, its inseparability, speaks to the role of microstoria in organization change antenarratives (Haley & Boje, 2014; Boje, Haley, & Saylors, 2015). An important contribution the chapter makes is to the ways in which antenarratives of negotiation are part of strategic practices and identity (Bülow & Boje, 2015).

Discussant References

Boje, D. M., Haley, U. C., & Saylors, R. (2015). Antenarratives of Organizational Change: The Microstoria of Burger King's Storytelling in Space, Time and Strategic Context. *Human Relations Journal*, 69 (2), 391–418.

Boje, D. M., & Henderson, T. (Eds.) (2014). *Being Quantum: Ontological Storytelling in the Age of Antenarrative*. Newcastle: Cambridge Scholars Press.

Boje, D. M., Svane, Marita, & Gergerich, Erika (2015). Counternarrative and Antenarrative Inquiry in Two Cross-Cultural Contexts. Accepted Nov 25, 2015 for publication of *European Journal of Cross-Cultural Competence and Management*.

Bülow, Anne Marie (Copenhagen Business School) & Boje, David M. (Management Department) (2015). The Antenarrative of Negotiation. Accepted Sep 8, 2015 in the Journal of Strategic Contracting and Negotiation (JSCAN), 1, 200–213.

Haley, U. C., & Boje, D. M. (2014). Storytelling the Internationalization of the Multinational Enterprise. *Journal of International Business Studies (JIBS)*, 45, 1115–1132.

Henderson, Tonya, & Boje, D. M. (2015). *Organizational Development Change Theory: Managing Fractal Organizing Processes*. London and New York: Routledge.

Hitchin, Linda. (2015). Method and story fragments: Working through untold method. In I. Michal, H. Linda, & A. David (Eds.), *Untold Stories in Organizations*. London: Routledge, 213–238.

Linde, C. (2001). The Acquisition of a Speaker by a Story: How History Becomes Memory and Identity. *Ethos*, 28 (4), 608–632.

Linde, C. (2009). *Working the Past, Narrative and Institutional Memory*. Oxford: Oxford University Press.

Saylors, R., Boje, D. M., & Mueller, T. J. (2014). Entrepreneurial Storytelling in Moments of Friendship: Antenarratives of Business Plans, Risk Taking, and Venture Capital Narratives. Tamara Journal for Critical Organization Inquiry, 12 (4), 3–15.

Varra, Eero, Sonenshein, Scott, & Boje, David M. (2015). Narratives as Sources of Stability and Change in Organizations: Approaches and Directions for Future Research. Academy of Management Annals. Nov 24, 2015, published on Taylor & Francis Online.

Chapter References

Barley, S. R., & Kunda, G. (2001). Bringing Work Back In. *Organization Science*, 12 (1), 76–95.

Belova, O. (2010). Polyphony and the Sense of Self in Flexible Organizations. *Scandinavian Journal of Management*, 26 (1), 67–76.

Belova, O., King, I., & Sliwa, M. (2008). Introduction: Polyphony and Organization Studies: Mikhail Bakhtin and Beyond. *Organization Studies*, 29 (4), 493–500.

Boje, D. M. (1991a). The Storytelling Organization: A study of Story Performance in an Office-Supply Firm. *Administrative Science Quarterly*, 36, 106–126.

Boje, D. M. (1991b). Consulting and Change in the Storytelling Organisation. *Journal of Organizational Change Management*, 4 (3), 7–17.

Boje, D. M. (1995). Stories of the Storytelling Organization: A Postmodern analysis of Disney as "Tamara-land". *Academy of Management Journal*, 38 (4), 997–1035.

Boje, D. M. (2001). *Narrative Methods for Organizational & Communication Research*. London: Sage Publications Ltd.

Boje, D. M. (2006). Breaking Out of Narrative's Prison: Improper Story in Storytelling Organization. *Story, Self, Society: An Interdisciplinary Journal of Storytelling Studies*, 2 (2), 28–49.

Boje, D. M. (2008). *Storytelling Organizations*. London: Sage Publications Ltd.

Boje, D. M. (Ed.) (2011). *Storytelling and the Future of Organizations: An Antenarrative Handbook*. New York: Routledge.

Brown, A. D. (2006). A Narrative Approach to Collective Identities. *Journal of Management Studies*, 43 (4), 731–753.

Bruni, A., Pinch, T., & Schubert, C. (2014). Technologically dense environments: What for? What next?. *TECNOSCIENZA: Italian Journal of Science & Technology Studies*, 4 (2), 51–72.

Chreim, S. (2007). Social and temporal influences on interpretations of organizational identity and acquisition integration: A narrative study. *The Journal of Applied Behavioural Science*, 43 (4), 449–480.

Coupland, C., & Brown, D. B. (2004). Constructing Organizational Identities on the Web: A Case Study of Royal Dutch/ Shell. *Journal of Management Studies*, 41 (8), 1326–1347.

Cunliffe, A. L., & Coupland, C. (2012). From Hero to Villain to Hero: Making Experience Sensible through Embodied Narrative Sensemaking. *Human Relations*, 65 (1), 63–88.

Czarniawska, B. (2004). *Narratives in Social Science Research*. London: Sage Publications Ltd.

Czarniawska, B. (2007). *Shadowing and Other Techniques for Doing Fieldwork in Modern Societies*. Korotan Ljubljana, Slovenia: Liber, Copenhagen Business School Press, Universitetsforlaget.

Driver, M. (2009). From Loss to Lack: Stories of Organizational Change as Encounters with Failed Fantasies of Self, Work and Organization. *Organization*, 16 (3), 353–369.

Eriksen, M. (2006). Antenarratives about Leadership and Gender in the U.S. Coast Guard. *Tamara: Journal of Critical Postmodern Organization Science*, 5 (4), 163–173.

Evans, J. A., Kunda, G., & Barley, S. R. (2004). Beach Time, Bridge Time, and Billable Hours: The Temporal Structure of Technical Contracting. *Administrative Science Quarterly*, 49, 1–38.

Flanagan, John C. (1954). The Critical Incident Technique. *Psychological Bulletin*, 51 (4), 327–358.

Hazen, M. A. (1993). Towards Polyphonic Organization. *Journal of Organizational Change Management*, 6 (5), 15–26.

Humle, D. M. (2013). *Fortællinger om arbejde*. Copenhagen Business School, Institute for Organisation, Department of Organization. Frederiksberg: Copenhagen Business School.

Humle, D. M. (2014a). The Ambiguity of Work: Work Practice Stories of Meaningful and Demanding Consultancy Work. *Nordic Journal of Working Life Studies*, 4 (1), 119–137.

Humle, D. M. (2014b). Remembering Who We are- Memories of Identity through Storytelling. *Tamara Journal for Critical Organization Inquiry*, 12 (3), 11–24.

Humle, D. M., & Pedersen, A. R. (2015). Fragmented Work Stories: Developing an Antenarrative Approach by Discontinuity, Tensions and Editing. *Management Learning*, 46 (5), 582–597.

Humphreys, M., & Brown, A. D. (2002). Narratives of Organizational Identity and Identification: A Case Study of Hegemony and Resistance. *Organization Studies*, 23 (3), 421–447.

Johansen, T. S. (2010). *Transported Essence of Collaborative Telling? Towards a Narrative Vocabulary of Corporate Identity*. PhD Series. Aarhus: Aarhus School of Business, Aarhus University, Centre for Corporate Communication.

Kornberger, M., & Brown, A. D. (2007). Ethics as a Discursive Resource for Identity Work. *Human Relations*, 60, 497–518.

Linde, C. (2001). The Acquisition of a Speaker by a Story: How History Becomes Memory and Identity. *Ethos*, 28 (4), 608–632.

Linde, C. (2009). *Working the Past, Narrative and Institutional Memory*. Oxford: Oxford University Press.

Mallett, O., & Wapshott, R. (2012). Mediating Ambiguity: Narrative Identity and Knowledge Workers. *Scandinavian Journal of Management*, 28, 16–26.

Mishler, E. G. (1999). *Storylines*. London: Harvard University Press.

Mitchell, T. R., Holtom, B. C., & Lee, T. W. (2001). How to Keep Your Best Employees: Developing an Effective Retention Policy. *The Academy of Management Executive*, 15 (4), 96–108.

Orlikowski, W. J. (2009). The Sociomateriality of Organisational Life: Considering Technology in Management Research. *Cambridge Journal of Economics*, 34, 125–141.

Orr, J. E. (1996). *Talking about Machines: An Ethnography of a Modern Job*. Cornell: Cornell University Press.

Pedersen, A. R. (2008). Narrative Identity Work in a Medical Ward—A Study of Diversity in Health Care Identities. *Tamara: Journal of Critical Postmodern Organization Science*, 7 (1), 38–53.

Pedersen, A. R., & Johansen, M. B. (2012). Strategic and Everyday Innovative Narratives: Translating Ideas into Everyday Life in Organizations. *The Innovation Journal*, 17 (1), 2–18.

Renemark, D. (2007). Varför arbetar så få kvinnor med finanser?'—*en studie av vardagen i finanssektorn*. Göteborg: BAS.

Rhodes, C., & Brown, A. D. (2005). Narrative, Organizations and Research. *International Journal of Management Reviews*, 7 (3), 167–188.

Sliwa, M., & Cairns, G. (2007). Exploring Narratives and Antenarratives of Graffiti Artists: Beyond Dichotomies of Commitment and Detachment. *Culture and Organization*, 13 (1), 73–82.

Smircich, L., & Stubbart, C. (1985). Strategic Management in an Enacted World. *The Academy of Management Review*, 10 (4), 724–736.

Thisted, L. N. (2003). *Mangfoldighedens Dilemmaer*. Copenhagen: Samfundslitteratur. PhD Series: 2003–2024.

Van Maanen, J. (1988). *Tales of the Field, on Writing Ethnography*. Chicago: University of Chicago Press.

Vickers, M. H. (2005). Illness, Work and Organization: Postmodern Perspectives, Antenarratives and Chaos Narratives for the Reinstatement of Voice. *Tamara: Journal of Critical Postmodern Organization Science*, 3 (2), 74–88.

Vickers, M. H. (2012). Antenarratives to Inform Health Care Research: Exploring Workplace Illness Disclosure for People with Multiple Sclerosis (MS). *Journal of Health & Human Services Administration*, 35, 170–206.

6 The Logic of Nursing Work

An Organizational Ethnography of Practice

Jette Ernst and discussant Davide Nicolini

Introduction

This chapter illustrates how combining ethnography with Bourdieu's practice theory offers a distinct analytical approach capable of providing a rich and contextualized understanding of work and organization. In the chapter I apply Bourdieu's concepts of field and habitus as an analytical framework for the examination of how standards impinge on nursing work. The organizational setting is hospital department E (a pseudonym) where nursing practices have been standardized to a large degree as part of quality-leveraging initiatives. Based on ethnographic fieldwork, the manner in which the standards are handled in practice is examined. The vignette in the chapter illustrates how the concept of logic is fertile for an understanding of standardized nursing practice. The practitioner thus effortlessly creates and restores logic in practice despite ambiguous situations that emerge.

Organizational Phenomenon: Standardized Nursing Practice and Its Background

Most health-care systems in the Western world are under considerable pressure to improve performance in terms of cost efficiency and the quality of services (Viitala, 2014). The development reflects common challenges of ageing populations and the perception that both costs and the quality of services are key problem areas (Andersen & Jensen, 2010). A predominant tendency is, therefore, that clinical work in hospitals is subjected to tighter steering (Kirkpatrick, Dent, & Jespersen, 2011; Hujala, Andri, & Kyriakidou, 2014). The development has been reinforced by recommendations to develop or adapt standards from transnational and influential actors such as the Organisation for Economic Co-operation and Development (OECD) and the World Health Organization (WHO) (Timmermans & Epstein, 2010). In consequence, standardization[1] has risen to prominence as a steering tool in the hospital sector, and standardization to enhance the accountability of clinical and caring processes is prioritized and promoted at the expense of individual autonomy and judgment (Jespersen & Salomonsen, 2009; Kirkpatrick et al., 2011).

Standards can be defined as specific types of rules in practice that require legitimacy for their implementation. This is often accomplished by reference to expert knowledge that gets integrated in the standards as decontextualized rules (Brunsson, Rasche, & Seidl, 2012). In the hospital sector, the legitimacy of standards is predominantly achieved through association with the scientific rationality of evidence-based medicine. Hospital services are thus increasingly standardized based on what is perceived as indisputable arguments of medical evidence (Timmermans & Kolker, 2004; Wears, 2015). Standards have achieved a status as a universal good, producing order, reason, and reproducibility in care (Wears, 2015, p. 90). They allow for quantification and comparison, and, accordingly, standardization seems to respond to the present challenges of the hospital sector.

Standardized nursing comprises predefined 'best practice' steps in practice (Baumann, 2010), as well as sets of nursing terminologies (Keenan, Tschannen, & Wesley, 2008) that enable electronic monitoring. While standards in nursing facilitate and rationalize practice, their reception in practice is often somewhat more ambiguous and complex. A reason for this can be found in professional self-understanding, which standards seem to both reinforce and contradict. On the one hand, standards collide with the autonomy embedded within the idea of a distinctive professional knowledge base for practice (Halford, Obstfelder, & Lotherington, 2010), but on the other hand, standards may also link with the professional ethos as a symbol of professional progress (Allen, 1998). Furthermore, standards are inherently political, reflecting interests and battles in the health-care field, and they embed assumptions about practices and the practitioners whose work they organize. This, in turn, can spark resistance with practitioners feeling controlled and strained (Bjørn & Balka, 2007). In the hospital context, standards work as both subtle and overt organizers of organizational life that carry strong normative dimensions because they coordinate practitioners, patients, and artefacts by distinguishing right from wrong in practice (Timmermans & Epstein, 2010).

In the department studied, standards materialize, for example, in schemes with clinical steps to be ticked off, which were designed to steer the practitioner. These schemes can be based on so-called algorithms that, on the basis of the data inserted into them, calculate and specify the next appropriate move in practice. However, as will be illustrated, this does not eliminate ambiguity in practice. The combination of ethnography and Bourdieu's practice theory in this study provides a perspective on standardized nursing practice in which the relation between workplace activities, clinical workers, and organizing processes comes to the fore and where the scope of the explanations arrived at extend beyond the immediate work situation (Nicolini, 2013). The approach, hence, has the ability to provide an in situ understanding of what happens in standardized practice and to connect this with the contextual factors of the field.

In the next section, I present the department where I conducted my ethnographic studies.

Organizational Setting: Department E and the Pursuit of Better Praxis

The management of department E supports the steadily increasing focus on quality and safety, which reflects a progressive line towards the agenda upon which the hospital board has decided. For example, the board decided that the hospital should opt to participate in the Patient Safe Hospital program as one of five national hospitals. The program is run by the National Society for Patient Safety, which was founded in 2001, and is part of the international Patient Safety Movement[2] (Travaglia & Braithwaite, 2009). The society has secured steadily rising influence in the Danish hospital sector, and it authors several projects to enhance patient safety. The Patient Safe Hospital programme aims to specify and advance best clinical practices (Travaglia & Braithwaite, 2009). The society's ambitions are explicitly high, thus objectives of 'changing the world' through the 'changing of systems', with analogies drawn to the Second World War, are stated on its home page.[3] Nursing practices in department E have been profoundly influenced by this program, as well as by the accreditation programs that are mandatory for all hospitals in the country.

The propagation of safe praxis according to the guidelines defined by the Patient Safe Hospital and accreditation programs is thus now pursued by the management at all managerial levels in the department using different means to prompt staff to incorporate the standards in their practice. In the field, it is commonly articulated that gaining clinical staff's acceptance of the standardization of their practices can be difficult, which is interpreted and verbalized as barriers to implementation (e.g., Taylor & Allen, 2007; Hauck, Winsett, & Kuric, 2013). Therefore, several strategies are employed to secure the standards a positive reception in the department, and both experienced and inexperienced nurses participate in the promotion of standardized practice, which is labelled 'quality work'. Under this heading, the nurses become spokespersons and advocates of standardized nursing practice, which many perceive as progression to practice.

A Bourdieuan Practice Theoretical Framework

Practice theories are concerned with the repetitive, routinized, and processual nature of social life. In a practice theoretical framework, the organization of work does not straightforwardly result from the application of plans, strategies, or standards (Nicolini, 2013). Consequently, while the phenomena of standards and standardization in relation to organizing could appear as the neat steering of work through formal rules acting as forecasting designs (Timmermans & Epstein, 2010; Brunsson et al., 2012), we must look beyond the standards to understand how they acquire meaning in practice. To look beyond the standards means to investigate them and to pose questions about their use. Studying organizing then means to examine, first, how these standards are handled in practice and, second, from where they originate and how their legitimacy is established. In this way, we allow the connection between standardization, practice, and organization to emerge.

Several theories are subsumed under the practice idiom[4] of which Bourdieu is a main exponent. Using the term *analytical approach* rather than, for instance, *lens* indicates that the practice idiom is not only a perspective, that is, a way of looking at the research object, but also a research attitude and the manner in which the research problem is investigated. We can say that the ethnographic and Bourdieuan practice approaches direct a way of knowing that knits together the methods for the exploration of practice and the theoretical lens so that they work together in a reciprocal and insepara-ble movement (Bourdieu & Wacquant, 1992, p. 35; Wacquant, 2004). The framing of the research problem and the methods for its study should, there-fore, be seen as one—an intertwined and mutually constitutive package.

Bourdieu's practice theory fundamentally deals with the explanations of the actions of agents in a field. For this purpose, Bourdieu adapted and developed his interdependent-working theoretical concepts. The concept of field serves to contextualize phenomena in Bourdieu's practice theory. Fields are structured spaces and sections of the social world held together by a common interest that works as an energy or a dynamic (Bourdieu, 1990). The field concept guided my ethnographic work and emerging theoretical understanding from the outset. I analyze nursing work in department E as organized entities embedded within the contextual and relational whole of the hospital and the health-care field in which standards have been adopted as organizational improvement tools. What takes place on the hospital shop floor must, therefore, be understood in light of this embeddedness within something larger that impinges on the experiences of staff.

Bourdieu's notion of logic is emblematic of his line of thinking. Logic is not of a rational and reflexive character; rather, it is 'fuzzy' (e.g., Bourdieu, 1990, p. 86), meaning that the logic of nursing resides where practice makes sense in relation to the contextual conditions pertaining to the field. Most of these conditions emerge at the pre-discursive level for the practitioner who has appropriated, learned, and internalized a given set of dispositions and ways of understanding the world—the habitus. Daily navigation in practice is, hence, piloted by habitus as the creative steering force that makes some actions likelier than others. The nursing practitioner in department E has been socialized in the nursing profession (Wicks, 1998) through education and ongoing job experience, and the learning thus acquired is stored in the body. The practitioner is thus predisposed with an ability to navigate the field and act with competence in taken-for-granted ways (Bourdieu, 1990, p. 68).

While the nursing practitioner enters the hospital as a work field with socialized dispositions, this work field, in turn, also socializes the nurse. Habitus is constantly under formation in the meeting with everyday organi-zational life in which some things remain relatively stable, while others are dynamic. In consequence, practices are constantly under construction and reconstruction (Bourdieu & Wacquant, 1992). The nursing habitus learns to match the demands of the hospital department as a specific workplace in the medical field. It learns the "rules of the game" (Bourdieu, 1990), and the nurses are, in turn, also co-definers of the game themselves. It follows that habitus is closely connected to the concept of field, and it is the interplay of these two that creates the fuzzy logic of work. Therefore, the sense of meaning in practice as that which seems natural to do results from this interplay, and the logic of practice resides in a complex relation between the immediate work situation and factors outside of it in both space and time (Nicolini, 2013).

The ethnography of practice approach can illuminate the complexity involved in mundane work (Nicolini, 2013). The methods employed in the study had to enable me to both capture the micro-level experiences of the nurses and connect these with the structuring macro-level from which the idea of nursing practice standardization originated. The ethnographic data were produced through various methods and means: First, to understand why standardization has won influence in the hospital sector, I read the literature that addresses the topic, including reports, government white papers, and research articles. Second, to understand why department E had adopted standardization, I interviewed the department's head nurse, studied regional policy documents, and examined the hospital intranet. Third, to understand the impact of standardization on the hospital shop floor, I employed a variety of fieldwork techniques throughout the course of 13 months. Before presenting the analysis of standardized nursing, I explain how I conducted my fieldwork and reflect on my role as a researcher in the hospital department.

Ethnography of Practice: Zooming in on Fieldwork

The notion of zooming was coined by Nicolini (2009; 2013), who takes it to mean a way of addressing how translocal phenomena are constituted. I use the term to introduce the reader to a specific part of my fieldwork by zooming in on it, namely, the coupling of observing participation (Hasse, 2015) with informal conversations to form the empirical basis of the forthcoming vignette.

Ethnography of practice inevitably involves the researcher's presence and engagement in the field. It is an engagement that can be demanding to tackle, but which is, at the same time, the key to the unique character of the research. Studying practice is indeed a practice in itself that involves epistemic choices on the part of the researcher. By wearing a name tag, saying "PhD student", and dressing like the individuals I was observing, I sought to immerse myself in the practices of the nurses and doctors whom I followed everywhere on their routes in the department to obtain insight into the multiple aspects of their work. The outset for my observations was thus the individual professional through whom I gained insight of daily practice in the department. In all, 25 nurses and 9 doctors were observed, totalling

118 hours in observation participation (Hasse, 2015). In this role, I participated in tasks that did not require specialized training such as getting food or blankets for the patients. The hospital department was a new and unfamiliar setting for me, not having been trained in health care, and I saw myself as learning the field (Hasse, 2015). Especially in the beginning of fieldwork, my prime concern was to gain acceptance from the staff as a legitimate researcher and participant in the field, because such acceptance was a provision of the research I was pursuing.

In the initial stages of fieldwork, I applied an open inductive approach to ensure that my theoretical assumptions would not hinder unexpected or surprising discoveries. I began my fieldwork with certain ideas on how to proceed based on the literature I had consumed, which I then adjusted along the way as I learned from my presence in the field and further readings. I thus allowed myself to respond to the circumstances I encountered and to apply the tools best suited for gaining the understanding I sought. The observations directed my attention towards the phenomenon of nursing standardization in the department since it seemed to have a profound influence on the work and the nurses. I therefore decided to grant it ethnographic focus while trying to work out a theoretical understanding of it. Theory was, in Gherardi's (2015, p. 121) words, "both a resource for guiding fieldwork and an outcome of the thinking process". Moreover, the observations significantly contributed to my general understanding of the work of nurses and doctors and their interplay with each other, patients, managers, physical outlets, and material artefacts. Granting nursing standardization ethnographic focus meant that I was seeking standards in my ethnographic work. Which standards had been adopted? Who worked with them? How did they achieve legitimacy? In which ways were they incorporated into work? How were they perceived and handled by the nurses?

During observations, I talked with the persons I observed as much as work allowed. Informal conversations or informal interviews (Agar, 2008) thus became a salient part my observations and a great source of learning in the field. I saw myself as what Lofland (1971) calls in Hammersley and Atkinson (2007, p. 79) an "acceptable incompetent" whose steadily increasing understanding of the field prompted more qualified conversations as I was able to ask better questions.

Generally, although especially in the beginning, my experience in the field was dominated by my own struggles to make sense of it, which often meant that my returning to the field was loaded with questions to which I was seeking answers. For example, I found myself surrounded by an entirely unfamiliar linguistic clinical lexicon and several medical artefacts that seemed like black holes in relation to my orientations. In that way, my ethnographic moves within the field, and outside it, were directed by the understandings I sought. Theory was built in the interplay between my experiences in the field, my readings of the literature, policy documents and so forth, and my theoretical assumptions. Through this interplay, it became clear that the notions of logic and habitus were productive for an understanding of standardized nursing practice in the department. Hence, through my observations of the nurses in their mundane practicing, it struck me how they had a brilliant ability to subtly uphold the meaningfulness of situations. I connected that ability to Bourdieu's concept of habitus, which emphasizes embodied knowing at the pre-discursive level in practice. I thus found that the nurses were indeed handling the standards and not merely following them, and I came to see the nurses as co-producers and creative jugglers of standardized practice in the department. However, this handling of standards was most often not verbalized.

Moreover, the theoretical concept of the field allowed me to contextualize the phenomenon to understand why and in what possible ways the nurses would embrace standardization of their work. The analysis thus focuses on the construction of logic in work through the concepts of field and habitus.

In the following vignette, in which I observe the nurse Mia on an evening shift, I invite the reader inside the lifeworld realm of practice (Schatzki, 2006) to experience how standardized practice in department E can unfold. The vignette illustrates how data were generated within a mesh of participant observation, informal interviews, discussions, and intersubjective constructions of sense in conjunction with the dynamics of the situation created by time (as a resource), patients, material artefacts, Mia's colleagues, and her position in the department. The observation began with a conversation concerning her involvement in the department's quality work. Then, as the pressure from incoming patients rose, I became predominantly an observer of her work. Later, during the same shift, I became both participant observer and conversational partner with Mia in a discussion about her practice.

Mia: Naturally Performing Standardized Nursing

Mia has recently been awarded a position as a key quality person—the cornerstones of quality work in the department. The position is closely connected to the promotion of 'best practice', where one of Mia's tasks is to disseminate and teach her colleagues the correct performance of practices and convince them to follow the standards. Because the department is quiet at the beginning of her shift, we seize the opportunity to have an informal chat in the staff's rest area, which is sealed off from patients. Mia tells me how she was 'headhunted' for the position, and how she understands her role in the department. Having been appointed a key nurse, Mia must promote the logics of standardized practice to her colleagues. This is natural for her, as she juxtaposes the correction of colleagues' individual practice with helping them become better nurses:

MIA: My manager asked if this position was something for me. She knows I like to set things in motion and also that I believe in order and structure. I accepted, although it gives me more work. It's now my job to teach my colleagues how we best comply with the standards and get ready for the second accreditation round approaching this autumn. Besides the national ones, which apply to all hospitals, we also have some local clinical guidelines here and they must be followed to the letter. It's a challenging task indeed, because many just do things their own way, the ways they are used to.

RESEARCHER (R): Is it, then, your job to correct your colleagues if they don't do things the right way?

MIA: Yes, my job is to *help* my colleagues. When I correct them, it is actually the same as helping them because they have a desire to improve their practice.

(Field notes, informal conversation)

Later the same evening, a man in his 50s is admitted by ambulance. "He is a strenuous patient", the nurse who coordinates the work tasks that evening tells me. "He comes in quite often . . . is a chronic alcoholic and absolutely not a dream patient", she continues. She decides that Mia should be assigned this patient. Mia accepts reluctantly but quickly sizes up the situation. "Come on, let's go to work", she says to me. We head for the computers where she retrieves the patient's medical records.

I have learned that the medical records that are produced and stored in the computer system are key tools in nursing practice. Mia encourages me to read the detailed medical records with her: "Not really prepared for cooperation", a "trouble maker", a "drunkard", and "leaves for a smoke when the urge becomes too pressing" are terms and sentences I understand. "And, on top of it, he is MRSA[5] positive, which is not a dangerous condition", Mia explains, "yet, it requires special provisions in practice". We then head for the ward to meet the patient.

It seems that that this patient is a challenge. In accordance with national clinical guidelines for MRSA-infected patients, we have to don a special protective uniform, including gloves and a mask, anew each time we enter the ward. Mia also has to negotiate access to the patient's body step by step, as he clearly demarcates his acceptable boundaries. In accordance with the Patient Safe Hospital program, Mia has to measure a number of clinical parameters for all patients, such as blood pressure, temperature, and pulse. In addition, for this patient, she has to administer a new MRSA test to see if he is still positive. Her negotiations are mixed with questions for the man, and her tone is light and humorous. Her interaction with the patient, who looks as if he is about to explode at any moment, resembles nursing on a tightrope. When she senses she is reaching a personal limit of his, she pauses and then regains her balance with him before continuing.

It turns out that both the patient and Mia have lived in Greenland. The conversation between them flows from this point on, and I cannot help but admire how Mia smoothly manages to measure all the parameters while I write down the values for her on my pad. "They drank booze up there in amounts you can't imagine", the man confides in us, and we can't help but laugh. He then asks for some tranquillizing medicine.

"Only the doctor can prescribe that kind of medicine for you", Mia says, "however, I can give you some of these less strong pills. Do you want that?" He accepts.

We remove our protective uniforms outside the ward and head for the department's central office space. We can hear the man shouting behind us in a husky voice, "Remember to bring me food. I'm hungry as hell".

On our way back to the office area, Mia tells me how important she thinks it is that nurses convey empathy and patience with this type of patient. I ask her if she, at some point, considered skipping measuring the clinical parameters or perhaps some of them since it was obvious that her patient was not very cooperative. "Absolutely not", she asserts. "It's important that we get this work done every time and with every patient". I then ask her how she assesses the standardization of practice. "There is tighter steering now and that's good", she says. "Variation was plainly too large earlier".

Arriving in the office space, Mia grabs what she explains is a scoring scheme for dosing the tranquillizing medicine for her alcoholic patient. I see her writing numbers on the paper: zeroes and ones, depending on the values of the clinical parameters she has measured. The following dialog takes place between us:

MIA: Through its inbuilt algorithm, the scheme will calculate the right dose of medicine for him.
R: What do you think about schemes such as this?
Mia: I like them. They make things easier. I just hope he scores enough points to get more than 50 milligrams because that will be too little for him.
R: How do you know that it will be too little?
MIA: He has been a chronic alcoholic for many years. I know from experience that he will need a larger dose than the one a low score will provide him.
R: But does that mean you have knowledge that the scheme cannot take into account?
MIA: No, no, the scheme works well, and I always follow it.
R: But when you say that you *hope* he will make a high score, isn't it because you feel you can't fully rely on the scheme?
MIA: [pauses and then looks at me] I haven't thought about it in that way before, but you may be right. The scheme cannot take into account the fact that he has been a chronic alcoholic for a long time and I know that matters.
R: So what will you do if the result comes out below the level you believe is needed. Will you give him a larger dose?
MIA: No, I am not allowed to do that, but I will surely consult a doctor and argue for a larger dose for the patient.

Mia's elevated position in the department results from her official appointment as one of the nurses who promote what is perceived as nursing excellence and safe praxis based on the most recent research-based knowledge of the field. Moreover, she is highly respected by her colleagues and superiors as a competent nurse, which was openly disclosed on several occasions during my fieldwork. This perception of her naturalizes and reinforces her elevated position and allows her to decide, without consulting any of the other nurses on shift, that she can withdraw to the sofa area with me to discuss her involvement in the department's quality work. In light of my other observations in the department, this autonomous act was relatively unusual.

Mia's appointment as a quality coordinator has granted her a semi-managerial function, where correcting the work of colleagues seems only natural to her because the standards separate right from wrong, which means that corrections can be made equivalent to helping. She is a firm believer of the quality-leveraging ability of standards and a proud frontrunner of their dissemination in the department, because her habitus is in accord with the changed conditions of the field. As Mia puts it, variation was too large earlier. Therefore, what for some nurses is a constraint on practice, is for Mia an opportunity to pursue new paths in her career and a natural advancement to practice. We can say that the logic of Mia's practice results from a good match between her dispositions (habitus) and the framework set for her work (the conditions of the field), which produces her pre-reflexive and naturalized relation to her world as it appears in the earlier dialog.

Because Mia's relation with the standards steering her work is a matter of course, she does not recognize that she actually compensates the medication scheme in practice. The scheme represents a pool of abstract knowledge in which she believes and firmly trusts, and the operating of the scheme is, for her, perfectly logical. The situation is illustrative of a gap between pre-reflexive embodied knowing in action (Bourdieu, 1990, p. 91) and the forecasted linearity of planned action. Brown and Duguid (1991) described this kind of professional situation as the gap between prescribed practice and actual practice that happens when organizational members take routes other than the ones they are supposed to, according to standards, in their efforts to solve problems in work. The efforts to solve problems in practice are often made pre-reflexively. Mia has a watchful eye on the scheme, ready to intervene if a faulty result arises, yet she believes the algorithm does the job and only recognizes the paradoxical situation when I question her way of making sense of the situation. By asking her to reflect on the scheme's properties and usefulness, the logic of her practice breaks down because the fuzziness and ambiguity by which sense is maintained in practice cannot be explained against the rationality that the scheme represents. Her hesitation implies that the situation I put her in is relatively uncomfortable to her. Paraphrasing Bourdieu (2003, p. 288), I can say that Mia does not have the scientific truth of her practice in her head that I am trying to extract from my observation of her practice. Bourdieu applies the concept of doxa to explain the state where things are characterized by their naturalness because agents are fully engaged in what takes place and therefore do not reflect on the rationale of it because no explanation is needed (Bourdieu, 1989). Mia can be said to be fully engaged in quality work in the department, therefore, she can only hesitantly recognize the missing logic of the situation.

The analytical approach applied facilitates an analysis that seeks to go beyond practice as it appears from the practitioner's point of view. Bourdieu (1973) describes this as a break with the self-evident and natural that takes into account that the representation of the social world will always reflect the perspective from where it is approached. Hence this approach allows an understanding that Mia's practice throughout reflects her embeddedness within a specific field at a specific time, when, for example, political interests directly and indirectly influence what is regarded as valuable and sound. In sum, with Bourdieu (1991), we can say that the whole structure of the field is embedded in Mia's practice.

Final Reflections

Standardization is under-represented in the scholarly literature concerned with the organization of work, and, paradoxically, its relevance is often overlooked despite the fact that the effects of standardized processes are often uncertain (Brunsson et al., 2012, p. 617). Standardization is rationalized organizing. It seeks to prescribe practice by pre-constructing a forecasted space of possibilities to delimit action which, however, often contrasts actual practice (Brown & Duguid, 1991).

In this chapter, I have sought to generate an understanding of the relation between standardization and the organization of nursing work through a Bourdieuan ethnography of practice in which I have been the prime tool of my own research (Wacquant, 2005). In my ethnographic fieldwork, I tried to situate myself at the point of practice production, to immerse myself to the extent possible in the nursing practices of department E. In this way, I took an epistemic position of learning the field through my engagement with it (Desmond, 2014; Hasse, 2015), and what I have termed my ethnographic moves—that is, the planned and unplanned decisions of data generation—were informed by my emerging understanding.

Among ethnographic researchers, the position of the researcher is the subject of much debate concerned with the truthfulness of research. However, rather than regarding the researcher as a problem of research, it seems generative to understand the researcher as "a vector of knowledge of the social world" (Wacquant, 2011, p. 88). From a Bourdieuan perspective, the research object is always a construction—a model of reality built by the researcher (Bourdieu, 1989). The ethnographic path of my research included various methods to build my research object, that is, to uncover where the standards applied to practice originate, how they impact work, and how the nurses handle them. The kind of research I have pursued is, however, particularly vulnerable to issues of access to the research site and the building of trusting relations with field agents.

From a practice perspective, understanding organizing is to understand what happens in practice and why it happens. To do so requires a firm eye for the subtle and complex layers of meaning in and of everyday work and working life. The case presented provides insight into how standards and standardization are experienced and handled in actual practice. Specifically, it exemplifies how standards can enter the terrain of innate logic in practice for the practitioner whose habitus is in accord with their inbuilt presuppositions. Moreover, it was illustrated that the rule-like nature of standards (Brunsson et al., 2012) creates a tension in practice that can be described as a tension between the linear logic of forecasted action and the fuzzy logic of practice. The case thus demonstrated how Mia's embodied nursing dispositions acquired through many years of work experience were bracketed to let the algorithm arrive at the appropriate dose of medicine. However, Mia's knowledge was only bracketed to the extent that she was alert, at a pre-discursive level, and ready to react if the algorithm had arrived at a result that conflicted with her knowledge.

From the case, it appears that, in practice, work is standardized under the watchful eye of a competent professional who will, if needed, compensate a standard shortcoming. This may seem like an optimum situation; however, it seems reasonable to question the apparent gap between precepts and practice. Standardization draws attention to the formal structuring of work, whereas the practitioners, patients, artefacts, colleagues, and all other things that impinge on how work is carried out are relegated to the background as stable variables. The Bourdieuan practice approach to organization illuminates why this is problematic and suggests that standardization implies a missing appreciation of the complexity of practice. Contrary to the belief that standards organize work, we have seen an example of how skilful decisions in practice result from the nurse's ability to size up emerging problems.

Seen through a practice lens, the organization of work happens through participants' immersion into several practices (Nicolini, 2013). Standardization is a mode of organizing these practices, a possibility among possibilities. The choice of this particular mode of organizing is not neutral (Timmermans & Epstein, 2010). Standardization addresses the perspective through which hospital services are scrutinized and evaluated. It addresses political choices related to the functioning of the hospital sector, in other words, and the resulting transformations to the field from these choices.

Comment by Davide Nicolini: On the Playful Relationship Between Theory, Practice, and Ethnographic Data

In her chapter on the logic of nursing, Ernst provides a brief yet vivid illustration of the mesmerizing nature of expert work when observed from close quarters. The author invites us to follow her into a hospital after dark. This is the time of the day when the hustling and bustling of modern medicine slows down and the humanity of both patients and carers takes central stage. Ernst invites us to observe the skilled activity of Mia, a nurse who has to walk the tightrope between standardized medicine, a difficult patient and her ongoing concern to provide the best care for this old and sick man.

Ernst shows us that while the nurse embraces the tools and conventions of standardized medicine, she follows a form of practical wisdom that is different from the mechanical logic of action inscribed in the algorithm she uses to calculate the dosage of the medication. Rather than thinking and acting, she seems to be acting thinkingly (Weick, 1983). Mia 'hopes' that the algorithm will agree with her judgment that the normal dosage is not enough to stop the suffering. She also tells the researcher, and us, that if the algorithm proves to be too stubborn, she will look for the support of another caring human, a doctor, so that together they can overrule the protocol. In the end, we are not told what happens, and the story remains open-ended. This nice trick forces the readers to reflect on the issue rather than simply take note of the story. What would you have done in Mia's shoes?

The paper is an interesting, albeit necessarily, succinct illustration of expert work and of how standards, rules, and algorithms enter the practice of consummate professionals. Ernst shows that many traditional theoretical dualisms dissolve when we zoom in on practice. Mia's expert conduct is, in fact, both embodied and discursive. Her activity is based on experience and mediated by tools and resources. Biographical trajectory and institutional demands are equally and carefully balanced. Most importantly, expert work is about weaving all these aspects together to produce a fluent performance. The chapter also illustrates how critical standards, algorithms, and rules are a part of the accomplishment of any human activity; however, the way in which they affect social conduct is different from the traditional mechanical and deterministic view still prevalent among engineers, politicians, and, often, clinicians, according to which rules determine behaviour. Thus Ernst joins an increasing number of authors, some of which are referenced in the chapter, who suggest that rules, standards, and algorithms do not externally determine conduct. Rather, they are used as one of the resources which practitioners draw upon in the flow of activity to come up with what to do next and to account for what they did (if they are asked to).

The piece is also a reminder that theory should work in dynamic tension with the empirical material throughout the research process. The chapter is, therefore, illustrative of the generative and constraining nature of theory in ethnographic research and of the necessity to establish a playful relationship between the two in general and with the theory produced by the great thinkers, in particular. It reminds us that concepts should always be used as sensitizing tools. When they get in the way, we must get rid of them.

This is visible especially in how habitus figures in the chapter and in Ernst's arguments. Bourdieu's idea of habitus has the great historic merit of suggesting that to understand large phenomena, we should look at small, mundane, and, apparently, unremarkable things. To understand crucial aspects of French society, for example, we need to look into ordinary settings, such as kitchens and dining rooms, rather than high places or abstract spheres populated with structures, functions, and the like (Bourdieu, 1984). Habitus also explains how large phenomena make themselves present in the 'here and now' of human conduct. Habitus is, in fact, a set of dispositions and "structured structures predisposed to function as structuring structures" (Bourdieu, 1990, p. 53). These are acquired during one's upbringing and secondary socialization and activated in the course of human activity, when the interaction between habitus and field conditions generates conduct. Through habitus, society manifests itself at any moment of our lives. Most importantly, such conduct stems from a sense of what to do next that is mostly pre-discursive and perceived as inescapable, an aspect that Ernst nicely captures in her chapter. This is because habitus implies a relation of commitment and belonging to a field, a total investment that is so strong that it becomes invisible to the initiator. In short, the value of habitus lies in the importance of placing attention on the processes and mechanisms through which orderly social practices are produced and reproduced without giving unduly priorities to the human carriers of such processes as in the traditional social theory.

The theoretical concept of habitus, however, also has analytical limitations. First, looking at Mia's case, it could be argued that habitus is less sequential than as imagined by Bourdieu. Mia's story is marked by several hesitations and doubts, while for Bourdieu, habitus just makes things happen. Second, and strictly related, Mia's conduct does not seem to be driven by the quasi-determinist and inescapable force that Bourdieu ascribed to habitus. In fact, there is a lot of thinking, tinkering, soul searching, and reflecting going on in the scene. Put differently, Ernst's description can be read as capturing elements of situated uncertainty and openness that are excluded by a strict understanding of habitus (see Schatzki, 1997, for a discussion) and that the ethnographic text makes visible. Finally, we are presented with an image of a nurse who is conflicted and is both in search of the 'right' dose of drug and in search of herself. According to Bourdieu, habitus and its relative tacit system of oppositions selects for us what is sensible and reasonable to say and do. However, in the case of Mia, there are several ways of being sensible and reasonable. Mia is carrying not one but many habitus: nurse, employee, champion of standards, carer, and object of Ernst's observations. Moreover, these different habitus do not sit well together (something that Bourdieu never addressed). The chapter is, therefore, a good demonstration of the necessity to keep theory and evidence in dialectic relation. The text asks us to reflect not only on expert practice and the role of standards in everyday practice, but it also invites us to treat theoretical concepts as playful tools in research. This does not mean rejecting established concepts such as Bourdieu's habitus, but taking them as living materials, ideas that can and need to be further expanded and developed.

Notes

1. I apply the definition of standardization put forth by Timmermans and Epstein (2010, p. 71) who, drawing on Bowker and Star (1999), explain it as "a process of constructing uniformities across time and space, through the generation of agreed-upon rules".
2. The National Society for Patient Safety describes itself as an independent organization receiving regional funding and grants from funds and membership fees. It

cooperates with partners abroad and engages in several projects and programs to enhance patient safety, including 'Patient Safe Hospital' (http://www.patient sikkerhed.dk/om-os.aspx accessed January 2016).
3. 'Patientsikkert Sygehus set fra helikopteren' [Patient Safe Hospital viewed from the helicopter] (author's translation) (http://www.patientsikkertsygehus.dk/media/31569/microsoft%20powerpoint%20-%20pss-horsens%208%20juni.pdf accessed January 2016).
4. The theoretical foundations of the practice theory label are indebted to Bourdieu, Giddens, Garfinkel, and Foucault (Corradi, Gherardi, & Verzelloni, 2010), who in turn are indebted to, notably, Wittgenstein and Heidegger (Nicolini, 2009). For a detailed account of what unites practice theories, see Rouse (2007) or Nicolini (2013, pp. 6–10).
5. The term *MRSA* stands for methicillin-resistant *Staphylococcus aureus*, that is, a drug-resistant staphylococcus (https://sundhedsstyrelsen.dk/en/disease-and-treatment/infectious-diseases/mrsa/guidelines accessed January 2016).

Discussant References

Bourdieu, P. (1984). *Distinction: A Social Critique of the Judgement of Taste*. Cambridge, MA: Harvard University Press.
Bourdieu, P. (1990). *The Logic of Practice*. Stanford University Press.
Schatzki, T. R. (1997). Practices and Actions a Wittgensteinian Critique of Bourdieu and Giddens. *Philosophy of the Social Sciences*, 27 (3), 283–308.
Weick, K. E. (1983). Managerial Thought in the Context of Action. In S. Srivastva (Ed.), *The Executive Mind: New Insights on Managerial Thought and Action*. San Francisco: Jossey-Bass, 221–242.

Chapter References

Agar, Michael H. (2008). *The Professional Stranger: An Informal Introduction to Ethnography, 2nd ed.* Bingley: Emerald Group Publishing.
Allen, Davina. (1998). Record-Keeping and Routine Nursing Practice: The View from the Wards. *Journal of Advanced Nursing*, 27 (6), 1223–1230. doi:10.1046/j.1365-2648.1998.00645.x
Andersen, Pernille Tanggaard, & Jensen, Jens-Jørgen. (2010). Healthcare Reform in Denmark. *Scandinavian Journal of Public Health*, 38 (3), 246–252. doi:http://dx.doi.org/10.1177/1403494809350521
Baumann, Steven L. (2010). The Limitations of Evidenced-Based Practice. *Nursing Science Quarterly*, 23 (3), 226–230. doi:http://dx.doi.org/10.1177/0894318410371833
Bjørn, Pernille, & Balka, Ellen. (2007). Health Care categories have politics too: Unpacking the managerial agendas of Electronic Triage Systems. In Liam J. Bannon, W. Ina, G. Carl, Richard H. R. Harper, & S. Kjeld (Eds.), *ECSCW 2007: Proceedings of the 10th European Conference on Computer-Supported Cooperative Work*, Limerick, Ireland, 24–28 September, 2007. London: Springer, 371–390.
Bourdieu, Pierre. (1973). The Three Forms of Theoretical Knowledge. *Social Science Information*, 12 (1), 53–80. doi:10.1177/053901847301200103
Bourdieu, Pierre. (1989). Social Space and Symbolic Power. *Sociological Theory*, 7 (1), 14–25. doi:http://dx.doi.org/10.2307/202060
Bourdieu, Pierre. (1990). *The Logic of Practice*. Cambridge: Polity Press.
Bourdieu, Pierre. (1991). *Language and Symbolic Power*. Cambridge, UK: Polity Press.

Bourdieu, Pierre. (2003). Participant Objectivation. *Journal of the Royal Anthropological Institute*, 9 (2), 281–294.

Bourdieu, Pierre, & Wacquant, Loïc J. D. (1992). *An Invitation to Reflexive Sociology*. Cambridge: Polity Press.

Brown, John Seely, & Duguid, Paul. (1991). Organizational Learning and Communities-of-Practice: Toward a Unified View of Working, Learning, and Innovation. *Organization Science*, 2 (1), 40–57. doi:10.1287/orsc.2.1.40

Brunsson, Nils, Rasche, Andreas, & Seidl, David. (2012). The Dynamics of Standardization: Three Perspectives on Standards in Organization Studies. *Organization Studies*, 33 (5/6), 613–632. doi:10.1177/0170840612450120

Corradi, Gessica, Gherardi, Silvia, & Verzelloni, Luca. (2010). Through the Practice Lens: Where Is the Bandwagon of Practice-Based Studies Heading? *Management Learning*, 41 (3), 265–283.

Desmond, Matthew. (2014). Relational Ethnography. *Theory and Society*, 43 (5), 547–579. doi:10.1007/s11186-014-9232-5

Gherardi, Silvia. (2015). Why Kurt Wolff Matters for a Practice-Based Perspective of Sensible Knowledge in Ethnography. *Journal of Organizational Ethnography*, 4 (1), 117–131. doi:10.1108/JOE-11-2013-0021

Halford, Susan, Obstfelder, Aud, & Lotherington, Anne-Therese. (2010). Changing the Record: The Inter-Professional, Subjective and Embodied Effects of Electronic Patient Records. *New Technology, Work and Employment*, 25 (3), 210–222. doi:10.1111/j.1468-005X.2010.00249.x

Hammersley, Martyn, & Atkinson, Paul. (2007). *Ethnography: Principles in Practice*. London: Routledge.

Hasse, Cathrine. (2015). *An Anthropology of Learning: On Nested Frictions in Cultural Ecologies, Vol. 2015*. Dordrecht: Springer Netherlands.

Hauck, Sheila, Winsett, Rebecca P., & Kuric, Judy. (2013). Leadership Facilitation Strategies to Establish Evidence-Based Practice in an Acute Care Hospital. *Journal of Advanced Nursing*, 69 (3), 664–674. doi:http://dx.doi.org/10.1111/j.1365-2648.2012.06053.x

Hujala, Anneli, Andri, Maria, and Kyriakidou, Olivia. (2014). Professional Autonomy under Pressure: Towards a Dialectical Approach. *Journal of Health Organization and Management*, 28 (5), 635–652. doi:http://dx.doi.org/10.1108/jhom-10-2013-0224

Jespersen, Peter Kragh, & Salomonsen, Houlberg Heidi. (2009). *Changing Professional Autonomy in Contexts of Institutional Change*. 25th EGOS Colloquium. Sub-theme 07: Organizing the Public Sector: Governance and Public Management Reform, Barcelona.

Keenan, Gail M., Tschannen, Dana, & Wesley, Mary Lou. (2008). Standardized Nursing Terminologies Can Transform Practice. *Journal of Nursing Administration*, 38 (3), 103–106. doi:10.1097/01.NNA.0000310728.50913.de

Kirkpatrick, Ian, Dent, Mike, & Jespersen, Peter Kragh. (2011). The Contested Terrain of Hospital Management: Professional Projects and Healthcare Reforms in Denmark. *Current Sociology*, 59 (4), 489–506. doi:http://dx.doi.org/10.1177/0011392111402718

Lofland, John. (1971). *Analysing Social Settings*. Belmont, CA: Wadsworth.

Nicolini, Davide. (2009). Zooming In and Out: Studying Practices by Switching Theoretical Lenses and Trailing Connections. *Organization Studies*, 30 (12), 1391–1418. doi:10.1177/0170840609349875

Nicolini, Davide. (2013). *Practice Theory, Work, and Organization: An Introduction, 1st ed.* Oxford: Oxford University Press.

Rouse, Joseph. (2007). Practice Theory. In Dov M. Gabbay, T. Paul, & W. John (Eds.), *Handbook of the Philosophy of Science*. Amsterdam, Elsevier BV. 499–540.

Schatzki, Theodore R. (2002). *The Site of the Social: A Philosophical Account of the Constitution of Social Life and Change*. University Park, PA: Penn State Press.

Schatzki, Theodore R. (2006). On Organizations as They Happen. *Organization Studies*, 27 (12), 1863–1873. doi:10.1177/0170840606071942

Taylor, Sue, & Allen, Davina. (2007). Visions of Evidence-Based Nursing Practice. *Nurse Researcher*, 15 (1), 78–83. doi:http://dx.doi.org/10.7748/nr2007.10.15.1.78.c6057

Timmermans, Stefan, & Epstein, Steven. (2010). A World of Standards but Not a Standard World: Toward a Sociology of Standards and Standardization. *Annual Review of Sociology*, 36 (1), 69–89. doi:http://dx.doi.org/10.1146/annurev.soc.012809.102629

Timmermans, Stefan, & Kolker, Emily S. (2004). Evidence-Based Medicine and the Reconfiguration of Medical Knowledge. *Journal of Health and Social Behavior*, 45, 177–193. doi:10.2307/3653831

Travaglia, Joanne F., & Braithwaite, Jeffrey. (2009). Analysing the "Field" of Patient Safety Employing Bourdieusian Technologies. *Journal of Health Organization and Management*, 23 (6), 597–609. doi:http://dx.doi.org/10.1108/14777260911001626

Viitala, Riitta. (2014). Leadership in Transformation: A Longitudinal Study in a Nursing Organization. *Journal of Health Organization and Management*, 28 (6), 602–618.

Wacquant, Loïc. (2004). Following Pierre Bourdieu into the Field. *Ethnography*, 5 (4), 387–414.

Wacquant, Loïc. (2005). Carnal Connections: On Embodiment, Apprenticeship, and Membership. *Qualitative Sociology*, 28 (4), 445–474. doi:10.1007/s11133-005-8367-0

Wacquant, Loïc. (2011). Habitus as Topic and Tool: Reflections on Becoming a Prizefighter. *Qualitative Research in Psychology*, 8 (1), 81–92.

Wears, Robert L. (2015). Standardisation and Its Discontents. *Cognition, Technology & Work*, 17 (1), 89–94. doi:10.1007/s10111-014-0299-6

Wicks, Deidre. (1998). *Nurses and Doctors at Work: Rethinking Professional Boundaries*. Buckingham: Open University Press.

7 Contexting the Patient

A Meeting Ethnography of Patient Involvement in Quality Development

Mette Brehm Johansen and discussant Anne Reff Pedersen

Introduction

In the last decades, government policies concerning increased user involvement have proliferated. Many different welfare sectors are faced with the requirement that users should be involved and heard in relation to the development of services provided. In health care, this is formulated in simple policy and strategy statements such as there is a need for "the patient perspective in quality work" (Sundhedsstyrelsen, 2002, p. 18; the author's translation) or that the patients' voice is heard (Terms of reference for the user panel, 2015; the author's translation). But even though patients are in abundance in the daily work in the clinic, it is not clear who to actually involve, include, or listen to when involving patients in quality development. Also it is not clear what to be involved in and in what ways. So the path from airy policy and strategy statements to the actual work performed in the clinic is long, and in order for patient involvement in quality development to become a consolidated practice, a lot of work is needed. The core interest of this chapter is focused on different aspects of this work. Through ethnographic fieldwork in an oncology clinic in a university hospital, I have studied patient involvement in quality development by looking at concrete activities taking place in concrete settings by concrete people. Through an analysis of empirical material in the form of both meeting observations and interviews with professionals, I will show how an ethnographic approach to patient involvement in quality development elucidates how involving patients in quality development is not a simple method-driven activity assuring the inclusion of 'the patient's voice' in quality development but requires contexting in order to be achieved. Through the use of the concept of contexting, the analysis points to the way tasks and patients continuously need to be related to other work processes and knowledge ideals in the clinic in order for patient involvement in quality development to be a doable endeavor.

Organizational Phenomenon and Setting: Patient Involvement in Quality Development in an Oncology Clinic

The organizational phenomenon taking centre stage in this chapter is patient involvement in quality development. Many methods for patient involvement in quality development exist and the methods are as different as conducting large national patient experience surveys, establishing patient panels with regular meetings, and using patients' photo diaries to gain insight into the patients' experiences in the hospital. All these methods are used in order to involve patients in discussing and sometimes choosing what needs to be improved in the clinic and how these improvements might be achieved. Patients' roles in these methods vary widely from being quite passive respondents to pre-formulated survey questions to being very active discussion partners with professionals around themes and topics in the patient panel. A core element of these activities is that some patients are involved—directly or indirectly—in developing organizational procedures and practices in order to improve conditions for future patients. Central to this are the ideas that 'the patient's voice' can be used to inform these practices and procedures and that some patients can speak on behalf of other patients and/or in some way guarantee patient interests.

But the largely method-driven character of patient involvement in quality development makes it quite invisible that involving patients is not just a question of choosing and using involvement methods. A whole lot of work is also required from both patients and professionals to actually involve patients in quality development *and* to connect both the concerns of the involvement activities and their outcomes with the practices and procedures in the clinic that patient involvement is supposed to inform and improve.

The existing literature on involving patients in quality development[1] is broad but three central themes will be discussed here: issues of representativeness, patient roles and patient-professional relations, and legitimacy relating to the use of patient knowledge and experiences. Regarding representativeness, Martin explores how representativeness is a concept understood in different ways by patients and professionals involved in public involvement in health-service management (Martin, 2008a). El Enany, Currie, and Lockett show how the professionalization of patients participating in these kinds of activities can make it hard to make the participation representative (El Enany, Currie, & Lockett, 2013). From these studies, we can see that understandings of representativeness and their workings in practice and the question of whether some patients can speak on behalf of others is thus a central theme in the existing literature. This issue relates to the theme of patient roles and patient-professional relations existing in the literature. The policy ideal of equal relations and partnerships between patients and professionals is discussed in the literature and also shows how both patients and professionals contribute to creating the divide between more expert patients and less-expert patients, depending on the knowledge and experiences they draw on (Brooks, 2008; Martin & Finn, 2011; El Enany et al., 2013). This categorization of patients as more-or-less experts relates to a third theme in the literature: negotiations of legitimacy and the use of patient knowledge and experiences. In this regard, El Enany, Currie, and Lockett show that patients regarded as expert patients typically do not solely draw on their patient experiences as the 'expert knowledge' used in patient involvement activities. They also draw upon other expertise such as educational background and work experience (El Enany et al., 2013). Solbjør and Steinsbekk show how professionals tend to value patient knowledge most highly when it can either be ascribed a function as an alternative to professional knowledge or when it is in accordance with what the professionals themselves regard as good professionalism, thus supporting professional knowledge (Solbjør & Steinsbekk, 2011). Van de Bovenkamp and Zuiderent-Jerak, in their study of patient participation in the development of evidence-based guidelines (van de Bovenkamp & Zuiderent-Jerak, 2013), show that patients gaining status as legitimate participants (e.g., because of their knowledge of research literature on the subject in question) at the same moment lose their credibility as representing what the professionals regard as 'real' patients (van de Bovenkamp & Zuiderent-Jerak, 2013, p. 9). As these studies demonstrate, the use of patient knowledge in quality improvement is thus not a straightforward or uncomplicated matter.

Through this short view of the literature, it is thus evident that no simple relationship between what counts as patient knowledge and what kind of involvement this knowledge makes possible exists. Not many of the existing studies have an ethnographic approach to the study of patient involvement in quality development, but Fudge, Wolfe, and McKevitt (2008) and Brooks (2008) are exceptions. Fudge et al. (2008) study a modernization programme aimed at improving stroke services in two London boroughs, and Brooks (2008) studies a specific patient council in a UK acute hospital, specifically the nurse-patient relationship. In contrast to these studies, I take the approach of studying ethnographically how patient involvement in quality development is carried out not as one method in isolation but as a phenomenon happening in different ways—and with quite diverse effects—in the same clinic.

In order to study this phenomenon ethnographically, a field site was needed. An oncology clinic in a Danish university hospital was chosen because the health-care staff in this clinic used different ways of involving patients in quality development. In this oncology clinic, tasks related to patient involvement in quality development are performed mainly by nurses, more specifically, nurses in managing or specialized functions (a rehabilitation nurse, a development nurse, a head nurse, and managing nurses). Also, this kind of work is largely project-based since involving patients in quality development is not a routinized and compartmentalized part of the organization and thus has no 'natural' or evident place or role in organizational life. In the oncology clinic, they work with both established and more formal methods for doing patient involvement, and they also experiment with involving patients in ways they develop through specific problems they need to solve in managing the life of the clinic. The established methods used are surveys, a permanent patient panel, and occasional feedback meetings. The more experimental and bottom-up driven activities primarily consist of involving patients from the existing patient panel in other tasks. These tasks include being part of a teaching programme for nurses, introducing new employees to the clinic, and using patient panel members for doing presentations on what it's like to be a patient in the clinic in different fora such as in management seminars or doctors' meetings. However, in order to explore the ways in which patient involvement in quality development is a lot more than the application of formal methods, I have chosen an analytical approach centred on work in order to widen the object of study.

Patient Involvement in Quality Development Approached Analytically as *Work*

When studying patient involvement in quality development ethnographically, what comes into view is a complex task requiring places, people, meetings, coordination, and considerations that need to be achieved to become an actual work practice, not just an airy policy or strategy statement. The ethnographic approach creates a widened room for understanding the phenomenon in question as something more than just formal involvement methods put into practice, thus complicating the alluringly simple picture of patient involvement methods as 'input-output machines' providing blueprints for action.

Work has become a renewed matter of concern in management and organization studies in the past decade (Barley & Kunda, 2001; Brannan, Pearson, & Worthington, 2007; Phillips & Lawrence, 2012). Barley and Kunda plea for bringing work back into the study of organizations in order to understand what they term 'postbureaucratic organizing' and study work practices and relations in situ in order to give attention to the dynamic aspects of organizing (Barley & Kunda, 2001, p. 84, 88). Even though hospitals can hardly be understood as 'postbureaucratic', it is still worth taking a closer look at some of the new kinds of work gaining prominence in health care. With the continuing emphasis on individualization and patient involvement in health care (paradoxically coinciding with a strong strive for standardization), involving patients in quality development in the clinic has become a matter of course and a political expectation, but *how* it is done is not since it is still a relatively new kind of work. This study thus also raises questions about how new tasks can gain a foothold in the landscape of existing ones—the answer being an empirical matter.

Work has also been prominent in ethnographic studies of hospital life and the workings of medicine (e.g., Berg, 1997; Strauss et al., 1997). Strauss et al. stress the importance of attention to the "analytic examination of work itself" (Strauss et al., 1997, p. xv) in opposition to work as a background for studying division of labour, professions, careers, etc. Through a thorough study of work in hospitals, Strauss et al. (1997) discern different kinds of work inherent in medical-nursing care. Inspired by Strauss et al., I study patient involvement in quality development as work tasks alongside other work tasks in the clinic rather than as formal methods. It is not my purpose here to create new generic categories of work in a hospital setting but solely to use the concept of work to point to the very practical doings of patient involvement in order to escape the heavy focus on formal methods.

One type of work central to the work done in and around patient involvement activities can be conceptualized as contexting. Contexting is a concept used by Asdal and Moser (2012) to discuss the reseacher's role in context-making. Asdal and Moser argue that contexts are not out there waiting to be found but instead are constantly being made: "By contexting we mean that contexts are being made together with the objects, texts, and issues at stake" (Asdal & Moser, 2012, p. 303). They point to the researcher's role in contexting, but, as I will argue, contexting is also a core part of the work done by the professionals and patients in patient involvement activities. This is done in selecting/deselecting and assembling relevant contexts for action in specific situations in order to make tasks, patients' knowledge positions, possible actions, and other work processes in the clinic be in accordance.

The two examples of analysis presented later in this chapter each deal with an example of contexting done by the professionals in order to turn patient involvement in quality development into concrete practices in the clinic. The first analysis shows how what is taken to the table in the patient panel needs contexting—both before and after the meetings—in order for the professionals to be able to both connect to and inform the everyday work practices in the clinic. The second analysis shows how the professionals also need contexting in order to create an understanding of what position the knowledge and experiences of the participating patients in quality development can take. This example of contexting is especially important since involving patients in quality development is not yet a routinized part of professional work in the clinic. In sum, the work approach to patient involvement in quality development thus makes it possible to discuss how the phenomenon studied is more complex than merely applying formal involvement methods. Let us now turn to the fieldwork.

Problems of the Everyday: How to Study an Episodic and Non-routinized Phenomenon Ethnographically

A strong ideal in organizational ethnography is striving for studying everyday life in organizations in order to capture the mundane, ordinary, routine, or, otherwise, unseen details of organizational life (e.g., Yanow et al., 2009; Yanow, 2012). In the oncology clinic studied in the fieldwork grounding this chapter, patient involvement in quality development as an organizational phenomenon has an episodic character since it is not a fully consolidated and routinized part of the organization and clinic in question. This circumstance made it much more difficult to find 'a suitable everyday' to position oneself in as a fieldworker than when the object of study is, e.g., consultations or treatments, where everyday work in the clinic occurs in more routinized, localized, and schematized ways. Clearly, when the clinic is a large organization with multiple settings and the phenomenon studied is episodic in character, finding out where to be at what time is not a trivial or simple task. Choosing a traditional approach of being in the clinic for six months full time would probably not have given me rich data on the workings of patient involvement in quality development or how it relates to other work processes going on in the clinic. Given that the phenomenon is not a formalized part of everyday life in the clinic and that the highly scheduled workday left very little unscheduled time in the daily life of the clinic, the classical fieldwork strategy of 'hanging around' would not have produced sufficient data to study patient involvement in quality development and how it is practiced as an organizational phenomenon. Therefore, the fieldwork was instead planned around three different involvement processes. These processes were identified through an explorative interview on the topic of patient involvement with the head nurse and the head of the clinic. The interview was initiated with the question: "Can you tell me, how do you work with patient involvement in this clinic?", and proceeded with elaborations hereof. After this interview and informal talks with a managing nurse in one of the diagnose-related teams in the clinic, I chose three empirical points of entry: an already established patient panel where patients meet with professionals and discuss issues or solve concrete tasks in order to get patients' input on specific themes or concrete tasks; an encompassing and, at the time of the fieldwork, newly initiated project aiming at creating a more patient-centred culture in the clinic; and, lastly, a collection of data from what was in the clinic termed 'naturally occurring feedback' from patients participating in an already existing patient education forum for cancer patients learning to live with late effects of cancer treatment. What these three processes have in common is that they are episodic in their constitution—they are not a routinized part of the everyday life of the clinic as are the treatment, care, and follow-up consultations in the outpatient clinic. Therefore, despite having three processes to study, the fieldwork was hard to conduct in a traditional sense. In order to actually 'meet' the phenomenon I set out to study, the fieldwork was thus—like the phenomenon—episodic in character. The fieldwork was episodic in the sense that it was largely organized around planned meetings of different kinds: patient panel meetings, preparation meetings, follow-up meetings, patient education meetings, quality council meetings, and different kinds of meetings and seminars in the project aiming at creating a more patient-centred culture in the clinic.

Meetings are a very common 'medium' for and main constituent of patient involvement in quality development and thus also turned out to be the central observation fora in the fieldwork discussed here. This study thus relates to a line of ethnographic work where meetings are a central object of study (Schwartzman, 1989; Thedvall, 2013; Nyqvist, 2015). While observing the meetings, I positioned myself—and was positioned by the others—as a silent meeting participant, a well-known role in the meetings I observed since the degree of (verbal) participation from the meeting participants varied greatly. I engaged in conversations with the other meeting participants during the breaks and before/after the meetings, but during the meetings, I would typically sit around the meeting table with the other meeting participants and write field notes on my iPad keyboard. The field notes written during the meetings were, as far as possible, the actual wording of the conversations taking place.

In order to go beyond the meetings, interviews with patients, professionals, and managers with experience in patient involvement in quality development were conducted during the fieldwork. These interviews can be understood as 'scheduled conversations' since there was little nonscheduled time to tap into as a fieldworker. I also viewed the interviews not as moments of extracting already existing information but as active interviews (Holstein & Gubrium, 2003) where data is created in interaction between the interviewee and the interviewer. I conducted, recorded, and transcribed 32 interviews in total. They can be grouped in three main parts relating to when they were conducted. At the onset of the fieldwork, group interviews with management teams were conducted in order to become familiar with the field and the large hospital centre (of which the oncology clinic was a part). After that, a cluster of interviews were conducted with members of the patient panel—both patients and professionals—and with professionals doing quality work in the clinic. The largest number of interviews was conducted at the end of the fieldwork after I had gained deep insight into the actual doings of patient involvement in quality development. The interviewees were nurses in managing or otherwise specialized functions and chief physicians.

As I mentioned at the beginning of this section, the practical fieldwork-related problem of knowing where to position oneself as a fieldworker when the phenomenon studied is episodic and non-routine in character can give rise to a problematization of the concept of the everyday in organizational ethnography and the trope (Rumsey, 2004) around this concept. When studying something ethnographically, researchers often strive for the informal, the behind the scenes, the everyday, the routine, and the ordinary. But what is this everyday exactly and what consequences does it have for the way we study the organizational phenomenon in question? In anthropology, the question has been pointed out, e.g. as a problem in the study of the lives of refugees in a refugee camp since a refugee camp can be understood as a transitory phenomenon in an 'unnatural' setting where stability, patterns, the ordinary, routine, and the everyday-like are not at the centre of attention (Malkki, 1997). But what does studying the non-everyday mean for the study of organizations and organizing? As with the discussion of the refugee camp and the study of extraordinary events, instead of patterns, routines, and the ordinary, the struggle to capture the everyday in organizational ethnography can be related to whether the fields studied are place-based or person-centred in their constitution. When studying phenomena that are not day-to-day endeavors, questions of where to actually be as a fieldworker—as has been argued in this section—become very important.

On an ending note, it can be argued that an empirical focus on the non-everyday gives way to considering whether something may or may not *become* everyday-like and routine, thus making the everyday-like an accomplishment rather than something taken for granted or something inherent in spatial conditions of organization or in types of work performed. But one could also go further and argue that when studying phenomena rather than places and a priori categories of work, in some way or another, all phenomena have everyday-like and routine elements in them.

Analysis: Taking a Closer Look at Patient Involvement in Quality Development

Let us now turn to the ethnographic data of the study and an analysis showing the advantages of taking an ethnographic approach to this topic. One advantage is that this approach makes it possible to see that patient involvement in quality development is not a simple method-driven activity assuring the inclusion of 'the patient's voice'. Rather, the analysis brings to the fore the contexting work needed in order for it to be carried out. The focus in the following analysis is thus on some of the work going on outside the formal methods for doing patient involvement, work needed in order to make the task of involving patients in quality development doable for the professionals.

Contexting Work Needed in Order to Go From Everyday Life in the Clinic to Patient Involvement Methods and Back Again

The data excerpts in this section come partly from a series of interviews with health-care professionals, mainly managing nurses and doctors in the clinic, and partly from observations from different kinds of meetings where discussions on patient involvement in quality development take place. In meetings and in other doings of patient involvement in quality development, competing agendas and requirements complicating this work are prominent, but this is also evident in the way the professionals talk about patient involvement in quality development. The following is an excerpt from a group interview with three nurses involved in the patient panel who talk about the work they do with the patient panel in the clinic and how it is related to other concerns in the clinic.

NURSE A: Also, it has been a considerable part of the balancing of expectations [with the patient participants in the panel] to make clear that not everything that is brought up [in the patient panel] we can go home and change. Some of it is processes that take time. Some of it is not on our level, it is important to consider, even though the patients are really keen on seeing things happen.

NURSE B: It is also an obligation to *get* all this information, which in some way or the other has to be put into action. Also, there are expectations from the patients that we do something about it and that really demands from us that we make things clear. But we are also aware that it should not necessarily affect our other prioritizing because what comes up in the patient panel should not necessarily override other activities we are doing even though the patient panel have an opinion of it, it is really a fine balancing act.

(Interview patient panel professionals: 3)

[. . .]

NURSE A: Actually, it requires a whole lot of work, managing and preparation for this group [the professionals] in order to avoid some of the shortcomings [of the patient panel method] and also in order to get a connection between what we discuss there and the other things going on in the clinic. So it is both a large responsibility and a comprehensive task for the ones responsible for the patient panel.

(Interview patient panel professionals: 12)

The ethnographic approach allows for noticing how the work done in the patient panel is not just compartmentalized as an isolated project in the clinic. In the excerpt, the nurses explain how the awareness of both patients' expectations and their own obligations to take action on issues or their deciding *not* to act on something brought up by the patients is central to the way they work with the patient panel. They say that they have to relate issues taken up or coming out of the meetings to other processes and concerns in the clinic when they decide which issues to take to the meetings and which ones to act upon after the meetings.

I find it fruitful to conceptualize this work as the contexting (Asdal & Moser, 2012, p. 303) continuously needed in order for the patient involvement in quality development to happen. Since patient involvement in quality development is not a 'natural' or routinized part of the work in the clinic, the professionals need to be very explicit in their contexting of issues brought to or coming out of the patient panel meetings. Contexting is a core part of deciding which of the issues to act upon and how to do it, as well as of deciding what not to act upon. Through contexting, the nurses relate specific issues to the broader life and work processes of the clinic. The issues need to be made relevant in relation to other concrete processes and actors in order for the professionals to be able to act on them. These actions might include, for instance, asking someone to fix the wheels of malfunctioning drip stands, sending an email to the regional office in order to pass on patients' comments about a poorly written pamphlet on patient rights, or pass on 'the patient perspective' to the quality council in order to discuss the patients' feedback on how waiting time is experienced from their point of view. Thus bringing together—or keeping apart—what in the specific situations is perceived as relevant contexts and issues is crucial in order to relate issues raised in the patient panel to other things going on in or outside the clinic. Deciding not to act upon an issue also involves contexting, as this happens through drawing in competing contexts made relevant in the decision situation. Thus contexts are not something to take for granted as background for action but something continuously being created and made relevant in specific situations. Patient involvement in quality development can thus be understood as requiring lot of contexting and making or dissolving connections in order for issues from the patient panel to be related to—or kept separate from—other processes in the clinic.

The Contexting Done by Professionals' in Order to Carve Out Knowledge Positions for Patients in Quality Development

The next empirical excerpts come from field notes from both agenda preparation meetings for the professionals in the patient panel and patient education meetings in one of the disease-specific teams in the clinic, as well as interviews with the managing nurses heading each of these two patient involvement activities. In the following excerpt, the managing nurse in one of the disease-specific teams in the clinic draws a contour of what constitutes a 'usable' patient for giving feedback.

> During an informal talk in her office, Louise is telling me about how she uses 'naturally' occurring feedback from patients participating in a patient education to 'catch' quality problems surfacing in the participating patients' exchange of experiences, which heavily structures the patient education sessions. Louise says: "What I like about it is the randomness. The patients have not signed up to participate in a feedback giving session and they are not all really resourceful patients that read all the pamphlets and want to help other patients", and she continues to explain to me that she needs to take care that the patient education sessions keep the format so that she can catch the 'natural' feedback from those patients with experience from the treatment and care in her team. She has considered using the forum to ask patients specific questions but as for now she doesn't want to influence the patients too much by asking pre-planned questions.
>
> (Managing nurse, informal interview)

A certain understanding of task, knowledge, and patients meet in this data excerpt. A wish for 'naturally' occurring feedback, a broad range of patients (being close to a wish for a representative patient), and the wish not to influence the patients by asking questions is at the heart of the managing nurse's considerations of what knowledge position patients can have in this kind of involvement. The nurse's ideal of knowledge as something naturally occurring, stemming from patients, and not influenced by pre-planned questions is evident in her explanation of how she uses patients' feedback on the treatment and care in her work. She is contexting the patient involvement activity by drawing on her knowledge ideal, thus also pointing to how the feedback gains its legitimacy and how a certain patient position is carved out through this contexting.

Let us now turn to another situation where contexting comes to the fore in order to see how a quite different patient is described in professionals' discussions of patients' roles when participating in the patient panel. The patient panel is a group of current or former patients in the clinic who meet with professionals four times a year to give their input on issues mostly selected by the professionals in the clinic. The patients decide to participate on the patient panel typically in response to a poster stating the need for new members to join. The patients are interviewed before entering the panel in order to ensure that they are able to 'free' themselves from their own course of disease and illness narrative and participate on somewhat more general terms in the panel. This is the professionals' framing of the primary requirement of the patients participating in the patient panel (Interview patient panel professionals: 2,6).

We enter the professionals' agenda preparation meeting during a discussion of what to put on the next meeting agenda. At this particular agenda preparation meeting, four professionals involved in the patient panel participated. In the discussion, patients' roles on the panel are brought up, and during this discussion, contours of what constitutes a 'usable' patient for giving feedback to the clinic emerge:

> *It is most successful when it [the task] is concrete, feedback on pamphlets for example; it is much more difficult when it comes to their subjective stances, things like communication is much more difficult to bring up in [other fora in] the clinic in a concrete way.*
>
> (Nurse A, agenda preparation meeting for
> the patient panel professionals)

The nurse explains that the results from concrete tasks taken up in the panel are the easiest to use in order to inform other areas of work in the clinic. It seems that when working on concrete problems, it is easier for the professionals to set aside that the patients on the panel participate with a more subjective perspective than when the professionals themselves have to bring a stance from the patient panel along to use in discussions in other fora or situations in the clinic. This fluctuating between the situational need for patients to represent a more general patient or contribute with very specific patient experiences is also central in the next field note excerpt from the same meeting:

> *Another nurse elaborates on the need for insight into the patient panel patients' experiences of concrete situations of treatment and care and the usefulness of this for developing interdisciplinary collaboration and*

other strategy-related issues [at the time of the meeting a process of renewing the strategy of the clinic was ongoing, and two of the nurses on the patient panel were also heavily involved in this process].

(Nurse B, agenda preparation meeting for
the patient panel professionals)

This nurse calls for the need for insight into the actual experiences of the individual patients, rather than wanting a unified stance from the patient panel when contexting the roles of the patients in relation to other processes in the clinic. This nurse's statement points to the situational character of what is a suitable role for the patients when involved in quality development. So even though one of the criteria for being a member of the patient panel—as mentioned earlier—is that you can free yourself from your concrete course of disease and participate on more general terms, this is not always the context chosen by the professionals to relate to in the work done on the panel. The nurse heading the panel also talks about another kind of task pointing even further away from a unified stance or a general patient position:

I am just really preoccupied with what Thomas [a doctor in the clinic] mentioned yesterday [at a management seminar about patient involvement in quality development], the question concerning the fact that right now we are arranging a new waiting room and is the furnishing good or bad? Well, why don't we just ask some of the patients there and just skip the question about the truth of it—even though we are in a natural science field—it is just one perspective. As professionals we don't have the absolute truth about the best way to arrange a waiting room either. It is just one perspective on something and the more perspectives we have, the more informed decisions we can make, so there is also a lot of opinion in this [matter].

(Head nurse, interview: 2)

The nurse explains that she is aware of the natural science ideal of knowledge underlying most areas of work in the clinic. However, she also turns away from this knowledge ideal with her reference to professionals not having an absolute 'truth' about these kinds of questions. In this case, the question of how best to arrange a waiting room is pushed outside the realm of both patients and professionals because she frames it as a question of perspective. This makes it more legitimate to have more perspectives on the question when deciding on a solution than when the question is closer to the core issues of treatment and care. In the negotiation of suitable tasks and the roles of the patients, the professionals fluctuate between the wish for a patient representing patients in general, the desire to capture unique patient experiences, and the view of patients as carrying just one perspective among many. This fluctuation demonstrates that the ideals of knowledge are situational and are connected to the difficulty of determining which patient is suitable for the task of giving feedback to the clinic. Through contexting, the professionals try to bring together the task, a suitable patient position, and a knowledge ideal in order to sort this out.

In sum, these analyses point to some of the contexting and other work required in order for patient involvement to be knit together with the rest of the life of the clinic and in order to carve out knowledge positions for patients in these activities where the patients have quite different positions than when being a patient undergoing treatment and care in the clinic. This analysis is focused on *professionals'* contexting, so whether the knowledge positions carved out are also taken by the patients in this kind of work is another question lying outside the realm of this chapter.

Conclusion

When studying patient involvement in quality development through ethnographic fieldwork, more than the methods-aspect of involving patients in quality development comes to the fore. With this approach, it becomes clear how patient involvement in quality development is an organizational practice entailing a lot of work in order to fulfil political and managerial demands. When studied ethnographically as concrete practices, it also becomes clear that even though the patient involvement activities studied are not fully consolidated or routinized parts of the daily life in the oncology clinic, they are also not isolated and compartmentalized. The phenomenon calls for the professionals to make new connections and/or change existing ones when dealing with specific questions or situations. Two elements of this have been discussed in this chapter: the contexting necessary for professionals in order to relate the involvement activities to other work processes in the clinic and the contexting involved in carving out knowledge positions available to patients when involved in quality development activities. This is not straightforward since 'the suitable patient' is a situational figure created and configured in different manners when involving patients in quality development. The contexting of knowledge ideals, patient roles and tasks to be solved is a complex job for professionals since no well-established and clear-cut knowledge position exists for patients in this kind of work. In light of this, it is relevant to point to the ways in which organizing through patients emerges when involving patients in quality development activities in the clinic. All in all, it is thus not a trivial task to answer the policy call for involving patients in quality development.

Comment by Anne Reff Pedersen: All That Work

Many studies of patient involvement in quality development are about *methods*: user panels, feedback meetings, public debates, patient surveys, or patient's videos, to mention some. These studies highlight the importance of bringing in patients' voices in health-care services with the goal of improving the quality of health care (Crawford et al., 2002; Bate &

Robert, 2007; Armstrong et al., 2013). The problem or drawback of these studies is the fact that they investigate single methods of how patient experience can inform the everyday of health care, but not how this knowledge becomes an integrated part of the everyday in health-care organizations, or how it might result in new interactions between patients and professionals.

Mette Brehm Johansen's study allows us to investigate patient involvement work as an organizing principle that affects health-care practices and as activities requiring a lot of meetings in order to plan, perform, and use these new involvement methods. In her fieldwork and in her "meeting ethnography approach", she focused not only on the performance of the patient involvement methods (the panel) but also on how they relate to other aspects and processes of the clinic. Her methods make visible some of the otherwise invisible work professionals and patients have to do when introducing these new methods in a clinic.

Here, three points of her chapter will be discussed to highlight the new knowledge they bring to the study of patient involvement: a) how the use of meeting ethnography was challenging classical anthropology ideas of making observations in one place for a long time, b) how contexting becomes the result of the analysis instead of a condition of it, and c) how patient-directed management is a new work practice that creates both possibilities and problems for health-care professionals and patients.

The methods of following the meetings of preparing and talking about patient involvement and how to perform it made it possible to capture some of the tacit patient-related work that few patient involvement studies have investigated before (Marchington & Wilkinson, 2005; Coulter & Ellins, 2006). Patient involvement is an everyday activity but not a daily activity, and this fact demands further reflection on how to do fieldwork in different ways, for example, by moving from one activity to another instead of staying in one specific place. Mette Brehm Johansen's chapter demonstrates this challenge and also the problems of finding your field as a researcher. Patient involvement is a complex type of organizing, which happens in different meetings and with different people and, therefore, classical virtues such as following the same person or the same ward over time, are difficult to fulfil. Instead, fieldwork becomes to follow an activity.

The other point is related to how health-care studies often become either very micro-oriented or very institutional and society-oriented. The micro-oriented studies often argue that their value and contribution result from the fact that they are situated in a living complex organizational context. The institutional and societal studies often claim to know beforehand the institutional condition of the organizational context. In Mette Brehm Johansen's study, the patient involvement context becomes the result of the analysis by adding the active use of the verb phrase *to do contexting*, a dynamic and processual view and understanding of doing contexting work. The relationship between the meetings and the work of the professionals in deciding which patients to involve and how to involve them demonstrates how contexting becomes an active, negotiated, and performed process, which requires new interactions between the concrete task, the patient understandings, and possible actions.

The last point is related to the further implications of the results of this kind of study, which uses ethnographical methods to demonstrate how patient involvement has become an organizing activity and how professionals are working with patients in new ways. The study stresses the development of how 'patient-directed management' is becoming a new kind of quality and management work in modern health-care organizations. Mette Brehm Johansen's study demonstrates that this new management style requires a lot of work and that patients are no longer just patients undergoing treatment and care but also meaningful 'professionals' who might potentially change the identities of health care professionals so that they become more patient-orientated health care professionals. This change occurs not just in one way but through exploring the many new roles and positions that are possible when inviting patients in.

It's very possible that the era of user influence in public organizations is just beginning (Thompson, 2007; Keating, McDermott, & Montgomery, 2013; Hardyman, Daunt, & Kitchener, 2015; Robert et al., 2015) and that, through these new studies, we have to learn about the possibilities but also the difficulties of bringing professionals and users to work together. Patients as users do not represent one type of user, or all the different patient types or roles, but just themselves as randomly selected patients. This is a condition that professionals have to accept and work with. The patients are informing the professionals, but they are also challenging the professional knowledge, so the borders and encounters have to be negotiated every time, and this is a time-consuming activity. Patient input helps institutions make important decisions, but also takes time away from other crucial health-care activities. Mette Brehm Johansen's work illustrates both the possibilities and limits of this work. As a reader, one wonders if all that work is necessary, leading to the possibility of adding some more critical reflections on patient involvement practices.

A final comment is related to the use of ethnography in studies of health care. In Brehm Johansen's study the ethnographic approach and the analytical concept of contexting brings a new aspect of patient involvement to the fore.

Note

1. I use the term patient involvement in quality development, but in the literature, many different terms are used: public participation in health-service management, user involvement in service development, patient participation, and patient and public participation, just to mention some of them.

Discussant References

Armstrong, N. G., Herbert, E. L., Aveling, M., Dixon-Woods, M., & Martin, G. (2013). Optimizing Patient Involvement in Quality Improvement. *Health Expectations*, 16 (3), e36-e47.

Bate, P., & Robert, G. (2007). *Bringing User Experience to Healthcare Improvement: The Concepts, Methods and Practices of Experience-Based Design*. Abingdon, UK: Radcliffe Publishing.

Coulter, A., & Ellins, J. (2006). *Patient-Focused Interventions: A Review of the Evidence*. London: The Health Foundation and the Picker Institute Europe, Quest for Quality and Improved Performance (QQUIP).

Crawford, M. J., Rutter, D., Manley, C., Weaver, T., Bhui, K., Fulop, N., & Tyrer, P. (2002). Systematic Review of Involving Patients in the Planning and Development of Health Care. *British Medical Journal*, 325 (1263), 1–5.

Hardyman, W., Daunt, K. L., & Kitchener, M. (2015). Value Co-Creation through Patient Engagement in Healthcare: A Micro-Level Approach and Research Agenda. *Public Management Review*, 17 (1), 90–107.

Keating, M. A., McDermott, A. M., & Montgomery, K. (Eds.) (2013). *Patient-Centred Health Care: Achieving Coordination, Communication and Innovation*. Basingstoke: Palgrave Macmillan.

Marchington, M., & Wilkinson, A. (2005). Direct participation and involvement. In S. Bach (Ed.), *Managing Human Resources: Personnel Management in Transition, 4th Ed*. Malden, MA: Blackwell Publishing, 398–423.

Robert, G., Cornwell, J., Locock, L., Purushotham, A., Sturmey, G., & Gager, M. (2015). Patients and Staff as Codesigners of Healthcare Services. *British Medical Journal*, 350 (g7714), 1–6.

Thompson, A. G. (2007). The Meaning of Patient Involvement and Participation in Health Care Consultations: A Taxonomy. *Social Science and Medicine*, 64 (6), 1297–1310.

Chapter References

Asdal, Kristin, & Moser, Ingunn. (2012). Experiments in Context and Contexting. *Science, Technology, & Human Values*, 37 (4), 291–306.

Barley, Stephen R., & Kunda, Gideon. (2001). Bringing Work Back In. *Organization Science*, 12 (1), 76–95.

Berg, Marc. (1997). *Rationalizing Medical Work: Decision-Support Techniques and Medical Practices*. Cambridge, MA: MIT Press.

Brannan, Matthew, Pearson, Geoff, & Worthington, Frank. (2007). Ethnographies of Work and the Work of Ethnography. *Ethnography*, 8, 395–402.

Brooks, Fiona. (2008). Nursing and Public Participation in Health: An Ethnographic Study of a Patient Council. *International Journal of Nursing Studies*, 45 (1), 3–13.

El Enany, Nellie, Currie, Graeme, & Lockett, Andy. (2013). A Paradox in Healthcare Service Development: Professionalization of Service Users. *Social Science & Medicine*, 80, 24–30.

Fudge, Nina, Wolfe, Charles, & McKevitt, Christopher. (2008). Assessing the Promise of User Involvement in Health Service Development: Ethnographic Study. *BMJ*, 2008 (336), 313–317.

Holstein, James A., & Gubrium, Jaber F. (2003). Active interviewing. In Jaber F. Gubrium, & James A. Holstein (Eds.), *Postmodern Interviewing.*Thousand Oaks: Sage, 67–80.

Malkki, Lisa H. (1997). News and culture: Transitory phenomena and the fieldwork tradition. In G. Akhil, & F. James (Eds.), *Anthropological Locations: Boundaries and Grounds of a Field Science.* Berkeley: University of California Press, 86–101.

Martin, Graham P. (2008a). Representativeness, Legitimacy and Power in Public Involvement in Health-Service Management. *Social Science & Medicine*, 67 (11), 1757–1765.

Martin, Graham P., & Finn, Rachael. (2011). Patients as Team Members: Opportunities, Challenges and Paradoxes of Including Patients in Multi-Professional Healthcare Teams. *Sociology of Health & Illness*, 33 (7), 1050–1065.

Nyqvist, Anette. (2015). The Corporation Performed: Minutes from the Rituals of Annual General Meetings. *Journal of Organizational Ethnography*, 4 (3), 341–355.

Phillips, Nelson, & Lawrence, Thomas B. (2012). The Turn to Work in Organization and Management Theory: Some Implications for Strategic Organization. *Strategic Organization*, 10 (3), 223–230.

Rumsey, Alan. (2004). Ethnographic Macro-Tropes and Anthropological Theory. *Anthropological Theory*, 4 (3), 267–298.

Schwartzman, Helen B. (1989). *The Meeting: Gatherings in Organizations and Communities.* New York: Plenum Press.

Solbjør, Marit, & Steinsbekk, Aslak. (2011). User Involvement in Hospital Wards: Professionals Negotiating User Knowledge: A Qualitative Study. *Patient Education and Counseling*, 85 (2), e144–149.

Strauss, Anselm L., Fagerhaugh, Shizuko, Suczek, Barbara, & Wiener, Carolyn. (1997) [1985]. *Social Organization of Medical Work.* New Brunswick, NJ: Transaction Publishers.

Sundhedsstyrelsen. (2002). *National strategi for kvalitetsudvikling i sundhedsvæsenet. Fælles mål og handleplan 2002–2006.* Sundhedsstyrelsen.

Terms of reference for the user panel. (2015). *Kommissorium for brugerpanel i Onkologisk Klinik ved Rigshospitalet.* Accessed September 3. https://www.rigs hospitalet.dk/afdelinger-og-klinikker/finsen/onkologisk-klinik/om-klinikken/Doc uments/brugerpanel_kommissorium_final.pdf

Thedvall, Renita. (2013). Punctuated entries: Doing fieldwork in policy meetings in the European Union. In G. Christina, & N. Anette (Eds.), *Organisational Anthropology. Doing Ethnography in and Among Complex Organizations.* London: Pluto Press, 106–119.

van de Bovenkamp, Hester M., & Zuiderent-Jerak, Teun. (2013). An Empirical Study of Patient Participation in Guideline Development: Exploring the Potential for Articulating Patient Knowledge in Evidence-Based Epistemic Settings. *Health Expectations*, 18, 942–955. doi:10.1111/hex.12067

Yanow, Dvora. (2012). Organizational Ethnography between Toolbox and World-Making. *Journal of Organizational Ethnography*, 1 (1), 31–42.

Yanow, Dvora, Ybema, Sierk, Wels, Harry, & Kamsteeg, Frans. (2009). *Organizational Ethnography: Studying the Complexities of Organizational Life.* London: Sage.

Part III

Public Organization Studies of Management and Collaborative Innovation

8 Meaning Negotiations of Collaborative Governance

A Discourse-Based Ethnography

Mie Plotnikof and discussant Danielle Zandee

Introduction

In this chapter, I explore the organizational phenomenon of collaborative governance through a discourse-based ethnographic approach. More
specifically, I explore how such an approach may offer methods and analytical insights concerning the constitution of such a governance form in
practice, not to argue for *one* best approach but to contribute to multi-
method approaches and multifaceted understandings of such a complex
phenomenon.

Collaborative governance is emerging currently in many welfare states to
involve stakeholders from across public, private, and/or nonprofit organizations in public problem solving by co-creating policy and service innovation
(Ansell & Gash, 2008). When interorganizational collaboration becomes a
governance means, the social interactions of involved actors become constitutive to the governing process and outcome, which demands new ways of
managing and organizing such. Thus governance literature seeks to identify
new organizational models and management concepts and to understand the
social dynamics affecting their practice. However, a recent literature review
argues, "Theory, empirical research, and practice all reveal that because
cross-sector collaborations are so complex and dynamic and operate in such
diverse contexts, it is unlikely that research-based recipes can be produced"
(Bryson, Crosby, & Stone, 2015, p. 658). Thus calls are made to advance
the understanding of such challenging multi-actor and multi-level practices
by bridging various theoretical and multi-method approaches.

I explore this form of governance and its complexities through approaching the negotiations and even struggles over meanings of its use and impact
in practice. In so doing, I use examples from the organizational setting of
education management. But first I will present my approach, which com-
bines theory and methods from governance research, discourse studies, and
ethnography. This extends existing studies of socially dynamic tensions and
discursive power in collaborations (Vangen & Huxham, 2011; Koschmann,
Kuhn, & Pharrer, 2012; Purdy, 2012; Vangen & Winchester, 2013). Considering both the potentials and challenges of collaboration identified in
theory, it becomes critical to understand its emergence in practice. One way

of doing this is studying locally emerging meaning negotiations and how they come to matter to involved actors' practices across time and space. This will elucidate constitutive processes and effects of such new governance form and unfolds their complexities as they come into existence locally. In conclusion, I will reflect on contributions of such an approach.

The Organizational Phenomenon of Collaborative Governance

Collaborative governance is broadly defined as processes of

> *public policy decision making and management that engage people constructively across the boundaries of public agencies, levels of government, and/or the public, private and civic spheres in order to carry out a public purpose that could not otherwise be accomplished.*
> (Emerson, Nabatchi, & Balough, 2011, p. 2)

This is often contrasted with hierarchical organizing of public policy and service associated with new public management (NPM). As such, it includes changes in public management practices from hierarchical to network-alike organizations, which is seen as needed to overcome public problems that are also as complicated (Ansell & Torfing, 2014). Despite the potential of interorganizational collaboration to enable co-creation, the literature is not naïve, rather it also considers the challenges. These include managing the complexity of diverse actors and interests, of different communication modes, of various organizational cultures, etc. In effect, collaborative governance is considered risky business, yet still necessary to deal with public problems (Bryson et al., 2015).

In particular, a few studies are concerned with unfolding such complications in terms of paradoxes, management tensions, discursive power, and communication. Such efforts address the social dynamics and issues related to multi-actor communication as central to this form of governance—and its success or failure. This stream argues to do so by combining governance research with other approaches to better grapple with the socially dynamic aspects. For example, Vangen and Winchester (2013) draw on earlier work (Vangen & Huxham, 2011) that bridges collaborative governance and action research to grapple with collaborative challenges and produce practice-based theorizing. In this case, they focus on diversity management, which they conceptualize as managing through various forms of multi-actor and multi-level tensions (Vangen & Winchester, 2013).

In the same line of argument, Purdy (2012) adds a focus on power and the power produced through discursive practices to legitimize specific interests in collaborations. This stresses the importance of studying the communicative interactions and discursive aspects to understand their effects on setting direction. Lastly, a thorough conceptualization of the communicative constitution of cross-sector collaboration is offered by Koschmann et al. (2012). Drawing on communication studies, they theorize the constitution of value during collaborative networks through text-conversation dialectics. They conceptualize this dialectic as ongoing communicative processes between interrelated texts that are (re-)produced and/or changed through participants' conversations and other communication modes, which shape collaborative processes, values, and events across time and space.

As the literature highlights both potentials and problems emerging from the diversity of actors involved and the possible conflicts of interest—or potential idea-generation—understanding inherent complexities of collaborative governance is fundamental to theory and practice. While some of the literature is primarily concerned with developing general models and concepts (Ansell & Gash, 2008; Emerson et al., 2011), the aforementioned studies dislocate focus to the socially dynamic, emerging aspects that become critical in practice by bridging governance research with other theories and methods (Koschmann et al., 2012; Purdy, 2012; Vangen & Winchester, 2013). Although collaboration may enable idea-generation and value-creation, its socially dynamic tensions and power imbalances are known to be conflicting and ineffective. This makes the communication between actors collaborating across time and space and the discursive aspects crucial to consider to strengthen this stream of studies. Thus this chapter adds a discourse-based ethnographic approach to grapple further with the meaning negotiations of such governance form and its matters to practice emerging across actors, space, and time.

The organizational setting of this study are two local governments' partnership to improve the local quality management of preschool education. In 2010, the local governments formed a partnership with an education union and involved a research team that I became a part of. Ambitions of collaborative governance in the education area are emerging along with political discourses of networks, partnerships, and co-creation, which manifest in many welfare states currently (Ansell & Torfing, 2014). The problem to be addressed through collaborative governance concerned existing quality-management methods, their report format, and one-way communication across the hierarchy, which was considered 'meaningless' by politicians, administrators, education managers, and teachers. The different languages and interests of stakeholders were seen as problematic, and so it was hoped that developing quality-management methods through collaboration would improve their communication, quality management, and development.

From 2010 to 2012, various collaborations emerged across the governments. In small- and large-scale workshops, diverse actors discussed existing and developed new quality-management methods. In each municipality, 4–6 workshops of around 20 actors from the education sector were enacted a year, including administrators, politicians, education managers, teachers, and, to some extent, children, and parents too. In between these events, meetings and workshops were held at city halls with management teams and at education facilities with education managers, teachers, and children. In both local governments, it was decided to continue collaborative governance practices resulting in annual collaborative quality-management events (including all stakeholders) and quality inspections (only preschool staff and administration) throughout 2013–2014. Soon I will return to the case, but first I will unfold the analytical and multi-method approach developed for the study.

Analytical Approach: Combining Governance Studies with Discourse and Ethnography

Initially, I was puzzled by how collaborative governance emerged as a solution, how its potentials/challenges came into play, and how it affects actors and practices concerning quality management in the two municipalities. To approach this, I needed empirical and analytical methods that would sensitize my work to the constitutive processes and effects emerging across actors, time, and space, rather than identified in general governance models and theory. With inspiration from the aforementioned stream of studies, I developed my approach by bridging these with organizational discourse studies and ethnographic methods.

Organizational discourse studies offer various analytical approaches to various phenomena (Philips & Oswick, 2012). By theorizing constitutive dynamics and effects of discourse, the role of communication and meaning production become critical to organizational issues such as identity, change, and governance processes. But discourse is considered more than a linguistic matter; it is defined as structured collections of texts and related communicative practices of production, dissemination, and consumption that bring organizational phenomena into being (Philips & Oswick, 2012, p. 436). As such, a discourse perspective on collaborative governance shifts the interest from general models and management concepts to their discursive construction and communication emerging within and across collaborative practices and spaces. Meaning formations become the central point of study, e.g. how actors from various organizational settings create and struggle over meanings of collaborative processes and outcomes to practice this type of governance.

This is in line with the aforementioned studies concerned with social dynamics, discursive power, and communication to this type of governance (Purdy, 2012; Vangen & Winchester, 2013). Like these, the ongoing interactions of actors and the communication during and between collaboration become central points of analysis to understand the constitutive processes and effects. In addition to Purdy's (2012) concern with discursive power and Koschmann et al.'s (2012) conceptualization of text/conversation dialectics, discourse studies concerned with collaboration and change offer fruitful analytics to study the meaning negotiations that affect collaborative actors and organizing processes (Hardy, Lawrence, & Grant, 2005; Thomas, Sargent, & Hardy, 2011). A study by Hardy et al. (2005) also conceptualizes text/conversation dialectics as constitutive to interorganizational collaboration through the ways in which discourse, as a set of interrelated texts and associated practices (re-)produces and changes collaboration. This study is concerned with how such dialectics enable effective collaboration and collective identity. Effective collaboration is discursively produced through two entwined processes: one involves constructing a collective identity between the actors, the other concerns the potential of collective identity to enable innovation by, e.g., speech styles and discursive tensions.

The studies that approach the complex emergence of collaboration through text-conversation dialectics include a perspective on dialogues as characterized by meaning negotiations and tensions between various, possibly conflicting, positions related to the subject at hand, rather than as consensus driven. Organizational discourse studies concerned with change (Grant & Marshak, 2011; Thomas et al., 2011) unfold this aspect on meaning negotiations and their tensions and constitutive effects to change events in, e.g., collaborative governance. They conceptualize change as an ongoing process of meaning negotiations producing discursive tensions that affect and may complicate events. For example, the meanings of a change initiative, such as collaborative governance, are negotiated through social interactions that include the use or production of relevant texts. Thereby, meaning negotiations are a necessary part of text-conversation dialectics, by which discursive tensions are produced between positions and interests made relevant. But these tensions may complicate matters by producing further negotiations. Through such communicative processes, the directions for change are emerging.

In developing my analytical approach, I combined governance studies on social dynamics with organizational discourse studies on collaboration and change by drawing on concepts of text/conversation dialectics and meaning negotiations (Plotnikof, 2015). This enables me to approach collaborative governance and its complexities by the ways they emerge in communicative practices across actors, time, and space. Analytically, it directs the attention to the negotiations and even struggles over meanings and matters of this type of governance and its challenges in everyday interactions, as well as through other communication modes such as written, visual, bodily, or spatial. Thus this analytical approach calls for certain empirical methods that have a multimodal focus during data collection. So another aspect of my approach became to elaborate methods sensitive to multiple communication modes concerning emerging complexities of this organizational phenomenon. This involved integrating ethnographic methods—rather than, for example, just interviews or document analysis often used in discourse studies.

Multimodality: Developing Empirical Methods to Approach Local Complexities

Although many discourse studies follow the discourse definition as a set of interrelated texts and associated practices that bring organizational phenomena into being, the overemphasizing of language at the expense of other communication modes and materiality remains a critique (Kuhn & Putnam, 2014). This critique has led to debates about

> *working across epistemological positions to move to a position that embraces the "discourse and materiality" and the "discourse as materiality" positions. By widening the methods used and bringing together methods that focus on the discursive and the material, organizational discourse analysis can make much more of a contribution to our understanding of organization and organizing.*
>
> (Philips & Oswick, 2012, p. 470)

So conceptual efforts are made to include materiality in discourse studies (Kuhn & Putnam, 2014; Putnam, 2014), which improves the understanding of discourse-material aspects of meaning formations and reality constructions. But the conceptual efforts also push for method-developments, although these are seldom central in the discussions (Iedema, 2007; Fairhurst & Grant, 2010).

When approaching collaborative governance, I was inspired by these ambitions. Thus I focused on multimodality to sensitize methods to various communication forms emerging as constitutive to local complexities. Such sensitivity is implied in the conceptual debates, but its empirical method implications are not discussed explicitly. Multimodality means multiple modes of expressions, which directs attention to various communication practices (human, non-human, verbal, non-verbal): "a multimodal focus pushes the data gathering and analysis to be sensitive to the symbolic, material, and/or the institutional—and future research looks to be headed in this direction" (Fairhurst & Grant, 2010, p. 197). To stimulate this, I developed multimodal methods to attend to various communicative modes and discourse-material infusions across collaborative governance practices. Such methods do not demand a priori definitions of discourse-materiality relationships (Kuhn & Putnam, 2014), but rather sensitivity to such relations as they emerge locally.

In the case of collaborative governance, I was inspired by ethnographic approaches to complexity (Yebema et al., 2009) and to "interactions in the field, captured through a blend of methods including field notes, recordings of talk and meetings, visual recordings of interactions and gestures, attending meetings, participant verbal or written accounts" (Cunliffe, 2009, p. 231). Although 'being out there' is not necessarily useful in itself, ethnographic methods can be fruitful to focus discourse approaches on multimodality. When I developed my approach, my fieldwork was not designed as a 'classic' ethnography of one organizational site, a pre-discursive entity to enter and uncover. Rather, my strategy was to approach collaborative governance through following the meaning negotiations and discursive constructions (including relevant materialities) emerging across actors, time, and space. Thus I integrated multiple methods, including exploratory single and group interviews and variations of participant observations in managerial meetings at city halls, in education facilities, at collaborative workshops, in hallways, in telephone conversations, etc. Data sources count field notes, audio/video recordings, photos, documents, emails, and mappings of local collaborative governance practices. The data collection was developed through intense fieldwork from 2010 to 2012 and occasional fieldwork from 2013 to 2014.

As mentioned earlier, my initial curiosity related to how potentials/challenges of collaborative governance emerged and their effects on involved actors and practices concerned with, in this case, quality management in the education sector. This affected my initial composition of multimodal methods. To explore emerging potentials and challenges, I started my fieldwork with observations and exploratory single and group interviews with the management teams (head of division, head of department, and consultants in the education departments of the two municipalities) and local managers and teachers in education centres participating in the collaborative governance work. These methods were to attend to locally produced meanings and matters concerned with existing quality-management problems and the potentials/challenges arising through collaboration.

Initial data analysis showed discursive constructions of certain quality-management problems associated with hierarchical roles and organizing, which collaboration was to help solve (Table 8.1). These constructions emerged across actors, practices, and spaces of city hall offices and education facilities. The former spaces embodied small square rooms filled with an array of computers, piles of paper, various people, coffee smells, and numerous sounds from Xerox machines. They were located in big buildings in town centres. The latter spaces comprised small rooms filled with children,

Table 8.1 Analytical display

Negotiations of challenges	Negotiations of potentials	Analytical & methodological focus on negotiations of:
"we use different languages", "we are down here, they are up there", "quality reports are meaningless", "top versus bottom", "hierarchy", "they think we don't care about staff and kids", "they don't know this reality, what education quality looks like"	"we need a common language for quality", "we need to collaborate to find better methods", "the ones making the decisions need to start listening", "the staff need to see the bigger picture", "we have to stop translating between education and political logics"	• Potentials/challenges: Which meanings and matters of collaborative governance are emerging? • Roles: How are certain 'roles' constructed and affected by collaboration? • Organizing: How is a local 'hierarchy' practiced and affected by collaboration?

toys, food, teachers, and smells of food and sweat. They were located in various buildings—some new public facilities, others old townhouses—and often surrounded by playgrounds in residential areas. Data on these multimodalities was gathered from photographs, audio/video recordings, and field notes/mappings of actors' movements. Occasionally, analyses were discussed with actors to nuance local constructions and research participation, both their impact in situ and as retrospective 'readers' of data.

I decided to follow the meaning negotiations of local problems and solutions regarding roles and ways of organizing collaborative governance as they emerged across diverse actors and spaces. In addition to the aforementioned methods, I developed a method called 'organizational mapping'. The original idea was to attend to actors' positioning of self and others and their organizing related to quality-management work by using discursive-material practices during and in between collaborations. Basically, the method consisted of a) mapping practices (who works where on what, communicating with who/how with what outcome, etc.) and b) communication about mapping practices (how do they see this, what kind of work are they enacting, etc.). Various versions of this method developed regarding specific situations and issues. Sometimes I did the mapping myself by following actors, tracking cases or quality documents, etc.; other times I asked actors to lay out working procedures and collaborative events and relations concerning quality management.

In the following section, I will discuss this method and its potential combined with the analytical approach to produce insights about the complex constitution of collaborative governance. But first I will briefly comment on the role of the researcher. From a discourse-based ethnographic stance, both empirical actors and researchers are co-productive of data—both on site, seeing particular things, asking specific questions, and when analyzing and writing. This demands a self-critical reflection of the researcher on ethical issues and potential biases, which I continually sought to include in my analytical and methodological work. As the partnership stressed challenges of the multiple actors and different languages as both the problem and potential solution, I approached this without positioning myself as an 'expert'. Rather, I told them that I saw them as 'knowledgeable' about their local reality. But as the actors worked to find answers and co-create new solutions, and I worked to approach complexities emerging through their efforts, I did take part in their explorations. I participated by talking about, questioning, and addressing the challenges that actors voiced, but not to define the answers. This enabled me to become sensitive to local issues of collaborative governance.

Organizational Mapping: A Multimodal Method to Approach Meaning Negotiations

The local governments included various stakeholders in collaborations across the education area, e.g., administrators, politicians, local managers, teachers, and sometimes children and parents. During collaborations, the actors discussed and developed quality-management methods and in so doing affected their working procedures, roles, and organizing across different contexts such as education facilities and city hall political and administrative offices. The collaborations included all sorts of expressions: laughter, frustrations, confusion, and conflicts, as well as technical breakdowns and solutions, creativity in human interaction, and material production. Some of this was 'easy' to access empirically; other events were more problematic to engage in as a researcher.

To approach matters that were considered problematic or conflicting, I hoped that organizational mapping could help me to avoid being rejected without intensifying local issues. The strategy of this method was to access problems or conflicts through actors' positioning and understandings of their own, others', and 'the organizations'' work with quality management and collaborative governance and thereby get insights to its complexities. I expected this might produce curiosity or self-reflections from actors about understanding local problems and solutions, and I hoped it would produce data with which to analyze emerging discourse-material dynamics (both linguistic meaning constructions and other discourse-material practices, images, and objects) constitutive to their work and 'mapping' of it. This method was thereby used to sensitize me to different modes of communication between multiple actors and spaces and the discursive-material aspects of certain 'problems', 'roles', and ways of 'organizing' that constituted the local collaborative governance practices.

During the collaborative governance events, the management teams in the local governments also had meetings of their own. The management team included a head of division, a head of department, and managerial consultants—all with managerial responsibility regarding the collaborative initiatives. Such meetings concerned managerial issues related to developing new quality-management practices through collaborative governance. During my fieldwork, I was sometimes asked to participate, and for a meeting on the managerial challenges of collaborative governance, I used organizational mapping to approach the managers' meaning negotiations of their role. This workshop consisted of the management team: Paul (head of children and youth division), Peter (head of preschool department), and Maria (quality-management consultant). As always, I wrote field notes about actors, practices, spaces, and atmosphere that 'set the scene'.

I meet Maria in the hallway at the city hall at 8:45. We walk into the office while chatting about traffic and another meeting, making coffee, checking emails and phones. Then Peter arrives and says causally, "Hi, guys", and then chats with the secretary at the front desk about a national TV show. Maria tells me about an issue with a preschool centre where a parent has complained without talking to the local manager and now demands political involvement. Paul hasn't arrived yet, and we talk about how rarely the team actually sits down together and discusses their work. Then Paul walks in, smiling and apologizing, then showing us a new iPad. He talks about using it as a logbook during collaborative events, and they start discussing the last collaborative workshop and how they struggle with their role and not knowing the outcomes.

Then Maria says "Well, let's get to it to discuss our role" and we all nod. I am asked to start, and I explain that my curiosity is concerned with the issues mentioned regarding their role during quality-management work and collaborative governance.

They nod and Paul claps his hands, smiles, and says "Let's get to work then". While giving them each a piece of paper, I ask them to do a two-minute brainstorm about their work and role. They look around smiling but then start writing in silence.

After a few minutes, I ask them to turn the paper around, and the head of department says "So we're done?" I reply by asking them to map out what they wrote. I stress that it is not to produce an aesthetic outcome, but to communicate how they each see their work and role. They all laugh a little nervously. One of them says, "No, come on . . . Are you serious?" I nod and smile. As they start, they look around but then quietly work on their own maps. A few minutes pass until they all look up. Afterwards I ask them to discuss their descriptions and mappings . . .

This led to a one-and-a-half hour conversation between the management team. Occasionally I was included, but mostly they talked to each other. As the workshop was ending, I was asked to sum up. Instead, I turned attention to some quotes I had from earlier fieldwork (interviews and observations) concerning the role of the manager, such as 'the translator', 'the mediator', and 'the facilitator'. I asked them to reflect on these in relation to their debate, their maps, and their work with collaborative governance. In conclusion, they decided to 'track' their future quality-management work, the emerging collaborations, and the case materials they found important to that work. In the next section, I discuss the data collected through such organizational mapping with the analytical approach presented earlier. For now, I will dwell a little more on the mapping method.

First, organizational mapping as a method may produce data on discourse-material aspects of collaborative governance by accessing conversations, texts, and related practices of local issues. In this version, the brainstorming asks actors to construct meanings of an issue in their own terms in relation to their work practice and position. This attends to locally constructed matters and multiple voices, which may show both dominating discourses and more marginal or silenced matters. Relational power dynamics (in this case, between management team actors) cannot be avoided—and neither should they be—as they are part of the organizational reality constructions. These can be studied in the following discussion about the individual mappings.

Second, the mappings materialize actors' discursive constructions of organizations, not as realistic representations, but as visualizations that make sense for actors in relation to a specific matter at a specific time and place. In addition, they may help dislocate focus from actors individually if critical or conflicting matters are expressed because actors tend to look at the maps instead of the person speaking. Furthermore, the mappings may indicate taken-for-granted organizational constructions of roles, organizational levels, or hierarchical structures. Third, the follow-up conversation invites actors to negotiate meanings—in this case, the negotiation of managerial roles and organizing in relation to collaborative governance by which they enact organizational discourses and materials crucial to local reality constructs.

Alongside other methods, this helped me approach the locally emerging collaborative governance roles and organizing and their inherent complexities. As the field note extract shows, a lot is happening at the same time; actors come from various spaces and multiple technological devices as well as different interests are in play, so this method can also focus attention, occasionally, to make sense of what actors do, where and with whom. That being said, I do not see it as representing a 'realistic' image of a static 'organization', but more as a discursive-material construction of what is at stake locally for certain actors at a certain time and place. It can be repeated if studying a process over time. In this case, it created both linguistic and visually materialized data with insights to managers' negotiations of their role and organizing of collaborative governance in the education sector. As such, this method helps with engaging in the working life and creating the local organization, which, in this case, was collaborative governance within education. Moreover, the method acts in a way that produces rich data of in situ discourse-material constructions critical to the organizational phenomenon in question.

Analyzing Negotiations of Roles and Organizing Within Collaborative Governance

The analyses of data during the local governments' collaborations showed discourse-material constructions and meaning negotiations of roles, quality-management work, hierarchical levels, collaborative organizing etc., including taken-for-granted assumptions and issues connected to these local constructions (see Plotnikof, 2015; 2016). Returning to the earlier example, this version of organizational mapping gave insights to meaning negotiations of managerial roles and hierarchical organizing as problematic, while collaborative governance was viewed as a challenging, but necessary solution. In Figure 8.1, we see the mappings. 1) is Maria's of managers as 'a rubber band' between education centres and politicians, in which the management team is the link; 2) Paul's of the managers as 'democratic orderliness and collaborators'; and 3) Peter's of the managers as 'secretariat' in a 'hierarchical triangle' between a political top and a welfare-service bottom. As the team discussed their work and the maps, they negotiated both different constructions of role and organizing, as well as the problems creating needs for collaborative governance and the challenges involved in collaboration.

In the following extract, Paul has explained his map and the managerial role as a traditional administration that 'exerts' the democratic power, an 'orderliness' he depicted as two people in dialogue (Map 2), which leads to the following conversation:

PETER: What I think this is about, well where you [Paul] have a general approach, we [pointing at himself and Maria] need legitimacy in the education contexts in order to link you [Paul] and them [pointing at the politicians on Map 1] with the education field.

Figure 8.1 Map 1 'the rubber band'.

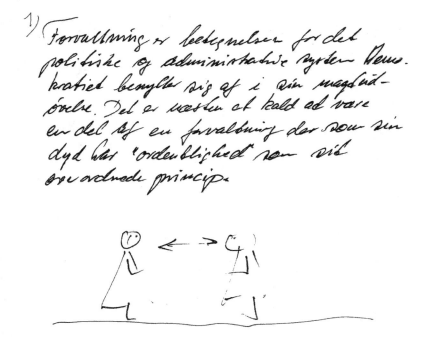

Figure 8.2 Map 2 'the democracy'.

1) Advokat for området
- Føre områdets interesser med læringens interesser
- udvikle området
- styre området
- Give oplysning til ledere, ansatte og brugere
- Ikke en forvaltning men et sekretariat
- Hjælpe området med at have fokus på kerneopgaverne.
- Give politikerne mulighed for at træffe politiske beslutninger.

Politiker/Byråd
Forvaltning
Institution

Figure 8.3 Map 3 'the secretary'.

PAUL: Yes.

PETER: So we are within another struggling area of interests. And that's why Maria talks about helping to translate and communicate changes in ways that make them understandable for the education actors. And that's why I talk about becoming a secretariat instead of an old-school hierarchical administration that commands. We are constantly negotiating. Negotiating our way with the stakeholders.

PAUL: And those [pointing at Peter's and Maria's maps] are your symbols of my orderliness.

PETER: Yes . . . We might have a hierarchy; we don't reject the hierarchy, but we say that it makes it necessary for us to service both upwards and downwards.

RESEARCHER: How?

PETER: Well, now we translate the messages from the top, no matter if it comes from local politicians or the law, new initiatives or whatever, to the bottom in ways that make it as easy as possible and logical as possible and as correct as possible in order to be performed down there [pointing at the education area at the bottom of his triangle]. And the same is intrinsic in my secretary idea of managing their interests upwards.

Paul and Peter negotiate the meanings of their maps and their matters in practices. Peter positions himself and Maria in a different role that 'links' and 'translates' between a top and bottom. Thereby, he places them in a 'struggling area of interests' between politicians and educators, which demands that they 'translate' his mapping constructs between the 'hierarchical levels'. Paul argues that this is the democratic 'orderliness' of the hierarchy, he mapped, but Peter uses the hierarchy as the problem that demands their translation and service between top and bottom. As such, the team constructs the managerial role in relation to their understanding of the organization of the education sector as a hierarchy which faces problems of detachment between 'levels' of different actors and spaces, hence the need, and legitimacy, of their 'translating' position. In the additional conversations, this becomes the argument for collaborative governance to solve their problem.

PAUL: As I said I visualized orderliness by two people standing in front of each other, communicating with each other, without crossing . . . without crossing transactions. Well, one tells the other one something, they adjust oneself to the other's situation. You talk differently when you talk to—we are sitting here talking professionally. We do this respectfully; we listen to each other . . . To me, really, to me orderliness is managing these non-crossing transactions.

RESEARCHER: So this visualizes such collaborative practices in this government?

PAUL: No, that would appear too naïve . . . [laughs] Because there are other interests of power in play.

RESEARCHER: And that's not part of that visualization?

PAUL: No, there'd be more people, and they wouldn't all be talking like that.

PETER: So she would have a knife in her back, right [pointing at Map 2]?

PAUL: Yeah, that might be [laughter]. Bottom line, it's a workplace with people. For people.

MARIA: Yeah, which is why mine [Map 3] is supposed to look like a rubber band, I didn't know how to draw a rubber band . . . Because in one way or the other, I'm thinking that this collaboration to qualify communication on quality, which I'm trying to enable, especially to the political level, and also to qualify the political decisions in relation to the education level that if the rubber band tightens, or if you imagine a total connection. Then it's like, it might be trivial, but if my work with these collaborations was successful, then in some way it ends with me not being necessary anymore, right? Or all of us. That they could just communicate directly. Eh, I think, well, I think there's still some translation needed now . . .

PETER: Yeah. I drew the old hierarchical triangle. And when I was sitting, philosophizing before instead of listening to what you [to Maria] were saying, I was thinking about doing a rectangle instead—because it's kind of clichéd, right? So, I'd rather have drawn yours [to Maria] because I'm much closer to that. I think a level to translate between the two positions is needed as it is between politicians, those in power, and the performing part. But my mission is that we may not need that link. There are still things to be done which is what we are struggling with in the collaborations, but I think—bottom line is that you don't really need that link, if they are communicating bloody well.

PAUL: And our job is to support . . . that the stakeholder positions reach each other.

In this extract, Paul and Peter negotiate the meaning of Map 2, which nuances Paul's construction of 'orderliness' as collaboration between actors in the hierarchy that he himself says is naïve. Along with Peter, Paul stresses that in a workplace 'with' and 'for' people, some 'interests of power' and 'back-stabbing' is to be assumed. Maria then enters the negotiation and brings them back to the need for collaborative governance, as she explains her mapping of a 'rubber band'. This she argues shows that now the managerial role is to translate between the two ends of the rubber band, which are described as politicians and educators, children and parents, and that her work to manage collaborative events is to qualify communication about education quality between politicians and educators to improve the political decision making in effect. These collaborations, she says, are to 'tighten' the rubber band, which then results in her existing role construction not being necessary anymore. The existing managerial role of 'translation' is part of the problem of the 'hierarchically organized' education sector and its detached 'levels' between educators, children, and parents on one side and politicians in the local governments on the other. This is affirmed by Peter, who also constructs the need for collaboration to overcome this problem and their practices of translation. He makes it his 'mission' to turn the triangle into better collaborations instead.

Through this communication, they are constructing problems of the 'hierarchy' and their 'translating' managerial role and collaborative governance as an alternative organizing that may be the solution, but which isn't easily accomplished and it questions their means of existence. One thing is that these negotiations give insights to local complexities connected to hierarchical organizing and collaborations by which actors negotiate the meanings of existing and becoming governance forms and their matter to practice as well as to the relationships between stakeholders in education. Another thing is that they also position themselves and each other, thereby giving insights to their social dynamics and discursive power production. For example, Peter and Maria stress their mapping as different from Paul's by referring to different hierarchical levels, which positions them in a different space—a struggling area—that enables them to question Paul's map and argue for the relevance of their own understandings of the local issues and collaborative work. This indicates that their internal social dynamics are not determined by their formal relationship, in which Paul is ranked higher than Peter and Maria. Rather, it shows that their middle position becomes central to the negotiations, as this embodies the 'struggles' and so the problem that makes them 'translators', which they try to solve by developing better collaborations.

Such data analyses can unfold constitutive processes about the managers' role constructions and the issues and needs for change associated with hierarchical versus collaborative organizing. This elucidates how meaning negotiations construct roles and ways of organizing, including actors' assumptions about organizational characteristics such as 'levels' or 'structure'. These are merely analytical examples that alone give limited insight into the local complexities, but combined with other data, this can show the effects of meaning negotiations of managerial roles and the organizing of collaborative governance in practice. This includes building analytical patterns of discursive constructions that may 'scale up' across actors, space, and time to explore constitutive processes and effects on a larger scale, which I have done elsewhere (Plotnikof, 2015; 2016). But the analytical and multi-method approaches presented here, including organizational mapping, support such efforts. This version, plus the mappings I did myself—and one the partnership did together (management teams, education managers, and teachers, as well as union representatives from both local governments) of their collaborative work and (dis-)organizing concerning quality management—became crucial entry points for me to engage with the local complexities that mattered to the development and impact of collaborative governance practices.

Critical Reflections and Concluding Notes

I have discussed the potential of bridging a stream of collaborative governance research with discourse and ethnographic studies to develop analytical and multi-method approaches. This directs attention to the meanings and matters of local complexities and thereby discourse-material constructions of collaborative governance. During my exploration, I developed empirical methods and analytics for multimodal communication, e.g. linguistics, visuals, bodily, and spatial. This helps with focusing on constitutive dynamics and effects without demanding a priori deterministic definitions; rather, it allows me to approach organizational phenomena as they emerge empirically. But it demands analytical sensitivity to the discursive and material relations that come to matter as the local complexities in question come into existence. Thus developing discourse-based ethnographic approaches engages the researcher in empirically embedded constructions that show (and help to think of) relevant communicative modes, meanings, and matters constitutive to organizing.

Rather than studying potentials and challenges identified in general governance models, I wanted to focus on the issues emerging as constitutive to practice. For this I combined governance studies with organizational discourse studies on collaboration and change (Hardy et al., 2005; Thomas et al., 2011; Koschmann et al., 2012). Analytically, this attends to the meaning negotiations of such governance form and its challenges in everyday practice. By using ethnographic methods, including different versions of organizational mapping, I produced data of actors' negotiations of significant organizational discourses by means of multiple communication modes and, thereby, of their construction of particular realities of collaborative governance in education. This enabled me to approach collaborative governance and its complexities as they emerged in communicative practices across actors, time, and space.

Regarding methods such as organizational mapping, the interactions of mapping and the following discussions gave insight to actors' taken-for-granted and strategic constructions concerning collaborative governance in practice. This showed how actors negotiated roles, agency, and hierarchical versus collaborative organizing dynamics. The actual mapping is not a realistic representation; rather, it is visualizations and their uses that were negotiated among actors at this specific time and space. Thereby the mapping produces discursive and material data of local issues.

During mapping and group discussions, actors negotiate meanings of their work and position in collaborative governance in education, including how they define this work in order to illustrate it and how they relate (or not) to each other in so doing. This shows individual voices or contrary group conformity, as it unfolds how a team constructs their work and positioning in relation to others. It unpacks relational power dynamics emerging between team members and their understanding of the organization—e.g., hierarchical or collaborative. The tensions between hierarchical and collaborative power are matters still uncovered in governance literature to which this chapter contributes (Purdy, 2012; Bryson et al., 2015). It is fruitful not because it confirms that collaborative governance is organized in networks rather than hierarchies, as is often argued (Ansell & Torfing, 2014), but because this captures constitutive processes of an emerging organizing of government practices by attending to actors' taken-for-granted assumptions and strategies through their negotiations of its meanings and matters.

The analysis also extends the insight of existing governance literature on the complicated social dynamics and discursive aspects of collaborative communication (Purdy, 2012; Vangen & Winchester, 2013) and the discourse-material formations that may constitute the organizing of such practices locally. The examples unfolded here shed light on managerial roles related to hierarchical versus collaborative governance and the changes implied for the manager, from being a link in a hierarchy to a facilitator of dialogues in collaborations. The meaning negotiations showed nuances in such complexities and their challenges to collaborations; they produced images and stories of hierarchical problems, collaborative governance as solutions, but also the more and less connected practices in which policymakers, management, and educators collaborate and discuss across multiple actors and spaces. But such negotiations do not necessarily produce convergence of meanings or complexity-reducing solutions, which is important to acknowledge since it is critical to theory and practice (Vangen & Huxham, 2011).

Without imposing representational arguments into 'being out there', I found that ethnographic fieldwork is valuable to produce data on discourse-material aspects. Actors negotiate meanings linguistically, but also as they move around, write, use objects, and, during mapping, construct images of local organizing processes. The latter point is valuable in producing data about collaborative governance because through the map, actors not only discuss whether or not the organizing of their work is shaped as a hierarchy or network, but they also visualize their (lacking) organizing across actors and spaces. The strength of the method lies in engaging with actors as they enact issues through multiple communication modes by which both taken-for-granted and strategic understandings of actors and organizing are enacted. Furthermore, it attends to the social dynamics and power relations emerging between actors and spaces. The weakness is that it is a research construction and as such offers a snapshot of a constitutive process, much like interviews or focus groups. However, if combined with other methods such as document analysis and everyday life observations, the researcher can approach the multimodality making up the organizing of collaborative governance.

Although my approach produced a multifaceted research identity—empirical actors described me as 'knowledgeable', 'weird', 'fly-on-the-wall', 'deconstructive', and 'valuable'—it also enabled a multimodal sensitivity. This is valuable because it helps to respond to local issues and to collect all sorts of data we might not know the relevance of before entering the field. However, it also challenges the researcher's identity and creativity. Critically reflecting on one's positioning when developing the approach on site is necessary both prior to and during fieldwork, but also when analyzing data. One critical aspect is that the researcher participates in framing the situation—like an interview. Another point is that by engaging in everyday life, the researcher can be included in both formal and informal work situations, thereby accessing central issues during naturally occurring communication, which nuance other data.

Developing discourse-based ethnographic approaches sensitive to multimodality when grappling with an organizational phenomenon such as collaborative governance implies engaging with a variety of empirically embedded issues and their discursive-material formation. This challenges the researcher to be curios to communicative modes that are not usually of interest, to engage in a workplace and co-produce a certain version of the phenomenon during fieldwork and analysis. Hence it remains necessary to critically reflect upon one's role, and in so doing, nurture multi-method approaches to the complexities emerging locally and constitute particular ways of organizing.

Comment by Danielle Zandee: Research That Enables Meaningful Action

In welfare states such as the Netherlands, there is a growing recognition that we live in a time of transition in which we experience the unsettledness of a fundamental shift to a new economy and society. In this shift, we are confronted with pressing issues such as affordable health care, green sustainability, refugee integration, and city livability. Such issues are seen as wicked, because they are highly complex, multi-factor, and multi-actor challenges. They evoke a search for innovative business models, novel approaches to leadership and organizing, and new practice repertoires. Reforms in modes of governance are commonly seen as an important focus of social innovation towards societal transformation. Hence Plotnikof's chapter makes a timely and relevant contribution to how we might move from an ingrained hierarchical perspective on public policy concerns to collaborative, inclusive forms of governance. With her discursive ethnographic approach that zooms in on the meaning making interactions of involved actors, Plotnikof gives ample guidance for how we might not only study but also enact collaboration possibilities in heterogeneous multi-actor settings around topics of shared interest. Her work inspires the question of whether ethnographic research can—and perhaps should—be deliberate in enabling meaningful transformative action. In what follows, I explore this question from the intertwined angles of theoretical lenses, research methods, and researcher positionings.

In theoretical framings of transition processes, a common macro-institutional focus is now partly replaced by an interest in the microdynamics that can be discerned in daily practice. When we zoom in on what goes on in practice, we become aware of the transformative potential of even seemingly mundane activities. We see how multiple conflicting logics (like cure, care, and control in hospitals) play out in daily interactions where they surely create friction, but also wiggle room for change. The field of practice theory uses ethnographic methods—such as shadowing—to study the sayings and doings of practices as they unfold across time and space. This is exactly what Plotnikof has done in her study of the development of collaborative governance in the area of preschool education. Her implicit practice lens made her move beyond more classic ethnographic one-site studies into the realm of emerging multi-actor settings. When we follow practice, we get close to the work that actually goes into social innovation. Such work can be seen as interplay of material and discursive components. With her focus on meaning making, Plotnikof draws from the field of organizational discourse, whilst simultaneously enriching that field with a clear sensitivity for materiality and context. Texts like public policies are performed in rapidly shifting contexts that request shared reflections on what is and should be happening. In order to successfully engage in constitutive processes of collaboration, involved actors need to understand the full complexity of what is going on. Researchers can help in the development of such reflexive competence through both the findings and methods of their studies.

Shared meaning making in ambiguous multi-actor settings implies openness to each other's positions and a willingness to not shy away from friction. How can one engage in such conversation and what methods may be helpful to constructively inquire into the opportunities, challenges, and tensions of working together in an underdeveloped terrain such as collaborative governance? Indeed, the study of novel phenomena in their contextual unfolding may necessitate innovative, more finely grained approaches. Plotnikof responded to the search of how to embrace the intricate complexity of practice shaping work when she developed 'organizational mapping' as a multimodal method to follow meaning negotiations over time. In her chapter, she describes how she uses this method not only as a research instrument for fieldwork but also as a discursive tool to invite meaning making conversations among actors in that field. In those instances, the individual maps seem to work as boundary objects for clarifying conversation because they enable translation and connection across multiple positions, logics, and spaces. Furthermore, the maps help actors to see differently because they intersperse the aesthetics of embodied knowing in a cognitive, discursive approach. When organizational mapping is used for reflexive conversation, it seems that the method workability shifts from a following into the framing of meaning making conversations. In dialogic approaches to change such as framing and reframing, activities are seen as important interventions for transformation. Thus the question arises whether Plotnikof is still acting as an ethnographic researcher when she facilitates conversations that enable novel action.

A well-known social constructionist premise is that "inquiry is intervention". This means that even when researchers position themselves as detached observers of organizational reality, their presence, assumptions, and questions will influence their findings. Indeed, what do we 'find' in the field when we impact the meaning-making dynamics that we study and are co-producers of the data that we "collect"? Plotnikof is aware of this knot in her discursive ethnography work and pays attention to her role and reflexivity as a researcher who participates in the explorations of the actors in her study. However, she refrains from positioning herself as—at least partially—an action researcher in an ethnographic tradition. Eschewing that combination seems to be a lost opportunity, especially when studying pressing issues such as governance reform. Organizational ethnography is well positioned to also engage in research *with* rather than *on* actors involved in everyday meaning-making actions. Long periods of observation in proximity to the nuanced fabric of organizational life build sensitivity, trust, and vocabulary to facilitate the co-creation of knowledge that is not only interesting but also actionable. Ethnographers can do so, precisely because they have learned to combine the closeness of deep familiarity with the distance of analytic skills. With its intent to democratize research processes, action research as collaborative practice can inform meaningful experiments with collaborative governance than can be shared and scaled through evocative ethnographic texts. In times of transition we need engaged, crafty researchers and thoughtful, creative approaches to study what might become. Plotnikof's chapter can be read as an example of such work.

Chapter References

Ansell, C., & Gash, A. (2008). Collaborative Governance in Theory and Practice. *Journal of Public Administration Research and Theory*, 18 (4), 543–571. doi:10.1093/jopart/mum032

Ansell, C., & Torfing, J. (Eds.) (2014). *Public Innovation through Collaboration and Design*. New York: Routledge Publishing.

Bryson, J. M., Crosby, B. C., & Stone, M. D. (2015). Designing and Implementing Cross-Sector Collaborations: Needed and Challenging. *Public Administration Review*, 75 (5), 647–663. doi:10.1111/puar.12432

Cunliffe, A. (2009). Retelling Tales of the Field in Search of Organizational Ethnography 20 Years On. *Organizational Research Methods*, 13 (2), 224–239. doi:10.1177/1094428109340041

Emerson, K., Nabatchi, T., & Balough, S. (2011). An Integrative Framework for Collaborative Governance. *Journal of Public Administration Research and Theory*, 22 (1), 1–29. doi:10.1093/jopart/mur011

Fairhurst, G. T., & Grant, D. (2010). The Social Construction of Leadership: A Sailing Guide. *Management Communication Quarterly*, 24 (2), 171–210. doi:10.1177/0893318909359697

Grant, D. and Marshak, R. J. 2011. "Toward a Discourse-Centered Understanding of Organizational Change". *Journal of Applied Behavioral Science*, 47 (2), 204–235. doi: 10.1177/0021886310397612.

Hardy, C., Lawrence, T. B., & Grant, D. (2005). Discourse and Collaboration: The Role of Conversations and Collective Identity. *The Academy of Management Review*, 30 (1), 58–77.

Iedema, R. (2007). On the Multi-Modality, Materially and Contingency of Organization Discourse. *Organization Studies*, 28 (6), 931–946. doi:10.1177/0170840607075264

Koschmann, M. A., Kuhn, T. R., and Pharrer, M. D. 2012. "A Communicative Framework of Value in Cross-Sector Partnerships". *The Academy of Management Review*, 37 (3), 332–354.

Kuhn, T. R., & Putnam, L. L. (2014). Discourse and Communication. In P. Adler, P. du Gay, G. Morgan, & M. Reed (Eds.), *Oxford Handbook of Sociology, Social Theory and Organization Studies: Contemporary Currents*. Oxford: Oxford University Press, 414–446.

Philips, N., & Oswick, C. (2012). Organizational Discourse: Domains, Debates, and Directions. *The Academy of Management Annals*, 6 (1), 435–481. doi:10.1080/1 9416520.2012.681558

Plotnikof, M. (2015). Negotiating Collaborative Governance Designs: A Discursive Approach. *The Innovation Journal: The Public Sector Innovation Journal*, 20 (3), 1–22.

Plotnikof, M. (2016). Letting Go of Managing? Struggles over Managerial Roles in Collaborative Governance. *Nordic Journal of Working Life Studies*, 6, 109–128.

Purdy, J. M. (2012). A Framework for Assessing Power in Collaborative Governance Processes. *Public Administration Review*, 49 (3), 675–689. doi:10.111/j.1540–6210.2012.02525.x

Putnam, L. (2014). Unpacking the Dialectic: Alternative Views on the Discourse-Materiality Relationship. *Journal of Management Studies*, 52, 706–716. doi:10. 1111/joms.12115

Thomas, R., Sargent, L. D., and Hardy, C. 2011. "Managing Organizational Change: Negotiating Meaning and Power-Resistance Relations". *Organization Science*, 22 (1), 22–41.

Vangen, S., & Huxham, C. (2011). The Tangled Web: Unraveling the Principle of Common Goals in Collaborations. *Journal of Public Administration Research and Theory*, 22, 731–760. doi:10.10 93/jopart/mur065

Vangen, S., & Winchester, N. (2013). Managing Cultural Diversity in Collaborations. *Public Management Review*, 16, 1–22. doi:10.1080/14719 037.2012.743579

Yebema, S., Yanow, D., Wels, H., & Kamsteeg, F. (Eds.) (2009). *Organizational Ethnography Studying the Complexity of Everyday Life*. London: Sage Publications.

9 Leadership of Collaborative Innovation in the Public Sector

An Engaged-Scholarship Ethnography

Jesper Rohr Hansen and discussant
Steven Griggs

Introduction

The organizational phenomenon studied in this chapter is leadership of collaborative innovation. I approach this phenomenon of leadership by exploring the constructionist nature of leadership in a local-government setting. I explain how this perspective on leadership was inspired by a three-year ethnographic study by means of engaged-scholarship ethnography. In particular, I illustrate the implications of using such an ethnography—namely, identifying uncertainty as the main explanation for leadership construction. The chapter is structured as follows. First I present the organizational phenomenon studied and subsequently describe my analytical approach. Next I explain the methodology used and give two empirical examples. Finally I reflect upon how the organizational ethnography deployed has contributed to existing knowledge of collaborative innovation leadership and touch briefly on the methodological implications of this approach.

Leadership of Collaborative Innovation

Collaborative innovation in the public sector is a research field that seeks to explore how this kind of innovation can be promoted and enhanced (Hartley, 2005; Moore & Hartley, 2008; Sørensen & Torfing, 2011). Collaborative innovation is called for especially when facing complex and wicked problems such as climate change, ageing societies, and financial crisis (Harris & Albury, 2009). With respect to the role of leadership in collaborative innovation, leadership is conceptualized by means of governance theory. Scholars have argued that a networked type of governance is useful, as it enables focus on effective coordination across government organizations, on self-organization, and on the integration of actors across sectors, all of which are central issues in collaborative innovation (Hartley, 2005; Eggers and others, 2009; Bland et al., 2010; Bommert, 2010; Sørensen & Torfing, 2011; Torfing, 2013). However, this conceptualization neglects issues of uncertainty and overstates assumptions of control, in that it assumes that leadership is able to remain disconnected from and safeguarded against innovation turbulence and, as a result, downplays the dynamic identity of such leadership. This neglect implies an inability to analyze the much more subtle and interdependent relationship that evolves between leadership and innovation throughout the innovation process (Hansen, 2015). In line with this, I demonstrate how to theoretically conceptualize an analytical approach within the research field of collaborative innovation, an approach that deals with uncertainty, direct leadership involvement, and leadership exposure to innovation turbulence.

The Organizational Setting

The organizational setting of the present study is the central-administrative level in a metropolitan municipality in the period 2009–2012. The municipality consists of seven administrations. In one of these, the Technical and Environmental Administration (TEA), a handful of professionals and their newly appointed middle manager set in motion a strategy and policy-development process. This process is aimed at addressing what they perceived was the main problem of the municipality's disadvantaged neighbourhoods: lack of cross-administrative coordination of project activities and services, lack of political ownership of the problem, and lack of a joint strategy involving the municipality's social housing organizations (Engberg & Larsen, 2010). This organizational setting was selected for empirical research because the setting enables a case study with elements of leadership and a wicked problem to be solved by means of a radically novel, collaborative problem-solving strategy.

Presentation of Analytical Approach

There are three focus areas to consider when constructing an analytical approach that implies a dynamic perspective of collaborative innovation leadership. One focus area is uncertainty, as uncertainty is a central facet of both innovation and wicked-problem studies. Thus leadership has to take uncertainty into account in a way that is compatible with organizational identity and resources available for exercising leadership. A second focus area is constructionist leadership theories, as these theories provide a post-structural vocabulary; accordingly, constructionist leadership theories make feasible the argument that leadership and a novel, emergent organizational order are interdependent in a post-structural fashion. Third, in terms of theory of science, constructionist approaches related to organizational discourse can be used to conceptualize leadership's ability to exercise control in a collaborative setting, collaboration defined here as an interorganizational setting that defies direct hierarchical control.

Concerning uncertainty, Koppenjan and Klijn's (2004) categories of 'network' uncertainty are tailored to a type of public problem that is 'wicked'.

Koppenjan and Klijn argue that governments, markets, and civil society are increasingly faced with controversies over complex societal problems. These problems are characterized by a high degree of wickedness, in that the involved parties not only disagree about the solution but also about the nature of the problem. These problems also entail a collaborative dimension because "they cut across the traditional jurisdictions of organizations and across the traditional boundaries between the private and public sector. Governments, businesses and civil society are unable to tackle these issues by themselves" (Koppenjan & Klijn, 2004, p. 1). According to Koppenjan and Klijn, the uncertainty of wicked problems has three manifestations: substantive, strategic, and institutional. These three manifestations involve uncertainties with regard to determining the nature of the problem, with regard to predicting which strategies other stakeholders will choose in order to influence the problem definition, and with regard to new ways of organizing across organizations, as well as taking into account each actor's different institutional background (Koppenjan & Klijn, 2004, pp. 6–7).

In innovation research, a study by Van de Ven et al. (1999) of innovation processes demonstrated yet another facet of uncertainty that stacks with those of wicked problems in collaborative processes: that these can be conceptualized as a 'journey' characterized by uncertainty, novelty, an unknown endpoint, and an unpredictable process (Van de Ven, 1999). In their study, the authors discovered how innovative ideas proliferate into many ideas that result in invention and reinvention. Many people were involved in these processes, albeit only partially. Stakeholder networks were constantly revised and multiple environments were enacted. Further, an innovation journey typically consisted of multiple tracks and spin-offs, making the final result indeterminate and blurring the identity of the innovation as the new innovation and old orders were integrated (Van de Ven, 1999, pp. 8–9). The authors also noted that the innovations did not develop through a simple linear sequence or predictable stages, but instead "a much messier and more complex progression of events" was observed (Van de Ven et al., p. 23), involving numerous setbacks and criteria shifts. This journey of uncertainty emphasizes the need for process studies of leadership.

More recently, with regard to constructionist leadership theory, the theory of complex responsive processes (Stacey, 2011) has proposed an organizational theory that pays specific attention to both the micro-level and post-structural nature of organizational change made visible by the central role the works of Norbert Elias and Herbert A. Mead play in this theory complex. Furthermore, Stacey's theory focuses explicitly on uncertainty and anxiety, rendering plausible that a relationship exists between leadership and the uncertainty aspects of wicked problems and collaborative innovation. In Stacey's work, the focus is on the quality of participation, conversational life, anxiety, and diversity, as well as on unpredictability and paradoxes (Stacey, 2011, p. 475). Contributing to the theory of complex responsive processes, Griffin (2002) understands leadership as something that is created through processes of recognition.

> *So what is the practice of effective leadership from the perspective of complex responsive processes? The practice is that of participating skilfully in interaction with others in reflective and imaginative ways, aware of the potentially destructive processes one may be caught up in. It is in this practice that one is recognized as leader, as one who has the capacity to assist the group to continue ethically, creatively, and courageously into the unknown. This is a very different way of understanding the role of leader from the mainstream perspective on which the leader stands outside the system, designing and manipulating variables, and pulling levers in order to stay in control.*
>
> (Griffin 2002, p. 13)

According to Griffin, that which leads to recognition as a leader is first and foremost the direct interaction in change processes, but also the improvement of a person's ability to articulate emergent 'themes' of sensemaking in an environment of insecurity, as well as the person's willingness to act in unfamiliar circumstances. 'Themes' are defined by Stacey as "continuously iterated patterns of intersubjective themes that organize the experience of being together" (Stacey, 2011, p. 340).

These considerations add to the analytical approach by emphasizing that in a context of uncertainty, leadership is something that emerges when developing new organizational themes that reduce the anxiety of organizational participants; however, it must also be noted that such anxieties and uncertainties are preconditions for leadership emergence in the first place.

In terms of theory of science, the uncertainty perspective towards leadership is rendered plausible in a collaborative context by being positioned within a relational leadership theory, a position of relational constructionism (Uhl-Bien, 2006). Such a position suggests focusing on processes, understood as "the influential acts of organizing that contribute to the structuring of interactions and relationships" (Uhl-Bien, 2006, p. 662). This relational ontology raises questions such as how the processes of leadership and management in organizations emerge, how realities of leadership are interpreted within the network of relations, and how decisions and actions are embedded in collective sensemaking processes (Uhl-Bien, 2006, p. 662). So the focus of relational constructionism is on processes of interaction, conversation, narrating, dialoguing, and multiloguing, meaning being constantly "negotiated and renegotiated within the context of its particular sociocultural location" (Uhl-Bien, 2006, p. 663). Across such relational perspectives, leadership is viewed as the processes through which a social order is constructed and changed (Uhl-Bien, 2006, p. 664). The contested, strategic power context of leadership within a collaborative context (Huxham & Vangen, 2005; Crosby & Bryson, 2010, pp. 211–230) can be further enhanced by drawing on a study by Phillips et al. (Phillips, Lawrence, & Hardy, 2004) on linking strategic action with discourse production and institutionalization in organizations.

In the following section, I draw on two examples to show how uncertainty and leadership produce a distinct perspective of organizing. This perspective emphasizes how a constructionist relationship between leadership and an innovation project enables leadership to overcome uncertainty by means of sensemaking (Weick, 1995) and informed the development of the leadership position. However, before doing so, I describe how my explorative and abductive fieldwork has inspired the development of such a perspective.

The Methodology Behind an Engaged-Scholarship Ethnography

In order to explore how my analytical approach can be developed and refined, I make use of Andrew Van de Ven's methodology of engaged scholarship (2007). This methodology has useful qualities for a study that wants to be inspired by practice in order to achieve a theoretical objective, in my case, contributing to the emerging research field of collaborative innovation leadership. Van de Ven argues that there is a theory-practice gap and that this gap is partly caused by a knowledge production problem that arises when the researcher recognizes that the different perspectives and types of academic knowledge are "partial, incomplete and involving [an] inherent bias with respect to any complex problem" (Van de Ven, 2007, p. 4). This problem can be solved by means of knowledge co-production among scholars and practitioners. As a result, engaged scholarship suggests a methodology in which the researcher perceives of her or himself as a participant, learning and understanding a subject by engaging in conversations with stakeholders (Van de Ven, 2007, p. 14). This is a pluralistic approach to knowledge, which requires a pluralistic methodology (Van de Ven, 2007, p. 15). An engaged-scholarship approach deems it necessary to operate with different theoretical perspectives in order to understand a complex phenomenon (Van de Ven, 2007, p. 15) and to compare different explanations to the same problem (Van de Ven, 2007, p. 21). In this way, engaged scholarship is an abductive approach that requires that the researcher is able to utilize the insights gained from fieldwork to inspire theory building.

The ethnographic fieldwork was conducted as part of a PhD project and was organized as a qualitative, single-case study (Flyvbjerg, 2006) with two embedded cases (Yin, 2008). The first embedded case was researched in the period 2009–2010 and the second case from 2010 to 2012. The purpose of the first embedded case was to conduct a pilot study which, in addition to gathering data, was also meant to further develop and adjust my overall case study, as well as my analytical approach.

The innovation project studied can be divided into two distinct phases. For each phase I selected an embedded case in order to track leadership development over time. The first phase was a strategy-development and implementation phase that was set in motion on the basis of a strategy report (Engberg, 2008) containing six recommendations. The report stated that implementing these recommendations would improve the coordination of area-based project activities in disadvantaged neighborhoods and thereby enhance municipal efficiency. The second phase was an unexpected consequence of the first phase, as leadership succeeded in lobbying in favour of a highly ambitious, cross-administrative policy for disadvantaged city districts. Accordingly, the strategic development project progressed into a policy-development phase that led to the activation of top decision makers across all seven municipal administrations, as well as decision makers from social housing organizations.

Leadership was distinguishable and located in the same office across the two embedded cases—i.e., the Neighborhood Development Office (NDO). This office comprised a handful of professionals and a middle manager at the central-administrative level with the responsibility for area-based programmes in disadvantaged neighborhoods, and it was located in TEA.

As a result of the pilot study, it became clear that leadership and the division of roles were the primary sources of conflict and collaborative inertia (Huxham & Vangen, 2005) between the representatives from the administrations. Furthermore, there was a clear link between the conflicts regarding role division and the substance of the project (i.e., increased coordination and joint strategy at the central-administrative level), as especially representatives from the Social Service Administration (SSA) had difficulties comprehending the added value of the development project and assessed that the project was a centralistic project that only served to stress their frontline, service-delivering staff in the disadvantaged neighborhoods.

Concerning methods, inspired by Yin's recommendations (2009), I made use of observations and field notes, thereby keeping myself up to date on developments in the NDO. There were several reasons for this approach: to document events and conversations, including issues dominating the process in this period of time; to qualify future qualitative interviews; to observe the points of conflict; to observe how leadership was enacted in certain interactions and by whom; and, finally, to identify what triggered inertia and what triggered progress. I also used in-depth, semi-structured qualitative interviews with participants from all the involved administrations, recordings of policy-formulation meetings in the second embedded case, and a focus group interview that enabled feedback on the pilot study by the NDO. In total, 45 field notes were compiled, 26 qualitative interviews were conducted, and 14 hours of policy-formulation recordings were gathered. Furthermore, a handful of essential policy documents were identified and used to document the line of events and outputs of the innovation project.

Ultimately, the research design was strong in regard to the gathering of data related to leadership adaptation and uncertainty and the interaction between these two research objects. It was also strong with regard to keeping abreast of sudden crises or content developments of the innovation project throughout the study period. I was able to identify when NDO staff positioned themselves in a new way and hence transformed their identities. In order to a) compensate for a potential 'going-native' bias as a result of the fieldwork in the NDO and b) to enhance the collaborative understanding of leadership, I attended as many meetings with administrative representatives as possible and conducted interviews across administrations in order to get their point of view concerning conflicts and to learn how they assessed the innovation project and leadership.

Next, two examples of analysis of leadership are provided, one from each phase of the ethnographic study. The first example is located within the context of a development project that the NDO had initiated, the purpose of which was increased coordination across administrations (first phase). Accordingly, the NDO was dependent on the consent and support of the six other municipal administrations. The second example is located within the strategic context of policy formulation, likewise led by the NDO, and concerned a process that ran across all seven administrations (second phase).

First Example of NDO Leadership: The Emergence of Coordinative Leadership

Vignette

An evaluation team across three administrations was to make a shared evaluation tool. This was one of six recommendations presented in a strategy report, the main purpose of which was to facilitate increased coordination between local governmental administrations when working with area-based initiatives in disadvantaged neighborhoods. The NDO was the project owner of this strategic development project. The other administrations displayed varying or no support for the project, with the exception of the Employment and Integration Administration (EIA) and SSA.

The evaluation tool was to form the basis for an ongoing, future evaluation practice. The strategic aim of this evaluation practice was to explore the pros and cons of the local-coordinative traits that these area-based initiatives display. However, for various reasons, making this cross-administrative evaluation tool was no easy task. Conflicts regarding leadership and uncertainty about the overall strategic objective of the entire development project increased the level of conflicts in the evaluation team, and this conflict-ridden context made it difficult to reach consensus about the desired purpose of the evaluation tool. Consequently, conflicts and inertia dominated the team's work.

Substantive and Institutional Uncertainties: What Is the Future Role of Area-Based Initiatives?

In terms of uncertainty, tricky substantive and institutional discussions surfaced (Koppenjan & Klijn, 2004), triggered by different administrative knowledge needs and mandates which reflected each administration's sectorial focus and position in the innovation process. This experience became a point of discussion for the team in autumn 2009, as two of the three involved administrations (SSA and EIA) were disappointed; they had expected that their institutional need to numerically document the effects of their engagement in area-based initiatives would be met. However, due to the complex composition of area-based initiatives and the wickedness (Rittel & Webber, 1973; Head & Alford, 2013) of 'what works' in disadvantaged neighbourhoods, these effects were difficult to document.

Institutionally, members of the evaluation team and the individuals generally involved in the development project needed to develop a shared understanding of what the area-based initiative 'was', what it should be in the future, and what problems such area-based initiatives should address. The current and future function of this cross-administrative programme was unclear, and this uncertainty was exacerbated due to the fact that the municipality did not have a firm political objective with regard to this policy field. Developing such a political objective was also part of the development project, but this parallel process had not had an impact yet. Accordingly, the institutional role of the area-based initiatives remained unclear in this phase, which had implications on the substantial content of the initiatives and hence made it difficult to establish an evaluation tool and practice.

Leadership Adaptiveness: Taking on the Position of a Coordinative Leadership

In terms of leadership, not just the administrative collaboration partners but also the NDO, tried, on a regular basis, to make sense (Weick, 1995) of how to further develop the understanding of area-based initiatives as a consequence of the strategy employed. Because the municipal-administrative context of these area-based initiatives changed due to the strategic development project, the purpose of the area-based initiatives also risked changing. Due to its role as project owner, the NDO had some crucial decisions to make in terms of the overall purpose and scope of its activities, because, potentially, a huge proportion of municipal resources could be framed within the spatial logic that area-based initiatives are based upon. Accordingly, in the years 2008–2010, a strategic discourse was launched by the NDO in local government, denoting a first step towards potential discursive embeddedness and institutionalization (Phillips et al., 2004); however, the NDO in this phase was faced with unexpected resistance due to the substantive and institutional uncertainties. Accordingly, in order to gain recognition from collaboration partners, the NDO had to find ways to reduce uncertainties, while maintaining core elements of strategic discourse.

As a result of the conflicts experienced in the evaluation team and the sensemaking such similar conflicts generated, three leadership options emerged for the NDO. Each option pitched leadership at different levels as regards ambition and sectorial breadth. Was the NDO a routine-oriented office that was merely to operate and supervise area-based initiatives as *efficiently* as possible? Was it an office that wanted to facilitate a certain *systemic* change in the way the municipal administrations coordinate their resources and strategies? Or was it an office that wanted to do all of this *and* wanted to focus on the much larger, cross-sectorial municipal problem, namely that of disadvantaged neighbourhoods?

Because of these in-process leadership reflections, the NDO conveyed mixed signals to its administrative collaboration partners, and this created blurry boundaries with regard to both the development project and the NDO's leadership. As a result, the NDO's development project about coordinating municipal resources in new ways was perceived as a threat by some of these administrative representatives. Collaborative inertia (Huxham & Vangen, 2005) became a serious risk in this part of the development project. The NDO was seen as a power-hungry actor that tries to take coordinative control of other administrations' sector-professional areas into which the NDO had no professional insight. For instance, the NDO was regarded by the SSA as a collaborative leader that merely pretended to be inclusive, while actually knowing all the answers in advance:

> *The reason why it has been a weird process is that it has been like: 'we do this together, but in-reality-it-is-us-who-decide' (. . .) you point towards a huge problem throughout the process that we have never actually articulated: 'who are you, who are we, what can you expect from us, what can we expect of each other across administrations'. It has constantly been running in an ad hoc kind of way.*
>
> (SSA, Civil servant, I5)

This role confusion among administrations created disappointment because the administrative representatives did not know what to expect of each other. Accordingly, the SSA did not recognize the NDO as their leader: they refused to be followers because the NDO failed to deal with fundamental uncertainties (Griffin, 2002).

So on the basis of several of these, and other, conflicts, the NDO regularly adapted its position over the next three years. In 2008, at the beginning of the project, the NDO has what the office members perceived to be a highly relevant, ready-to-go, strategic development project with six firm recommendations, which were outlined in a highly detailed and well-prepared report. However, as the project proceeded, they discovered that the *value-based* outset (i.e., "We want to do something radical to improve

disadvantaged neighborhoods".) was too weak to function as a collaborative foundation to gain support across the entire municipality.

In the quote from the NDO that follows, several understandings of the
NDO's own leadership are presented, exemplifying the first time leadership
takes on a new leadership position in the organization discourse (Phillips
et al., 2004, pp. 635–652) of the office through the development project (see
Hansen, 2015 for a full analysis of these leadership positions). In the quote,
the middle manager from the NDO explains how office staff has become
more aware of their own roles: they are an office capable of handling issues
related to organizing and collaborating.

> *This has been an exercise which is also about shutting things down—what
> we should not do. As regards other municipal strategies and projects, we
> have the same academic reflections which are what can we do here, how
> far can we go, what is our role? (. . .). I think this might also be a relief for
> some of the other administrations—the fear of whether we would spread
> all over the place and have an opinion about everything. Here we say,
> "No, this is your field of responsibility—this is what you do best". I defi-
> nitely think that some of our professionalism lies in being capable in the
> field of organizing and collaborating.*

(NDO, middle manager)

Ultimately, the example demonstrates how the NDO reduced uncertainty
and related conflicts by redefining its leadership position from being concerned with substantially related issues to being in a coordinative leadership
position; the NDO as leader was itself on a 'journey', just as the innovation
process was (Van de Ven, 1999).

Second Example of NDO Leadership: The Emergence of Strategic Leadership

Vignette

In the period 2010–2012, the NDO managed to influence a parallel-
running, cross-administrative process of implementing new legislation, the so-called Governance Dialogue. This legislation transferred
the supervisory obligations of the social housing sector from central
government to the local-government level. As a result, the municipality
in this study and the involved social housing organizations needed a
way to cooperate in a coordinated partnership fashion. Part of the influence exercised by the NDO was to give sense (Gioia & Chittipeddi,
1991, p. 433–448) in such a way that the future organizational partnership structure for the Governance Dialogue was in accordance with

the concepts and recommendations already introduced previously in the strategy report for area-based initiatives, as both of these policy streams revolved around issues of disadvantaged neighbourhoods, coordination, and cooperation with social housing organizations. The NDO ensured that these conceptual linkages were communicated, thereby further expanding the scope of their strategic discourse (Phillips et al., 2004). The NDO did this by lobbying for support for a policy for area-based initiatives in disadvantaged neighbourhoods to guide the activities of such a new cross-administrative partnership structure. As a result of additional sensemaking triggered by the subsequent process of policy formulation, the NDO had a growing ambition: that the policy should not just be a toolbox policy for area-based initiatives, i.e., one programme type out of many, operating in small-scale disadvantaged neighbourhoods. Instead, the policy should be an overall policy framework that should comprise larger, disadvantaged city districts and as such involve numerous cross-administrative activities and services.

Uncertainty as an Enabling-Constraining Condition: Creating a Demand for Leadership

In terms of uncertainty, what informed and enabled a decisive strategic reorientation from the NDO was to a high extent a combination of substantive, strategic, and institutional uncertainties that paralyzed the newly established policy-formulation team. Brainstorming sessions held at the onset of the process only led to disappointment. Administrative representatives found it difficult to relate area-based initiatives to their own administrative strategies, as the problem to be solved had not been clearly defined due to institutional limitations: At this point in time, the policy field of disadvantaged neighbourhoods was non-existent in the municipality. Accordingly, the team initially had only been granted the mandate to make a policy for a type of programme—the area-based initiatives. Just as in the previous vignette, the NDO development project created institutional changes in parallel with the unfolding of strategic discourse. Consequently, institutional uncertainty was generated, resulting in numerous discussions in the team on the wishes of the decision makers (the Lord Mayor, a newly established 'intra-municipal steering committee' and the NDO's director) and on what was expected of the team. This led to increasing frustration:

Heck, I don't know what they want [Steering Committee], specifically not with regard to this neighborhood. But I do know what my politicians want, and how it should be presented to them, and if it is to progress further through the system, it must be tolerable. And it will not do any good if we then choose a solution that transcends the policies and strategies we already have.

(Group interview 11, part 3)

Consequently, despite being a collaborative process facilitated by the NDO, an increasing demand for leadership emerged as the policy process continued fruitlessly.

'To Take on Leadership': The Emergence of a Strategic Leadership

In terms of leadership, the discussions in the policy-formulation team contributed to the leadership sensemaking (Weick, 1995) and, ultimately, to a change in leadership positioning. An NDO employee ('Sam') reflects on the initial terms of reference for the policy and the unarticulated relationship between the function of area-based initiatives and disadvantaged neighbourhoods. This relation also caused some frustration in the evaluation team as described earlier. Consequently, Sam and the NDO consultant begin to realize that the terms of reference for policy should perhaps be different. The NDO consultant explains this change of perception in the NDO:

It was a time of transition, when all of a sudden Sam begins to say, well, "Shouldn't we rather call the Policy something else?", because what we constantly ended up talking about [in the Policy Formulation Team] was those neighborhoods, but we are constantly telling ourselves that we are only looking at the area-based initiatives. So why not call it [the Policy] what it was supposed to be called? And that point, I must admit, no one else has questioned. So again it is, in a way, plainly to take on leadership.

(NDO, special consultant, I19)

The quote shows that, at the outset, the NDO did not have all the answers with regard to how to solve the uncertainties that surfaced within the initial terms of reference for the policy for area-based initiatives. Instead, they had to rely on their own ability to make sense (Weick, 1995) of what they were doing in the process; they had to reinterpret their original strategic development project and to interpret the numerous discussions with collaboration partners; finally, they had to come up with new solutions and concepts, and in this respect, they had to give sense to collaboration partners (Gioia & Chittipeddi, 1991).

However, despite the NDO's initial success with regard to lobbying for policy support and breaking the initial paralysis of the team by means of a more firm leadership position, the occurrence of strategic uncertainty proved to be a challenge throughout the process, putting the entire policy process at risk. When the NDO mobilized hierarchical support in its own administration to change the terms of reference for the policy, the policy became much more powerful, but also more vulnerable to strategic considerations. This created a demand for a more strategic, steady leadership behaviour and leadership profile. For instance, in an interview, a former level-3 director in TEA mentioned an example demonstrating this strategic element. The example highlights that it was essential that all the mayors involved in the new organizational partnership structure felt that the present, now more powerful policy was relevant to them, which required hard work on the part of the NDO:

> *Where there might be a little skepticism, someone asked: Haven't we created a huge complicated organizational structure here, which is almost larger than what we had before? Remember, we [in NDO, TEA] used the argument that we needed to clean up the mess about organizational proliferation. So we insisted, "No, we believe this structure is transparent and therefore usable". I remember when we were having the first meeting [in the board of mayors] . . . If it had seemed meaningless to the actors involved in some of these sessions, we would have lost it, and there were signs of this. For example, the mayor for children and youth said, "Why am I sitting here?" And the mayor for culture and leisure was perhaps also present. In this case, we then made a speedy decision and opted for a culture theme the next time the board of mayors was supposed to have a meeting. So if people could not see that this was very important, we wouldn't have been able to move up [to that policy level]. So it was really, really important that the meetings were prepared in detail and that there was some substance in it.*
>
> (TEA, director, I29)

What this quote shows is how vulnerable the policy process had become for the NDO in terms of maintaining and sanctioning support at the top decision-maker level, as the office had to rely on soft power tools (making and giving sense across numerous stakeholders) in order to maintain hierarchical support. Moreover, the quote hints at the constant, and growing, workload that is required to give sense as the uncertainty of collaborators mounts and as the numbers of collaborators increase.

As a consequence of the changes in policy scope and content triggered by the NDO, the NDO was forced to alter and clarify its leadership position towards a less developmental and, hence, more strategic, leadership position in which uncertainties were reduced and a steady, strategic leadership was displayed.

Reflections

The present chapter has described how an engaged-scholarship ethnography has contributed to knowledge about leadership of collaborative innovation in the public sector. Due to its abductive nature, the ethnography has done this by being highly sensitive towards the dominant challenges of leadership and collaboration partners. This ethnography was made possible by observing those challenges on a daily basis, as the professionals struggled with an innovation project in a wicked-problem policy field. This has resulted in a theoretical inspiration that has informed the analytical approach, combining in a novel fashion theoretical concepts of uncertainty, collaborative innovation, constructionist-relational leadership theory, and organizational discourse analysis. This analytical approach has enabled me to explain leadership of collaborative innovation in a process language that allows for strategy and power, yet also conveys insights of uncertainty and identity-related issues.

In terms of findings, four stand out. First, the analytical explanation has yielded insights in, above all, the pervasiveness of uncertainty and the transformative impacts this has on leadership and the way that leadership exercises influence. As the examples demonstrate, uncertainty mounts throughout the innovation process as leadership partly by being strategic, partly by muddling through, keeps pushing the innovation agenda forward, while simultaneously making sense of what leadership and collaborators are doing. This leadership practice has qualities that existing research assesses as crucial: qualities of adaptation and flexibility (Torfing, 2013), as well as 'emergence' (Griffin, 2002; Vangen & Huxham, 2003, p. 63). However, this combination of qualities also results in leadership conveying mixed signals about its own leadership role and the overall purpose of the innovation project. Although collaborative conflicts and inertia (Huxham & Vangen, 2005) are mitigated and utilized, these challenges are not avoided.

A second finding is that leadership redefines its leadership throughout the innovation project. Leadership does so in order to reduce uncertainty: Redefining leadership in the light of dominant uncertainties makes possible the conceptual construction of specific distinctions and activities of influence, resulting in clear divisions of labour between leadership and collaborators. In this study, this has the effect of reducing fear of turf colonialism within the studied municipal central administrations.

Third, the engaged-scholarship ethnography has helped to uncover the highly dynamic, post-structural relationship between leadership and innovation project. As the content of the innovation project is altered, for example, by expanding policy scope and introducing new rhetoric, other uncertainties are triggered. The constant production of new bundles of uncertainties creates a collaborative demand for a new type of leadership that is able to match this new trajectory of the innovation journey. Accordingly, collaborative innovations can be understood as organizational discourses at the micro-level (Alvesson & Kärreman, 2000; Phillips et al., 2004) in which leadership is first of all an interdependent subject position in that very same discourse, and, second, the prime producer of this discourse. Accordingly, both discourse and leadership display their own 'innovation journey' (Van de Ven, 1999). The examples have highlighted that the relationship between these two independent, yet also *inter*dependent, organizational phenomena are by no means predictable, but exactly constructionist (Uhl-Bien, 2006) in nature. Leadership has to decide on one out of several possible leadership positions, the range of these being limited by the self-initiated discourse as well as the sense made throughout the innovation process.

Finally, the study has made clear the overall nature of the relationship between leadership and uncertainty: Leadership triggers specific types of uncertainty, sometimes even deliberately seeking out such sources of uncertainty, and in this respect, demonstrates leadership traits of influence related to employee-driven, bottom-up innovation (Borins, 2002), public entrepreneurship (Klein et al., 2010), and strategic sense-giving (Gioia & Chittipeddi, 1991). Consequently, uncertainty is not a structural, deterministic condition, but rather a self-generated framing condition that leadership generates partly deliberately, partly unintentionally.

Such ethnography warrants methodological considerations. First of all, it helped a great deal that I was experienced in terms of the substantial content of the innovation studied—in this case, area-based initiatives and the NDO strategic development project. Had this knowledge not been acquired before fieldwork was begun, I would have been much less sensitive to when additional layers of discourse concepts were added to the innovation and hence would not have been able to detect the relational impact of the innovation project on leadership or to detect when a new leadership position was introduced. Second, the engaged-scholarship ethnography is demanding in terms of theory building; sensitivity towards observations in the field requires much patience and time in terms of exploring relevant literature. Obviously, this challenge might be reduced if one is a very experienced researcher. Third, such an approach may be most suitable in novel research fields; leadership of collaborative innovation in the public sector is an emerging and, therefore, explorative, academic field to work with as the researchers committed to the field seek to combine organizational phenomena typically divided in specific academic research disciplines, such as public/private, micro/meso, administrational/organizational, leadership/management/governance, intra-/interorganizational, emerging/discourse/institutional, and process/static descriptions. In order to detect which of these combinations has empirical relevance and explanatory power, and how the elements causally are related, the present ethnography is useful.

Comment by Steven Griggs: Leading Innovation Through the Mess of Collaboration

Collaborative innovation is hard to get a handle on. Seasoned observers in the field know it when they see it. But it means different things to different people. It comes in different guises, travels down many different paths, and crosses multiple boundaries and frontiers. Leading such a 'shape shifting' collection of practices challenges public sector professionals, managers, and politicians. It demands that they take on multiple styles of leadership, possess skills of reflexivity, persuasion and visioning, and exercise the capabilities to span the boundaries of different organizations whilst addressing head on politics and conflict (Ansell & Gash, 2008; Hartley, Sørensen, & Torfing, 2013). But in practice, how do public leaders tackle such tasks? How do they navigate the processes of collaborative innovation? And how do we communicate that to others?

Jesper Rohr Hansen's ethnography study of urban administrators and planners helps us to answer these questions. Organizational ethnography examines the everyday practices of those who work within, and come to constitute, organizations (Ybema et al., 2009, p. 1). Having experienced 'being there' (Miettinen, Samra-Fredericks, & Yanow, 2009, p. 1315), meeting administrators and planners in their own context, observing and reflecting on meetings, conversations, and interviews, Hansen offers us valuable insights into what it means to be a 'collaborative leader', encouraging us to bridge theory and practice and to reflect on just what it is that practitioners 'do' when they lead collaboration (Wagenaar, 2004). Challenging existing studies, and their tendency towards simplified or parsimonious narratives of collaboration which impose too much order and post hoc coherence on events, Hansen opens us up to the messiness that comes from accepting "a reality that [is] multiple, slippery and fuzzy. Indefinite" (Law, 2003, p. 9).

In fact, what Hansen gives us is a picture into how the leadership of collaborative innovation is a continuous exercise in the craft of puzzling, dealing with 'mess', and managing uncertainty. In short, he brings out the concept of the 'journey' towards innovation as one of learning and adaptation as pressures, partners, and positions shift and change. As Hansen's urban planners and administrators move forward in the construction of a novel evaluation framework, or act strategically to influence new 'Governance Dialogue' legislation, these actors do not necessarily know where they are going and what they are seeking to achieve. These traditional endpoints of any policy process become at best temporary settlements that are generated as the programme itself takes shape. As Hansen reminds us, collaborative leadership is about taking advantage of opportunities as they emerge, a practice that requires professionals on an almost daily basis to reflect upon, and communicate, where 'we' are in the process of collaboration and where 'we' are going: be it second-guessing the wishes of the steering team, knowing what 'political masters' want or responding appropriately with a new discussion theme when one mayor says "Why am I sitting here?" In other words, Hansen surfaces that the leadership of collaborative innovation is a craft, a set of tacit political skills that we struggle to codify or capture in any straightforward way.

But what Hansen also surfaces through his observations is how far uncertainty and the management of uncertainty figures in the everyday leadership of collaborative innovation. These different spaces of uncertainty enable leadership to happen, to emerge, and to come forward. Indeed, as Hansen shows, during moments of uncertainty, leaders from outside established hierarchies can step up to the plate and offer themselves up as leaders. Uncertainty can be tapped into by leaders, or even generated, as a means of moving projects forward. And once such uncertainty is removed from the collaboration, troubles can emerge, for such moments can spark opposition and conflict as it becomes clear where the programme is heading and how it might contest certain institutional positions.

Yet uncertainty is a double-edged sword, as it places constraints on leadership. As we discover through the everyday practices of the administrators in the spotlight of Hansen's study, collaborators or followers do not always appreciate uncertainty. In fact, we learn that leadership has to deal with the 'fundamental uncertainties' of partners, revealing something of a paradox, in that uncertainty creates spaces for leadership, but too much uncertainty risks breaking down collaboration and dialogue. Followers, as Hansen foregrounds, want certainty and order, as revealed by one civil servant expressing her displeasure to him that the process "has been running in an ad hoc kind of way". In other words, if collaborative innovation as a leadership challenge is a process of puzzlement and uncertainty, you can have too much puzzlement, at least in public; followers expect leaders to know where they are going and get frustrated when they do not.

Importantly, this unease brings to the fore the emotional labour of collaborative innovation. Hansen peppers his study with recognition of 'disappointment' and 'frustration'. Leading on a daily basis is emotional work; it surfaces issues of personal identity, and it demands that practitioners critically reflect on their own limitations. It also demands authenticity, which administrators and professionals have to constantly reproduce and evidence for others. When the SSA threatens to leave the entire process, it does so because the NDO might make reference to collaboration and dialogue, but it does not put those principles into action; they talk the talk, but they do not walk the walk.

Where does that leave us? Leading collaborative leadership, as Hansen helpfully contributes, is a craft, a craft that puzzles its way through 'mess' and uncertainty, often without an end in sight. The paradox is that, despite the strategic opportunities raised for leaders in exploiting uncertainty, followers or collaborative partners often want certainty, but not too much. Hansen thus points us in the direction of the mess of leadership and the political art of twists and turns, of critical reflection. These twists and turns create conflicts and inertia, but this is not always a barrier to innovation; it can be an opportunity if taken, and most times people just want to know that there is a direction of travel. As such, Hansen makes us aware that in everyday practices, leadership emerges over time, adjusts to shifting contexts that in part it brings into being, and that leadership is at best a temporary settlement. The challenge is how we communicate these lessons to practitioners in terms that meet with their underlying desire to rid themselves of uncertainty. This new dialogue is the challenge raised by Hansen's timely intervention.

Discussant References

Ansell, C., & Gash, A. (2008). Collaborative Governance in Theory and Practice. *Journal of Public Administration Research and Theory*, 18 (4), 543–571.

Hartley, J., Sørensen, E., & Torfing J. (2013). Collaborative Innovation: A Viable Alternative to Market-Competition and Organizational Entrepreneurship. *Public Administration Review*, 73 (6), 821–830.

Law, J. (2003). *Making a Mess with Method*. Centre for Science Studies, Lancaster University, Lancaster. Accessed February 7, 2016. http://www.lancaster.ac.uk/fass/resources/sociology-online-papers/papers/law-making-a-mess-with-method.pdf

Miettinen, R., Samra-Fredericks, D., & Yanow, D. (2009). Re-Turn to Practice: An Introductory Essay. *Organization Studies*, 30 (12), 1309–1327.

Wagenaar, H. (2004). "Knowing" the Rules. Administrative Work as Practice. *Public Administration Review*, 64 (6), 643–655.

Ybema, S., Yanow, D., Wels, H., & Kamsteeg, F. (2009). Studying everyday organisational life. In S. Ybema, D. Yanow, H. Wels, & F. Kamsteeg (Eds.), *Organisational Ethnography: Studying the Complexity of Everyday Life*. London: Sage, 1–20.

Chapter References

Alvesson, M., & Kärreman, D. (2000). Varieties of Discourse: On the Study of Organizations through Discourse Analysis. *Human Relations*, 53 (9), 1125–1149.

Bland, T., Bruk, B., Kim, D., & Lee, K. T. (2010). Enhancing Public Sector Innovation: Examining the Network-Innovation Relationship. *Public Sector Innovation Journal*, 15 (3), 1–25.

Bommert, B. (2010). Collaborative Innovation in the Public Sector. *International Public Management Review*, 11 (1), 15–32.

Borins, S. (2002). Leadership and Innovation in the Public Sector. *Leadership & Organization Development Journal*, 23 (8), 467–476.

Crosby, B. C. and J. M. Bryson. 2010. "Integrative Leadership and the Creation and Maintenance of Cross-Sector Collaborations." *Leadership Quarterly*, 21 (2), 211–230. doi:10.1016/j.leaqua

Eggers, W. D., Singh, S. K., Goldsmith, S., & Ash Institute for Democratic Governance and Innovation. (2009). *The Public Innovator's Playbook: Nurturing Bold Ideas in Government*. Cambridge, MA: Ash Institute, Harvard Kennedy School.

Engberg, Lars A. (2008). *Den Horisontale Søjle: Et Strategisk Udviklingsperspektiv for Koordinering Af Områdeindsatser i Københavns Kommune*. 1, udgave ed. Statens Byggeforskningsinstitut.

Engberg, Lars A., & Norvig Larsen, Jacob. (2010). Context-Orientated Meta-Governance in Danish Urban Regeneration. *Planning Theory & Practice*, 11 (4), 549–571.

Flyvbjerg, Bent. (2006). Five Misunderstandings about Case-Study Research. *Qualitative Inquiry*, 12 (2), 219–245.

Gioia, Dennis A., & Chittipeddi, Kumar. (1991). Sensemaking and Sensegiving in Strategic Change Initiation. *Strategic Management Journal*, 12 (6), 433–448.

Griffin, Douglas. (2002). *The Emergence of Leadership: Linking Self-Organization and Ethics: Complexity and Emergence in Organizations*. London: Routledge.

Hansen, J. R. (2015). *A Bottom-Up Perspective on Leadership of Collaborative Innovation in the Public Sector: The Social Construction of Leadership for*

Disadvantaged City Districts in the City of Copenhagen. PhD Thesis. Aalborg: Aalborg University Press (PhD Series).

Harris, Michael, & Albury, David. (2009). *The Innovation Imperative*. London: Nesta.

Hartley, J. (2005). Innovation in Governance and Public Services: Past and Present. *Public Money & Management*, 25 (1), 27–34.

Head, B. W., & Alford, J. (2013). Wicked Problems: Implications for Public Policy and Management. *Administration & Society*, 20 (10), 1–29. doi:10.1177/00 95399713481601

Huxham, C., & Vangen, S. (2005). *Managing to Collaborate: The Theory and Practice of Collaborative Advantage*. New York: Routledge.

Klein, P. G., J. T. Mahoney, A. M. McGahan, and C. N. Pitelis. (2010). Toward a Theory of Public Entrepreneurship. *European Management Review*, 7 (1), 1–15.

Koppenjan, J. F. M., & Klijn, E. H. (2004). *Managing Uncertainties in Networks: A Network Approach to Problem Solving and Decision Making*. New York: Routledge.

Moore, M., & Hartley, J. (2008). Innovations in Governance. *Public Management Review*, 10 (1), 3–20.

Phillips, N., Lawrence, T. B., & Hardy, C. (2004). Discourse and Institutions. *Academy of Management Review*, 29 (4), 635–652.

Rittel, H. W. J. and Webber M. M. 1973. Dilemmas in a General Theory of Planning. *Policy Sciences*, 4 (2), 155–169.

Sørensen, E., & Torfing, J. (2011). Enhancing Collaborative Innovation in the Public Sector. *Administration and Society*, 43 (8), 842–868.

Stacey, Ralph D. (2011). *Strategic Management and Organisational Dynamics: The Challenge of Complexity to Ways of Thinking about Organisations, 6th ed.* Harlow, Essex: Financial Times/ Prentice Hall.

Torfing, Jacob. (2013). Collaborative innovation in the public sector. In Stephen P. Osborne, & B. Louise (Eds.), *Handbook of Innovation in Public Services*. Cheltenham: Edward Elgar, 301–316.

Uhl-Bien, M. (2006). Relational Leadership Theory: Exploring the Social Processes of Leadership and Organizing. *The Leadership Quarterly*, 17 (6), 654–676.

Van de Ven, A. H. (1999). *The Innovation Journey*. New York: Oxford University Press.

Van de Ven, A. H. (2007). *Engaged Scholarship: A Guide for Organizational and Social Research*. Oxford: Oxford University Press.

Vangen, S., & Huxham, C. (2003). Enacting Leadership for Collaborative Advantage: Dilemmas of Ideology and Pragmatism in the Activities of Partnership Managers. *British Journal of Management*, 14, S61–S76.

Weick, Karl E. (1995). *Sensemaking in Organizations*. Thousand Oaks: Sage.

Yin, R. K. (2008). *Case Study Research: Design and Methods*. Thousand Oaks: Sage Publications, Inc.

10 Montage Ethnography
Editing and Co-Analyzing Voices from the Field

Morten Arnfred and discussant Mike Rowe

Introduction

Generally, ethnography requires a strong authorial voice in the form of a researcher who represents the different perspectives and actions of his or her informants and proceeds to analyze, contextualize, and interpret these actions and perspectives. The empirical material is viewed through different theoretical lenses in order to come up with new angles, concepts, and arguments. This chapter will explore a slightly different approach to the representation and analysis of ethnographic material, where informants to a greater extent are allowed to speak for themselves and where the analysis is done collaboratively. The approach is inspired by montage—the cinematic principle of juxtaposing different images to create new meaning. The concept of montage was originally introduced into ethnographic methodology by the anthropologist George Marcus (see Marcus, 1990; 1992). This chapter will discuss a specific kind of ethnographic montage called polyphonic sound montage (Arnfred, 2015). In this approach, recordings of semi-structured interviews are analyzed and edited into themed sound montages. These montages can then be played to relevant groups of people, who can engage in collaborative interpretation and analysis of the material. The approach thus contains two main elements: a format for presenting qualitative research in the form of polyphonic sound montages and a strategy for analyzing these montages through a process of 'co-analysis'. I define co-analysis as a cooperative, retroductive process, where empirical material is discussed and analyzed (Arnfred, 2015, p. 356). The aim is to propose possible social structures and mechanisms that can explain apparent patterns in the material. The chapter will illuminate how the polyphonic sound montages can be crafted, how the process of co-analysis can be structured, and how this can lead to ideas for service innovation.

The chapter investigates the organizational phenomenon of user involvement in a health-care setting. How can patient perspectives and experiences be captured and used to develop and improve health-care services? Polyphonic sound montages are explored here as an approach to patient involvement. What does this approach allow the researcher and the health-care staff to see, and what are some of the strengths and weaknesses of this approach? The approach was developed at a cardiology department at a public hospital where it has been used in several user-centred innovation projects. The chapter analyzes a project which focused on the department's pacemaker out clinic ('pace-clinic' from now on) where patients with pace-makers and implantable cardioverter defibrillators (ICDs)[1] come to get their devices[2] checked regularly. The overall aim of the project was to help the staff generate new ideas for organizing the pace-clinic by involving the patients' perspectives.

The crafting of polyphonic sound montages and the process of co-analysis, as described in this chapter, is a new approach to ethnographic representation and qualitative analysis. It is argued that the role of the researcher becomes more like that of an editor when the qualitative interviews are turned into montages. The chapter will illustrate how working with polyphonic sound montages can be an engaging way to present qualitative findings, enabling the researcher to include more people in the analysis of the material. In the case discussed in this chapter, the montages highlighted a tendency for the patients to feel like the employees focused too much on the technology and in various ways lacked a focus on them as individual human beings.

First, the chapter briefly discusses different approaches to user involvement in a health-care setting before describing the background and conditions for the pace-clinic innovation project. The use of montage in ethnography will be illustrated with a few examples. Second, the chapter goes on to discuss the concrete considerations and challenges of crafting polyphonic sound montages from ethnographic interviews. Finally, the chapter describes the process of co-analysis and gives some examples of the findings in the pace-clinic project, while discussing the epistemological underpinnings of using sound montages in organizational ethnography.

User Involvement in Health Care

User involvement has recently become much more common in health-care organizations, where it is seen as a way to achieve more efficient, more integrated, and more patient-focused health-care services (Greenhalgh et al., 2010, p. 10). There are many different related concepts and approaches, and the language within this field is rapidly changing and contested. In health research, the term 'service user' is generally used to mean patients, carers, and members of the public, but terms like 'consumer', 'citizen', and 'public' are also used (Morrow et al., 2012, p. xii). In this chapter, user involvement means capturing and representing how patients experience health-care ser-vices and using these insights for service transformation.

Research is emerging which suggests that users can be involved in health-care innovation projects with good result (Bate & Robert, 2006; Groene et al., 2009; Longtin et al., 2010). Bate and Robert (2006) have developed what they call the experience-based, co-design approach, which draws on the field of service design. They argue that previous approaches to service improvement have emphasized the performance and engineering aspects of design, but not the experience aspect, which they define as "how well people understand it, how they feel and how well it fits into the context in which they are using it" (Bate & Robert, 2006, p. 309).

A wide range of methods can be applied to capture the experiences of patients and staff in order to redesign health services. This chapter discusses the use of polyphonic sound montages, but in the following, I will briefly outline a few alternative approaches to highlight how different approaches have different strengths and weaknesses. It is a matter of the specific project and context for which that approach is best suited. A range of approaches and models for service improvement by way of user involvement were tested in the so-called Modernization Initiative, which began in 2003 in the British National Health Service. In one project, a 'mystery shopper' approach was used. This meant hiring and training patients to visit a given service incognito and write up their experiences of certain parts of the system (Baraitser et al., 2005; 2008). The mystery shoppers were briefed on the level of quality they could expect from the clinics. After their visits, they would meet up with a member of the project team to evaluate their experience. This type of feedback was generally well received by staff and used to reduce waiting times, reduce the number of visits, and redesign the physical environment at the clinic. One of the challenges of the approach was that it was quite time consuming to train and coordinate the group of mystery shopper patients (Greenhalgh et al., 2010, p. 30). Another approach in the Modernization Initiative was 'whole system events'. These were workshops where patients and staff worked together to map out all the individual steps in the provided care. The staff included everyone from ward cleaners and managers to porters and clinical staff. This gave the staff insights into how the patients experienced the services and, additionally, provided an overview of the entire user pathway through the system. Greenhalgh et al. note that it is important that the patients who participate are representative of the wider patient population and that their views seem to reflect this. Otherwise the events can become an outlet for personal agendas and single issues (Greenhalgh et al., 2010, p. 31). The final approach in this brief review stems from a Swedish research project in which diaries were employed as a way to involve patients (Elg et al., 2010; 2012). Patients were recruited to keep a diary and asked to write about their contact with health-care institutions, everyday situations relating to their health status, and note any ideas and suggestions for service improvements they might have. These diaries were kept for 14 days after which they were collected, anonymized, and analyzed. Elg et al. identify three ways to learn from the diaries. First, the ideas and suggestions from the diaries can be used directly as input for service-innovation projects. Second, the diaries can be used to identify strong and weak areas of the care process by analyzing the entries of multiple diaries. Third, individual patient stories from the diaries can be used as the basis for discussion within health-care teams and thereby initiate change processes. These aforementioned are just a few of the ones possible for involving patients in service improvement. What polyphonic sound montages have to offer will be explored in the coming sections.

The Pace-Clinic Innovation Project

The pace-clinic innovation project had three partners: a cardiology department at a large public hospital, a cross-governmental innovation unit, and a university department. The aim of the project was to investigate how pacemaker and ICD patients experienced living with a device, coming to consultations, and sending data through telemedicine.[3] The staff would then use these insights to transform current services or develop new ones. One of the managers at the department framed the project like this: "The voice of the patients will help us to rethink the way we think about the pace-clinic". But how do you locate and capture the "voice of the patients"? Who do you include and how? To answer these questions, the project employed polyphonic sound montages.

The organizational setting was the cardiology department's outpatient clinic, which included many different sub-clinics specializing in different heart conditions and tests. One of these sub-clinics was the pace-clinic where patients came to get their devices checked and where the technicians monitored data sent via telemedicine. The staff at the pace-clinic had been through quite a bit of organizational change leading up to the project. For many years, the pace-clinic had been located in a different part of the hospital than the rest of the cardiology department's outpatient clinic. Right about the time this project started, they had been moved to the same location as the other clinics. The small group of about nine technicians had been a relatively autonomous unit, but now they had been put under the same daily management as the rest of the cardiology clinics. All this marked the upstart of the innovation project. The technicians were still trying to find their bearings in the new setting. After all, their old routines had been disrupted. They were a little sceptical about starting a new innovation project because their new responsibilities and assignments were still being negotiated and organized. The managers at the cardiology department had a different perspective. They were well aware that the technicians were under pressure, but they saw the relocation as a good opportunity to try and reorganize the clinic. Additionally, the managers had received some complaints from both patients and other staff about a harsh work environment among the technicians, and they hoped the innovation project could help disrupt this culture.

The consultants from the government innovation unit focused on the patients and their experience with the clinic. They wanted to show the staff at the clinic how the patients were affected by everything from the way the waiting room was designed to the way they talked to the patients. They used the metaphor of holding up a mirror in front of the organization to show the employees: This is how you are perceived, and this is how the patients are affected by your services. The consultants would then work with the staff at the clinic to develop new ideas and concepts that could somehow improve the patients' experiences.

My role was to do research both *for* and *of* the project (Kjærsgaard, 2013, p. 51). As a researcher for the project, I provided the polyphonic sound montages about the patients' perspectives and experiences of their treatment at the clinic. This material was used in the innovation project, and I, therefore, became an active change agent in the organization. As a researcher in the project, I studied the innovation process itself. I had a particular interest in the way patients were involved, how their experiences and perspectives were communicated to the organizational staff, and how insights were transformed into design concepts.

Ethnographic Montage

In this section, I will briefly discuss the concept of montage and what approaches based on this principle allow us to see. The concept of montage was introduced into ethnography by anthropologist George Marcus who had been one of the defining figures in the linguistic turn of the 1980s (Clifford & Marcus, 1986; Marcus & Fischer, 1986). Marcus (1990; 1992) identified montage as a possible strategy for dealing with some of the problems he saw with ethnographic representation. He argued for what he called modernist ethnography, while critiquing traditional, realist ethnography. The ambition was to modernize ethnography's "apparatus of representation" (Marcus, 1990, p. 3). Marcus highlighted that moves away from realist representation at the time had been done in the name of montage. Montage, according to Marcus, is a way to break with undesired rhetorical conventions and narrative modes, because it exposes their artificiality and arbitrariness (Marcus, 1990, p. 4). In other words, Marcus views montage as a way to challenge a coherent finished narrative. Anthropologists Suhr and Willerslev (2013) have recently re-vitalized the idea of montage based on Marcus's original articles. Like Marcus, they praise montage for its disruptive potential. A tool for "the destabilization and rupture of our common-sense perception" (Suhr and Willerslev, 2013, p. 2). Suhr and Willerslev define montage in its broadest sense as "the joining together of different elements in a variety of combinations, repetitions, and overlaps" (Suhr and Willerslev, 2013, p. 1).

Suhr and Willerslev position themselves explicitly against what they call "realist schools of anthropological writing", and claim that this orientation sees montage as a disruptive principle that pollutes the representation of the social world. I argue that even though montage techniques have traditionally been associated with these social constructivist positions, they do not have to be. From a critical realist perspective (Bhaskar, 1975; 1979), montage is an interesting approach to ethnographic representation because it can highlight the complexity of the multicausal open system of social reality and the possible co-existence of conflicting and contradicting social trends and currents (Arnfred, 2015, p. 363). In this chapter, I seek to combine realist and disruptive approaches to ethnographic representation. I will pursue this idea in the second part of the chapter in which I will discuss how the montages can facilitate a process of co-analysis.

A recent, interesting use of textual montage is Nina Holm Vohnsen's text *Labour Days: A Non-linear Narrative of Development* (Vohnsen, 2013). The text analyzes a programme called 'Active—Back Sooner' developed by the Danish National Labour Authority for citizens who receive sickness benefit. The text is not structured with an introduction, review, analysis, etc. Instead it consists of 31 paragraphs, each with their own headline. The paragraphs describe and analyze a fieldwork experience among bureaucrats, frontline social workers, or clients, or they elaborate on a theoretical perspective, a newspaper article, or a policy paper. Vohnsen offers no definitive conclusion, however, and the text ultimately appears open-ended. It is up to the reader to find meaning in the juxtapositions and create an overview of the fragments. The text is a good example of how "montage as presentational form can be used to keep the paradoxes of fieldwork experience alive in the subsequent production of academic text" (Suhr & Willerslev, 2013, p. 97).

Another anthropologist who has experimented with montage as a presentational form is Karen Lisa Salamon (2009; 2010; 2013). For Salamon, ethnographic montage is a way to acknowledge the lack of continuity between different people's experiences—what she calls the "gaps" (Salamon, 2013, p. 145). She argues that often these gaps are smoothed out for the sake of a consistent narrative or convincing argument (Salamon, 2013, p. 147). By taking notes written by war refugees about crossing a border in 1943 and juxtaposing them with later texts and images by holiday and business commuters who crossed the same border, Salamon has constructed a montage for an anthology about a national frontier region (Salamon, 2010). Salamon writes that she wished to highlight the "absence of a single, graspable border experience" (Salamon, 2013, p. 146). In a study of cultural civic centres, Salamon put together a montage consisting of quotes from people who speak about the role of their local centres (Salamon, 2009). The material was organized under thematic headlines which came partly from the speakers themselves and partly from Salamon through her analysis. Salamon writes that she did not wish to bridge the variations, contradictions, disagreements, and gaps that she encountered in her study. Instead the material was to "function as documentation and inspiration for further debate, involving also the interviewees themselves" (Salamon, 2013, p. 154).

Both Vohnsen and Salamon use montage to emphasize the contradictions and the complexity of social reality. They highlight the gaps in the empirical material and leave the interpretation open-ended to a degree. Polyphonic sound montages are based on the same principles, but the medium is different. How this affects their construction will be explored in the following section.

Crafting Polyphonic Sound Montages: The Ethnographer as Editor

When working with sound montage as an ethnographic approach, the ethnographer's efforts in the field are ultimately focused on getting 'rich material' on tape—i.e., good recordings of informants who tell interesting anecdotes and share personal perspectives. Everyday life needs to be caught on tape or it cannot be edited and presented as part of a sound montage. This differentiates the approach from other ethnographic approaches where the ethnographer can reconstruct overheard conversations and situations.

In the pace-clinic project, participant observation was carried out among the technicians, nurses, secretaries, and doctors. These observations were supplemented by interviews with key employees to get a nuanced impression of the work done at the clinic. As the anthropologist Agar (1996) points out, the informants will always assign a social category to the ethnographer (Agar (1996, p. 91). This category may change over time, but it will always be there, and it greatly influences the ethnographer's role in the field and how the informants react to him or her. When doing fieldwork in an organization, the category of management consultant is readily assigned. As David Gellner and Eric Hirsch (2001) write: "Large organizations often have experience of management consultants. This may mean that the anthropologist is regarded as a potential enemy by staff, who assume that he or she is a management consultant whose report will recommend redundancies" (p. 5). As mentioned, the technicians felt that the managers were already too involved in their work at the time. Therefore they were understandably a little apprehensive when an external researcher was suddenly introduced by one of the managers. Some of them later reported that they had been quite suspicious at first. A few never seemed to warm to the idea of a researcher at the clinic. The majority, however, did eventually become very interested in the project and were glad to participate in interviews and allow observation of consultations.

Patients were randomly selected from lists of the scheduled consultations and contacted by phone. Interviews were scheduled after an already planned consultation at the clinic. The patients were informed that the interview would be about their personal experiences of living with a device and how they experienced their visits and general contact with the pace-clinic. All the informants had at least one thing in common: They had to live with a small machine under their skin, which connected to small wires that went into their heart. To make sure this machine operated ideally, they had to visit the hospital on a regular basis.

Thirty-two patients were interviewed for the project. Interviews took place in a small office in the building next to the clinic. This allowed for a minimum of interruptions and a quiet environment to get good recordings. The interviews varied in length from just eight minutes to well over an hour. People were asked to tell the story of what had led them to first have contact with the cardiology department. Based on this story, they were asked to talk about specific experiences related to the consultations, the reception at the clinic, the letters they received, the way telemedicine worked, etc. Fifteen hours of conversation was recorded.

Because the material will be edited and played back to an audience, there are a few things the researcher should consider when interviewing. It is important to encourage the informants to be as concrete as possible and describe specific situations instead of general impressions. This way the people listening to the montages are better able to understand what the informant thought in different situations and what actually happened. Apart from uncovering the process, these step-by-step descriptions or anecdotes also make it fundamentally more captivating and interesting to listen to the accounts. Anecdotes draw us in as listeners and activate our empathy for the informant's perspective. Anecdotes also have the advantage of being able to stand on their own. When writing ethnography, it is easier to contextualize and fill in the gaps of a conversation. When editing sound montages, one can only use what has actually been recorded (Arnfred, 2015, p. 358).

The next step is to edit the recorded material into polyphonic sound montages. Here the aim of the researcher is not to analyze the material in order to formulate a theory, but rather to categorize it in a way that creates a loyal overview of what the informants have said. This can then be presented to the employees in the organization who partake in the analysis with the researcher. The main criteria guiding the researcher in the editing process will therefore be how to best represent the most important trends in the perspectives and experiences of the informants relating to the specific focus of the given project. First and foremost, the specific sound clips that are kept in the montages are the ones that somehow best capture the theme of each montage. However, two additional considerations contribute to the exact composition of the final montages. These are aesthetic and ethical considerations.

First, in the editing process, the montages are also viewed as 'experiences' that should be engaging. Effort is devoted to finding catchy titles for the montages, and there is some consideration as to which of the sound clips are the most engaging or perhaps even the funniest. The rationale is that the more engaging the montages are, the more the listeners will be motivated to discuss the issues they highlight. This consideration also drives the way the individual sound clips in the montages are edited, where excessive pauses are cut out to keep the clips short and pointed. In this way, each clip is 'distilled' down to its essence.

Second, there are ethical considerations when deciding how to compose the montages. First and foremost, it is important to be aware of how sensitive it can be for the staff to be presented with user feedback on the care or service they provide. The researcher should be careful that the montages do not become counterproductive by leaving people feeling exposed and therefore dismissing the feedback in order to protect themselves. This is where the knowledge that the researcher attains through the initial fieldwork becomes important. Generally one should try, both in editing and in interviewing, to focus on the organization or the topic and not on specific individuals (Arnfred, 2015, p. 359).

In the end, each montage appears as a collection of voices—fragments of interviews—tied together by an overarching theme. Polyphony is prioritized over narrative arch. The listener does not get to linger with each of the informants, but is instead presented with different perspectives revolving around a theme (Arnfred, 2015, p. 360). Barbara Czarniawska writes that as ethnographers we act as spokespersons for others, and we "translate" their speech into what we think they mean (Czarniawska, 1999, p. 107). With the montage technique, however, the researcher becomes more like an editor than a translator. Instead of adding layers of interpretation, the researcher adds a thematic structure and lets the informants 'speak for themselves'. The researcher acts as an intermediary between the informants and the listeners, and the task is essentially one of communication: to accurately and fairly structure and convey the most significant perspectives from the users to the employees. Meinert et al. (2014) liken this way of editing to artistic work. The artist's interpretation is inherent in the artefact, but not made explicit. This makes the interpretation of the work open-ended and encourages the audience to make their own associations and conclusions. As they write, "The effect sought is affect in the sense of moving someone else to reflect or feel or make meaning" (Meinert et al., 2014, p. 4).

In the pace-clinic project, the 15 hours of recorded material was first turned into 7 themed montages which were up to 8 minutes long. This is typically too long to keep peoples' attention in a workshop situation. In order to select the best themes to work with, a meeting was set up with the two workshop facilitators from the innovation unit. Here the unfinished montages were played and the thematic structure and composition of the montages were discussed. The most important issue was whether some of the sound clips would be too hurtful for some of the staff to listen to in a room full of their colleagues. References to specific employees had already been edited out, but still a few of the patients had quite harsh criticisms, and while these were important, it was discussed whether their points were still contained in some of the other clips that were perhaps not as pointedly formulated. A balance had to be found where the most significant of the patients' perspectives were presented, but in a way that did not make the staff feel unnecessarily uncomfortable, leading them to perhaps take a defensive position. The montages had to be disruptive, but not so destabilizing that they became destructive. Just enough to act as the starting point and motivation for innovation.

The final result was five montages varying in length between a minute and a half and three minutes. The montages were given the titles "Half Robot", "The Consultation Moment", "Accessibility", and "Telemedicine". The final montage was named after a famous athlete who had a device and was referenced by many of the patients, because she had been shocked during a TV-transmitted event. In "Half Robot", the selected clips were about both the experience of living with a piece of technology inside one's body and how some patients felt that the staff sometimes treated them as if they only saw the technology and not them as individual human beings. In "The Consultation Moment", the patients talked about not being completely sure about what the consultations were about beforehand and about the experience of sitting in the examination chair at the clinic feeling there was a lack of communication about what was going on. In "Accessibility", the patients shared different perspectives on the difficulty and confusion about when and how to contact the clinic. In "Telemedicine", the clips were about living with different telemedicine solutions in one's home. The patients talked about being confused about how the devices actually worked and not understanding the sounds and lights produced by the technology at seemingly random times. Finally, in the last montage, the selected clips all referenced the famous athlete. Either because the patients had seen or heard about the TV-transmitted event, or because they had discussed the event with the staff at the clinic. The event had appeared quite dramatic to some, and they were afraid that something similar might happen to them as well.

These montages were the end result of a long, iterative process as outlined earlier. They did not, however, present a finished analysis or a coherent narrative. They were still open to interpretation and further analysis. This process will be discussed in the next section.

The Process of Co-Analysis

This section will discuss the second element of using polyphonic sound montages as an ethnographic method: how the montages can be used to facilitate a process of co-analysis. In the pace-clinic project, two workshops were held with 20 employees from the cardiology department. The group consisted of managers, doctors, nurses, secretaries, and technicians who were all connected to the pace-clinic. The overall aim of the workshops was to come up with new ideas that could be implemented to improve the service experience of the patients. The first workshop focused on identifying and understanding the problems and challenges, and the second workshop focused on formulating ideas for solutions to meet these challenges. The polyphonic sound montages were the starting point for the process. They represented the "voice of the patients".

The process of making the montages was briefly explained, and they were then played one by one for the group. The participants were asked to silently reflect and write down any thoughts and associations they might have listening to the voices of the patients. Between each montage, they shared and discussed these reflections. In the montage "Half Robot", a patient had the following to say about his experience with telemedicine:

> *In the beginning, I got a letter every time—I think it is every third months, I send these data via telemedicine—then I got a letter 3 or 4 days after, in which it said: "We can confirm that the technology works". And then I thought: "The technology works . . . How do I work? Has there been any episodes[4] where it [the device] has been active?" To find out, I had to call the clinic. But the fact that the technology works is no surprise to me. It would be horrible if it didn't work . . . When the letter about the technology then stopped coming, I nevertheless thought: "That's strange . . . I've sent these data . . . " No reaction was almost worse than irrelevant information . . . and that's a little peculiar*

After this montage played in the workshop, one of the technicians commented:

> *I think it reflects a technology-focus. But we have to have a patient-focus. That's what they're saying. We have to make sure the technology is a hundred percent all right, but we also have to see the whole picture. We have to become better at that, I think.*

The montages lead to a lively discussion in the workshop. The staff supplemented the anecdotes and perspectives from the montages with their own everyday experiences from the clinic, to try to figure out why the patients felt like they felt, or experienced the consultations the way they did. After the workshop, one of the doctors reflected on the process:

> *The montages caused surprise. Is it really perceived like this? Then a lot of discussion. How can we avoid it? How and why is it like that? What do we do wrong? So they introduced some challenges that was then explored, and then we started to think. How can we make this better?*

Based on the discussions, the groups formulated a problem or challenge they wanted to explore further. One of the groups formulated the following problem: "The patients feel they lose control over their own life". The group then tried to come up with possible consequences of, as well as possible causes for, the problem. As consequences they proposed: "Need for more control", "denial", "a lack of motivation to come to all the appointments at the clinic", "a need to be recognized". As causes they proposed: "A lack of focus on the psychological aspect", "fear of dying", "lack of continuity", "experts have more knowledge about your illness than you do yourself", "incomprehensible technology", "lack of inclusion" (Arnfred, 2015, p. 362). The anthropologist Kjærsgaard (2013) uses the term 'knowledge pieces' to describe the Post-it notes and pictures produced in interdisciplinary design workshops. She describes how new design concepts are generated through the combination and juxtaposition of various types of data, ideas, insights, technology, people, skills, perspectives, and knowledge traditions (Kjærsgaard (2013, p. 65). Nuanced and contested perspectives are translated into a few key words and written on Post-it notes. Although this process is extremely reductionist, it also makes all the different perspectives manageable and facilitates new combinations and possibly new ideas for solutions. Kjærsgaard argues that creativity and design concepts arise through the dynamic composition of these knowledge pieces and the gaps and frictions between them.

The polyphonic sound montages raise a lot of questions, and as a listener, one needs to talk to somebody after hearing them. In a cooperative process, the participants in the workshop start with the anecdotes and perspectives from the montages and try to illuminate structured social relations. In this way, the analysis of the qualitative data becomes a collaborative, multidisciplinary project. The aim is to identify some possible social structures or mechanisms in order to possibly be able to modify the status quo (Arnfred, 2015, p. 362).

This analytical approach resembles the retroductive approach applied in the philosophy of science known as critical realism (Bhaskar, 1975; 1979). Instead of deducing the conclusion from the premises, the task is to find the premise when the conclusion is given. In other words, the starting point is a given trend, action, phenomenon, or event, and the aim is to describe social structures and mechanisms that would explain it. In the pace-clinic project, the sound montages identified and represented some trends or themes in the patients' experiences. These had to be explained. As Porter (2002) points out, the role of ethnography, in this worldview, becomes to describe the manifest interactions of the social world and then to subject these to the transcendental process of generating theories about the structural premises of those interactions. Finally, these theories should be tested. Critical realism, then, is not confined to a focus on individual experience, but uses ethnographic material to illuminate structured social relations. Furthermore, critical realist scholarship will often try to point to actions that can be taken to make these relations less oppressive (Porter, 2002, p. 65).

So why use sound recordings to facilitate this collaborative retroductive process? Instead one could imagine a scenario where informants were actually invited to the workshop to tell about their experiences. Some concerns quickly arise in this thought experiment, however. It would not be possible to include more than a few informants before it would take up too much time. Furthermore, most informants would probably be nervous if they had to tell their story in front of a room full of people. They would also not be able to be anonymous, which would probably put a damper on what they felt they could say. By using the sound montages as mediator, it is possible to do a lot of work before one reaches the workshop and thereby present concentrated excerpts of the most significant perspectives (Arnfred, 2015, p. 363).

Instead of just using audio, it is of course possible to add the visual dimension and do video montages instead. Just using audio, however, has a number of advantages. First, most informants will be more comfortable and relaxed if they are just talking to the interviewer and an audio recorder on the table instead of a video camera. Second, there is the issue of anonymity again. In an organizational setting, the informants are more likely to be honest, and perhaps critical, if they know the staff will not be able to easily recognize them the next time they visit the organization. Third, it might short-change some of the listeners' prejudices if they cannot see the user, thereby nudging them to listen more to the content of what is actually being said (Arnfred, 2015).

The sound montages work partly because they activate the listeners' emotions. As one of the doctors said in the pace-clinic case: "They work because they hurt. There is a self-image among the staff that we deliver the highest possible quality, and the montages challenge this a little. Therefore you take it in". Kotter and Cohen (2002) pinpoint this when they write, "People change what they do less because they are given analysis that shifts their thinking than because they are shown a truth that influences their feelings" (Kotter and Cohen, 2002, p. 1). By hearing their actual voices, the listener experiences a relation to the informants. Anthropologist Salamon (2013) supports this claim in her discussion of montage. She argues that montages can invoke a kind of intimacy because the direct authorial voice of the ethnographer is peeled away, and the informants' voices are kept relatively intact. The listener therefore feels a more powerful connection and relation to the informants (Salamon, 2013, p. 154). Of course, the ethnographer lurks behind the curtains having orchestrated the voice fragments, but the montages preserve much of the identity of the informants (Salamon, 2013, p. 146). By hearing their voices, you clearly feel the human being behind the utterances and perspectives, which makes the process more engaging and moving (Arnfred, 2015, p. 363). You hear the nuances in the way the perspective is expressed.

The first workshop ended with the groups formulating a list of questions, which, if answered, could be part of solving the problems they had identified based on the sound montages. At the beginning of the second workshop, the groups had to choose one or two of these questions to pursue. They were then given time to come up with as many ideas as they could to answer this question. The workshop facilitators stressed that the participants should be as concrete as possible. After the ideation process, the participants presented their ideas within the groups. One of the groups worked with the following question: How can we make sure the patients receive the most relevant information both before and by the end of the consultation? Many ideas were discussed: varying the length of consultations to suit the patients' different needs, grouping patients who came in for their first consultation, changing the physical layout of the consultation rooms, and making cartoons which explained how to use the technology.

After an exercise where all the ideas were sorted based on how easy or difficult they were to realize and how beneficial they were to the patients, the group voted for the best idea. They ended up with an idea about developing a system where letters to patients could be individualized by ticking off relevant topics from a list, thereby copying a few prewritten lines into the letter. This idea then had to be explored and expanded. Each group was asked to make up a patient with a name and backstory. Then they had to construct a story. They had to start with a concrete reason why the patient showed up in the pace-clinic. Then they had to illustrate step by step how the idea they had come up with could help this patient.

Finally, the groups had to present their ideas. Each group had three minutes followed by questions and comments from the other participants. The aforementioned group had made a scenario where a 55-year-old CEO receives a letter asking him to come in for a consultation. The data he has sent through his home transmitter has indicated that his device is not working properly. Before he comes in, he receives a letter with information specifically about this scenario, what he can expect from the consultation, and how he should prepare. The group's scenario focused on how to better prepare the patients for consultations so they know what is going to happen. The aim was to make the patients feel more at ease and make the consultations more efficient. After the group's presentation, there were questions and comments from the other participants before the next group presented a scenario.

In this way, the perspectives from the polyphonic sound montages were transformed into scenarios for possible future practices at the clinic. The employees were asked to devote their full attention to listening, and a group of patients were given the chance to communicate their experiences and perspectives to people with the power to change the conditions for their treatment.

Conclusion

This chapter has discussed the use of polyphonic sound montages as an ethnographic approach to involving users in health-care service improvement. The sound montages are a way to present ethnographic material and facilitate a shared analysis and interpretation with the staff in an organization. This can then inspire new ideas for re-organization and service improvement. The sound montages draw the listeners in and affect them emotionally because they consist of real human voices telling stories from their own lives. The listener is included in the analysis and interpretation because the metanarratives are reduced to a minimum. They are open-ended.

Using polyphonic sound montages is about communicating an experience more than it is about communicating an assessment. Like all qualitative research, the method is not representative, but explorative. It identifies certain trends and novel perspectives, but does not indicate exactly how many hold these beliefs or share these experiences. Compared to a quantitative survey that can say something about the satisfaction of an (non-existent) average user, the montages deal in insight: to understand how things look and feel from another point of view. They can act as 'eye-openers', pose new questions, and show people new perspectives on their social reality (Arnfred, 2015, p. 364). In the pace-clinic case, the montages provide an idea of what it would feel like to live with a pacemaker. What one notices when one comes to the clinic for a device. What one thinks. The staff heard the patients' honest perspectives, and the format helped them to see the world through the patients' eyes and thereby to see themselves and their everyday routines in a new light. It made them aware of some of the conditions and practices they no longer noticed themselves and how some of the things they said could be perceived in a very different way than intended. Because it is engaging to hear the montages, the employees become more invested in trying to figure out what is behind the perspectives they are hearing. They feel a relation to the informants and become motivated to identify possible causes for any problems or issues.

Comment by Mike Rowe

The past 20 years have been exciting ones for ethnographers, and we can look forward to a bright and variegated future. Just as innovation becomes a major theme in studies of corporations, of public agencies, and of economic activity, ethnographers are innovating at a pace. We have seen experiments with photographic and other visual methods, the use of smell to prompt memory and reflection, and ventures into the virtual worlds of netnography and autonetnography. There is no shortage of innovative methods to explore the ways in which others understand and make sense of their worlds and to open up aspects of daily life that have proven hard to observe in a more traditional fashion.

The innovations in technique and technology help us, as ethnographers, as we engage in discussions with our collaborators/informants. But we confront dilemmas when we wish to represent this raw material, the images and smells, to other audiences. There are very real ethical issues, perhaps particularly ones of consent and anonymity. But there are also artistic/aesthetic questions. That is, the photos taken by our participants may not in themselves communicate much in the way of meaning. They do not easily convey to a third party, the distant reader, what they might to the researcher and, more particularly, their subject. We glean deeper insights in discussion with informants about the meanings they associate with images and smells. But we are left with the questions of translation, selection, and authenticity.

As we reflect upon our field notes, interviews, and, perhaps, photos and other materials, we seek to represent, to translate, and to interpret in ways that, we hope, will convey some insight, some fragment of our informant's truth. But in that process, we are always aware that we, as researcher and author, stand between the reader and the field. Arnfred doesn't offer a way out of this perennial dilemma. Instead, after that process of editing and selecting, looking for items that will hold the attention of the audience while not offering a false image, montages and specifically polyphonic sound montages still convey the voice, the sounds of the original, and offers it directly to another audience. We all know of the story, told to us alone, full of emotion and meaning. We can repeat that, offering it up with our own interpretations taken as authorized readings. What would others make of the story as told, with inflection and emotion, with imagery, with pauses and hesitations? I tell one story that I cannot complete without tears, but my audience all too often look uncomfortable and embarrassed. How would they respond were they to hear the story as told to me? Where my emotion might feel inauthentic, the original recording would convey something more directly affecting.

In this chapter, Arnfred is not only concerned with one more innovation in method, but he is also concerned with the way this innovation offers insights into the very process of innovation in a health-service setting. Representing the experience of users, consumers, clients, or customers to those with the power to make changes that will affect that experience is fraught with methodological and ethical challenges. The shortcomings of approaches that employ mystery shoppers, surveys, or citizens' panels have become familiar. Each, in different ways, struggles with questions of veracity, legitimacy, authority, authenticity, and representativeness. There are also serious questions of power, perhaps particularly in a health setting. Given these difficulties, how might we, as ethnographers, present the client perspective to those with professional and institutional power in ways they will hear?

The polyphonic sound montage offers a way of allowing users to speak and be heard by professionals while allowing for some of the issues of power to be neutralized. It allows for more than the few voices that can be heard in more traditional consultation formats. And it allows the voices to convey the depth of feeling and authenticity that is often lost in extracts and text. The technique still requires an intense process of editing and analysis, a process that is also in part an aesthetic one, creating a sound montage that is more than a cacophony of contradictory voices. But in that montage, some of the tendency to impose order and structure on our data is tempered by the more nuanced ways in which informants actually express themselves.

There are perhaps contexts in which the polyphonic sound montage is more appropriate than others. Arnfred discusses its value in the process of innovation in a health setting. This is very explicitly action research. As a collaborative process used, in this context, to inform professionals, there would be potential for harm in a total institution. Voices could not be anonymous in the way they might be for outpatients. And in other contexts, perhaps where the audience is not genuinely prepared to listen, the potential for challenge, destabilization, and rupture become less innovative and more dangerous.

We might also ask what the value of polyphonic sound montages might be outside of an action research context. As an editor of a journal, one who always encourages authors to experiment with the way they present their fieldwork, it does strike me that there is further potential for montages to convey some of the sound and emotions of the field. As printed output declines and as articles are increasingly accessed and read in electronic formats, should we be incorporating sound clips embedded in articles? Might we replace indented bodies of text, lengthy quotes, and tales told by ethnographers with the voices of the field?

Notes

1. Implantable cardioverter defibrillator (ICD). Just like a pacemaker, the ICD is implanted under the patient's breast muscle. Simply put, the pacemaker assists a heart which is beating too slow, whereas an ICD stops a heart from beating too fast. The ICD can ultimately administer a concentrated burst of electricity in order to 'reset' the heart.
2. A term for both pacemaker and ICD.
3. Patients with ICDs have a transmitter in their home that sends data periodically from their device to a database at the hospital. The staff at the pace-clinic then checks this data.
4. An instance when the heart has been beating too fast is called 'an episode'. The patient does not necessarily feel these episodes.

Chapter References

Agar, M. (1996). *The Professional Stranger: An Informal Introduction to Ethnography, 2nd ed*. San Diego: Academic Press.

Arnfred, M. (2015). Polyphonic Sound Montages: A New Approach to Ethnographic Representation and Qualitative Analysis. *Journal of Organizational Ethnography*, 4 (3), 356–366.

Baraitser, P., Pearce, V., Blake, G., Collander-Brown, K., & Ridley, A. (2005). Involving Service Users in Sexual Health Service Development. *The Journal of Family Planning and Reproductive Health Care*, 31 (4), 281–284.

Baraitser, P., Pearce, V., Walsh, N., Cooper, R., Brown, K. C., Holmes, J., . . . Boynton, P. (2008). Look Who's Taking Notes in Your Clinic: Mystery Shoppers as Evaluators in Sexual Health Services. *Health Expectations: An International Journal of Public Participation in Health Care and Health Policy*, 11 (1), 54–62.

Bate, P., & Robert, G. (2006). Experience-Based Design: From Redesigning the System Around the Patient to Co-Designing Services with the Patient. *Quality and Safety in Health Care*, 15 (5), 307–310.

Bhaskar, R. (1975). *A Realist Theory of Science*. London: Routledge.

Bhaskar, R. (1979). *The Possibility of Naturalism*. London: Routledge.

Clifford, J., & Marcus, G. (1986). *Writing Culture: The Poetics and Politics of Ethnography*. Berkeley: University of California Press.

Czarniawska, B. (1999). *Writing Management: Organization Theory as a Literary Genre*. Oxford and New York: Oxford University Press.

Elg, M., Engström, J.,Witell, L., & Poksinska, P. (2012). Co-Creation and Learning in Healthcare Service Development. *Journal of Service Management*, 23 (3), 328–343.

Elg, M., Witell, L., Poksinska, B., Engström, J., Dahlgaard-Park, S., & Kammerlind, P. (2010). Solicited Diaries as a Means for Involving Patients in Development of Healthcare Services. *International Journal of Quality and Service Sciences*, 3 (2), 128–145.

Gellner, D. N., & Hirsch, E. (Eds.) (2001). *Inside Organizations: Anthropologists at Work*. Oxford: Berg.

Greenhalgh, T., Humphrey, C., & Woodard, F. (2010). *User Involvement in Health Care*. Chichester, West Sussex, UK and Hoboken, NJ: Wiley-Blackwell and BMJ Books.

Groene, O., Poletti, P., Vallejo, P., Cucic, C., Klazinga, N., & Sunol, R. (2009). Quality Requirements for Cross-Border Care in Europe: A Qualitative Study of Patients', Professionals' and Healthcare Financiers' Views. *Quality and Safety in Health Care*, 18 (Suppl 1), i15–i21.

Kjærsgaard, M. (2013). (Trans)forming knowledge and design concepts. In W. Gunn, T. Otto, & R. C. Smith (Eds.), *Design Anthropology: Theory and Practice*. London and New York: Bloomsbury, 51–67.

Kotter, J. P., & Cohen, D. S. (2002). *The Heart of Change: Real-life Stories of How People Change Their Organizations*. Boston: Harvard Business Press.

Longtin, Y., Sax, H., Leape, L. L., Sheridan, S. E., Donaldson, L., & Pittet, D. (2010). Patient Participation: Current Knowledge and Applicability to Patient Safety. *Mayo Clinic Proceedings*, 85 (1), 53–62.

Marcus, G. E. (1990). The Modernist Sensibility in Recent Ethnographic Writing and the Cinematic Metaphor of Montage. *SVA Review*, 6 (1), 2–12.

Marcus, G. E. (1992). Past, present and emergent identities: Requirements for ethnographies of late twentieth-century modernity worldwide. In S. Lash, & J. Friedman (Eds.), *Modernity and Identity*. Oxford: Blackwell, 309–330.

Marcus, G. E., & Fischer, M. M. J. (1986). *Anthropology as Cultural Critique: An Experimental Moment in the Human Sciences*. Chicago, IL: University of Chicago Press.

Meinert, L., Obika, J. A., & Whyte, S. R. (2014). Crafting Forgiveness Accounts after War: Editing for Effect in Northern Uganda. *Anthropology Today*, 30 (4), 10–14.

Morrow, E., Boaz, A., Brearley, S., & Ross, F. (2012). *Handbook of Service User Involvement in Nursing and Healthcare Research*. West Sussex: Wiley-Blackwell.

Porter, S. (2002). Critical realist ethnography. In T. May (Ed.), *Qualitative Research in Action*. London: Sage, 53–72.

Salamon, K. L. (2009). *En etnografisk montage om huses lokale kultur og forankring*. Copenhagen: Huse i Danmark.

Salamon, K. L. (2010). Bro over tid og grænse: En montage. In Orvar Löfgren and Frederik Nilsson (Eds.), *Regionauterna: Öresundsregionen från vision til vardag*. Stockholm: Makadam Forlag, 199–213.

Salamon, K. L. (2013). Mind the gap. In C. Suhr, & R. Willerslev (Eds.), *Transcultural Montage*. New York, NY: Berghahn Books, 145–158.

Suhr, C., & Willerslev, R. (2013). *Transcultural Montage*. New York, NY: Berghahn Books.

Vohnsen, N. H. (2013). Labour days—a non-linear narrative of development. In C. Suhr, & R. Willerslev (Eds.), *Transcultural Montage*. New York, NY: Berghahn Books, 131–144.

Index